Disability, Sport and Society

Disability sport is a relatively recent phenomenon; yet it is also one that, particularly in the context of social inclusion, is attracting increasing political and academic interest. The purpose of this important new text – the first of its kind – is to introduce the reader to key concepts in disability and disability sport and to examine the complex relationships between modern sport, disability and other aspects of wider society.

Drawing upon original data from interviews, surveys and policy documents, the book examines how disability sport has developed and is currently organized, and explores key themes, issues and concepts including:

- disability theory and policy;
- the emergence and development of disability sport;
- disability sport development in local authorities;
- mainstreaming disability sport;
- disability, physical education and school sport;
- elite disability sport and the Paralympic Games;
- disability sport and the media.

Including chapter summaries, seminar questions and lists of key websites and further reading throughout, *Disability, Sport and Society* provides both an easy to follow introduction to and a critical exploration of the key issues surrounding disability sport in the twenty-first century. This book is an invaluable resource for all students, researchers and professionals working in sport studies, disability studies, physical education, sociology and social policy.

Nigel Thomas is Head of Sport and Exercise at Staffordshire University, UK, where his research focuses on the history, mainstreaming and media coverage of disability sport. He previously worked for ten years with young disabled people as a sports development officer in local authorities and national governing bodies.

Andy Smith is a lecturer in the Sociology of Sport and Exercise at the University of Chester, UK. He is a co-editor of the *International Journal of Sport Policy*, and a co-author of *Sport Policy and Development: An Introduction* and *An Introduction to Drugs in Sport: Addicted to Winning?* Both books are published by Routledge (2009).

Disability, Sport and Society

An introduction

Nigel Thomas and Andy Smith

Routledge
Taylor & Francis Group

LONDON AND NEW YORK

First published 2009
by Routledge
2 Park Square, Milton Park, Abingdon, Oxon OX14 5RN

Simultaneously published in the USA and Canada
by Routledge
270 Madison Ave, New York, NY 10016

*Routledge is an imprint of the Taylor & Francis Group,
an informa business*

© 2009 Nigel Thomas and Andy Smith

Typeset in Goudy by Swales & Willis Ltd, Exeter, Devon
Printed and bound in Great Britain by CPI Antony Rowe,
Chippenham, Wiltshire

British Library Cataloguing in Publication Data
A catalogue record for this book is available from the British Library

Library of Congress Cataloging-in-Publication Data
Thomas, Nigel.
Disability, sport, and society: an introduction / Nigel Thomas and Andrew Smith.
p. cm.
Includes bibliographical references and index.
1. Sports for people with disabilities. 2. Athletes with disabilities. I. Smith, Andrew. II. Title.
GV709.3.T46 2008
796.087—dc22
2008026694

ISBN10: 0–415–37818–4 (hbk)
ISBN10: 0–415–37819–2 (pbk)
ISBN10: 0–203–09936–2 (ebk)

ISBN13: 978–0–415–37818–5 (hbk)
ISBN13: 978–0–415–37819–2 (pbk)
ISBN13: 978–0–203–09936–0 (ebk)

Contents

List of tables

Acknowledgements

We would like to thank the many people who, over many years, have encouraged us and contributed, directly or indirectly, to our development during the course of writing this book and to the development of our thought in relation to disability sport. Particular mention should be made of colleagues in Sport and Exercise at Staffordshire University for their longstanding support and encouragement. We would also like to thank our colleagues at the University of Chester, especially Daniel Bloyce, Ken Green, Katie Liston, Helen Odhams and Chris Platts for their encouragement and good humour. In addition, we would like to acknowledge the ongoing support of Barrie Houlihan (Loughborough University), Ivan Waddington (Visiting Professor at the University of Chester and at the Norwegian School of Sport Sciences, Oslo) and Fiona Reid (Federation of Disability Sport Wales).

We would like to express our particular gratitude to the various Chief Executives and Senior Officers who kindly gave their time to be interviewed during the course of the research for this book. In particular, we should like to thank Colin Chaytors (English Federation of Disability Sport), Philip Craven (International Paralympic Committee), Jeff Davis (Football Association), Tim Marshall (Minister's Review Group), Gordon Neale (Disability Sport Events), David Sparkes (British Swimming), Sue Wolstenholme (Tennis Foundation), and those interviewees who wished to remain anonymous.

Finally, each of us would like to pay a particular tribute to our friends and family. Nigel Thomas would like to thank his parents and owes an enormous debt of gratitude to his wife, Julia, for everything and to Jake and Esme for making a grumpy man very happy! Andy Smith would like to pay special thanks to his parents and sister, Jenny, for their support and for always wondering why he had been working so late!

List of abbreviations

ASA	Amateur Swimming Association
BALASA	British Amputee and Les Autres Sports Association
BASA	British Amputee Sports Association
BCODP	British Council of Disabled People
BLASA	British Les Autres Sports Association
BBS	British Blind Sport
BDSC	British Deaf Sports Council
BPA	British Paralympic Association
BPSS	British Paraplegic Sports Society
BS	British Swimming
BSAD	British Sports Association for the Disabled
BTF	British Tennis Foundation
BTTAD	British Table Tennis Association for the Disabled
BWSF	British Wheelchair Sports Foundation
CAS	Court of Arbitration for Sport
CCPR	Central Council for Physical Recreation
CCT	Compulsory Competitive Tendering
CGF	Commonwealth Games Federation
CPD	Continuing Professional Development
CP-ISRA	Cerebral Palsy International Sport and Recreation Association
CP Sport	Cerebral Palsy Sport
DCMS	Department of Culture, Media and Sport
DDA	Disability Discrimination Act
DfES	Department for Education and Skills
DNH	Department of National Heritage
DPI	Disabled Peoples' International
DRC	Disability Rights Commission
DSE	Disability Sport England / Disability Sport Events
DSO	Disability Sport Organization
EB	English Basketball
EBA	English Basketball Association
EFDS	English Federation of Disability Sport
EHRC	The Equality and Human Rights Commission

ETTA	English Table Tennis Association
FA	The Football Association
GBWBA	Great Britain Wheelchair Basketball Association
IBSA	International Blind Sports Association
ICF	International Classification of Functioning, Health and Disability
ICIDH	International Classification of Impairments, Disability and Handicap
INAS-FID	International Sports Federation for Persons with an Intellectual Disability
IOC	International Olympic Committee
IOSD	International Organization of Sports for the Disabled
IPC	International Paralympic Committee
ISMGF	International Stoke Mandeville Games Federation
ITT	Initial Teacher Training
LSA	Learning Support Assistants
LTA	Lawn Tennis Association
MCGOC	Manchester Commonwealth Games Organizing Committee
NCPE	National Curriculum for Physical Education
NDP	National Demonstration Project
NDSO	National Disability Sport Organization
NGB	National Governing Body
ODI	Office for Disability Issues
Ofsted	Office for Standards in Education
PE	Physical Education
PESSCL	Physical Education and School Sport Clubs Links strategy
SEN	Special Educational Needs
SSC	Specialist Sport Colleges
TF	Tennis Foundation
UKSAPMH	United Kingdom Sports Association for People with Mental Handicap
UNESCO	United Nations Educational, Scientific and Cultural Organization
UPIAS	Union of the Physically Impaired Against Segregation
WHO	World Health Organization
YST	Youth Sport Trust

Introduction

Disability sport as it exists in its modern form is a relatively recent phenomenon that first emerged in Britain, specifically England, during the immediate post Second World War period. More specifically, as we shall explain elsewhere in this book, the roots of the emergence and early development of disability sport can be traced back to the request made by the British government that Sir Ludwig Guttmann (a Jewish neurosurgeon) should open the National Spinal Injuries Centre (NSIC) at the Stoke Mandeville Hospital in Aylesbury, England, in 1944. Once the NSIC was established, a range of sports and physical activities were used as a means of physical and psychological rehabilitation of large numbers of soldiers and civilians who had acquired a range of impairments following their involvement in the Second World War. Despite this initial motivation for encouraging the war-injured (especially those with spinal cord injuries) to engage in sport and physical activities, the perceived benefits that competitive, organized sports could have for war veterans and for challenging attitudes about the abilities of disabled people were quickly recognized by Guttmann and other hospital workers. The first formally recognized national event in disability sport was subsequently held for athletes with spinal cord injuries in 1948 at Stoke Mandeville Hospital. From these early beginnings, disability sport has since developed rapidly and disabled people with a range of physical, sensory and cognitive impairments now participate in sport and physical activity from the grassroots to elite level in many countries. Such has been the growing internationalization, globalization and competitiveness of disability sport at the elite level, for example, the thirteenth Paralympic Games held from 6–17 September 2008 in Beijing was the largest Paralympics ever with approximately 4,000 athletes participating in 20 sports.

Despite its relatively short history and increasing prominence in the world of modern sport, there is currently very little literature that has explored the emergence and development of disability sport and the associated issues which surround it. In fact, disability sport has been largely ignored in the sport and exercise sciences (especially in the social sciences of the discipline) as well as the mainstream disability studies literature. Indeed, with the exception of the American-based book titled *Disability Sport* by DePauw and Gavron (2005), and other texts written from an adapted physical activity perspective (e.g. Sherrill, 2004; Winnick, 2005), there are currently few social science texts dedicated solely to an examination of disability sport. This is, then, a book that we hope begins to fill this gap and our intention here is to make a small modest contribution to our understanding of disability sport. Set in this context, it is worth making clear to the reader what this book is about and, equally importantly, what it is not about.

The purpose of this introductory text is to examine some of the complex relationships between modern sport, disability and other aspects of the wider society. It is also primarily intended for those either studying disability sport or who work in the disability sport movement in various capacities. In this regard, it is hoped that the content of the book will appeal to those who are following courses in a diverse range of subjects, including sports studies, sport and exercise sciences, sport policy and development, physical education (PE), as well as sociology and disability studies. The book is not intended, however, to be a comprehensive survey of all the possible issues which may have been explored; indeed, it is likely that we have left many stones unturned and there will be some readers who would have liked us to have included chapters on subjects such as the use of performance-enhancing drugs. Other readers may feel – quite rightly – that much more could have been said about each of the various topics that are covered in the book. Themes such as the emergence and development of disability sport, PE and school sport and elite disability sport among other things are, for example, deserving of books themselves. It is also the case that whilst many of the case studies and examples provided in many of the chapters come from Britain and, in some cases, primarily England, we have wherever possible sought to incorporate international research in order to demonstrate the cross-cultural and international relevance of the various topics to an understanding of disability sport. If these are, in fact, perceived as limitations by some readers, then we would like to think that these have been offset, to some degree at least, by the fact that the book includes, for the first time, original data from interviews (with several high profile Chief Executives and Senior Officers, including the current President of the International Paralympic Committee) conducted by the authors between 2000 and 2008, surveys of organizations involved in disability sport, and documentary analysis of several policies and minutes of meetings that are not widely available.

The perspectives of the book

It is important at this point to say something about the theoretical perspectives which inform the book. The general approaches which underpin this book are expressive both of the authors' different theoretical and disciplinary backgrounds, as well as the balance between their practitioner and largely research-based involvement in disability sport. Before pursuing a career as a university lecturer, Nigel Thomas previously worked for 10 years with young disabled people as a sports development officer in local authorities and national governing bodies. He is now interested in researching disability sport from the perspective of political science and has a particular interest in policy analysis perspectives (especially Marsh and Rhodes' typology of policy networks). As a lecturer in the sociology of sport and exercise, Andy Smith, by contrast, has a largely research-based background and the theoretical framework on which he draws is that of figurational or process sociology, which has grown out of the work of Norbert Elias (1897–1990). However, for the most part, these perspectives have been used here implicitly in order to limit the more explicitly theoretical aspects of the book and to make it as accessible as possible to those who have an interest in sport and in disability sport, but who may not have a grounding in sociological theory or models of policy analysis.

Notwithstanding the different theoretical and disciplinary backgrounds of the authors, the book starts from the premise that despite the general lack of literature which explores many of the issues surrounding disability sport, some of the literature that does exist has tended to be highly emotive and heavily value-laden in character which has had the effect of hindering, rather than helping, the development of a more adequate understanding of disability sport. In this respect, we have sought in this book to develop a more realistic and adequate understanding of disability sport and, where relevant, to question some of the taken for granted assumptions which surround many of the various topics that we discuss. We would stress, however, that in doing so we have not attempted to provide *the* definitive account of disability sport but *an* interpretation of it and we hope that, if nothing else, the book provides a starting point on which others can build and that it may encourage others to undertake greater systematic study of disability, sport and society.

Terminology

Each of the chapters in this book explores, and where necessary, defines those concepts which are central to the analysis being presented. For the purposes of the book, however, we use the term 'disability sport' to describe those sports activities that have been developed for the specific involvement of disabled people and which provide opportunities for disabled people to compete with or against other disabled people. We also prefer to use the term 'disabled people' rather than 'people with disabilities' (the preferred usage in the United States, for example) for, as we noted earlier, much of the core material on which we have drawn here has tended to come from Britain and the phrase 'disabled people' has tended to dominate much of the British disability studies literature over the last half century or so. We are acutely aware, however, that the use of these terms has generated considerable debate and that some key terms, including 'disability' and 'disabled people', are often not easily translated into other languages and have been subject to various interpretations over time and vary from one society to another. Nevertheless, we are confident that our usage of these terms does not detract substantially from the general points that we wish to make, or to an understanding of disability sport more generally.

The structure of the book

Given that until now few texts have attempted to bring together in one volume a range of topics which begin to reflect some of the key issues to be found within the disability sport literature, we have deliberately sought to ensure that each chapter provides the reader with an introductory guide to a number of key issues which begin to help us make sense of the relationship between modern sport, disability and aspects of the wider society. Whilst we hope that some readers would be interested in reading the book from cover to cover, to try to make the book as accessible as possible to the reader, we have deliberately set out to provide a text that contains chapters on discrete topics that can be read in any order and which could be used as part of a broader area of study than disability sport. The one exception to this is Chapter 1 – titled 'Disability Theory and Policy' – which should be read in conjunction with each of the other chapters, for it is our contention that in order to understand something about the other key issues that are explored in the book, it is helpful for the readers to have some appreciation of the various theoretical explanations of disability and to explore some key developments in disability policy. In all cases, however, each chapter begins with a series of objectives which indicate the content to be explored and concludes with a list of further readings, useful websites and a series of revision questions that may be used as part of further discussions on the issues raised.

As we noted above, in Chapter 1 we explore some of the major theoretical explanations of disability and outline the emergence and development of disability policy that have been intended to enhance the lives and experiences of disabled people. In particular, we consider the medical and social models of disability and examine the relationship between disability and impairment. A consideration of these and related issues, we argue, are vital pre-requisites for understanding how disability sport has developed and is understood. Chapter 2 then examines the emergence and development of disability sport from its origins in Britain, and particularly England, during the 1940s. It also considers some of the major changes to the organization and administration of disability sport over the last half century or so before focusing, in particular, on the development and role of the English Federation of Disability Sport. Chapter 3 builds on the analysis presented in the previous chapter and discusses the role played by local authorities in the provision of disability sport by drawing on three case studies of local authorities in England. The analysis reveals that there currently exists differential policy and practice between individual local authorities in the provision of disability sport and that, as a consequence, the sporting experiences and opportunities available to disabled people often vary from one local authority to another.

A case study approach also forms the basis of the analysis presented in Chapter 4, which explores how the principle of mainstreaming disability sport has come to impact on the policy and practice of the national governing bodies of four professional sports: football, swimming, tennis and wheelchair basketball. We conclude by suggesting that governing bodies of sport have variable commitment towards mainstreaming disability sport, and some, at best, have played only a peripheral but supportive role to the disability sports organizations with whom they work. Chapter 5 continues with the theme of mainstreaming and examines the increasing use of PE and school sport in many countries as vehicles of social policy targeted at promoting the inclusion of young disabled people and those with special educational needs (SEN) in mainstream (or regular) schools. In doing so, we suggest that while the inclusion of young disabled people and pupils with SEN has tended to be uncritically accepted as an unambiguously desirable policy response designed to enhance those pupils' experiences of PE and school sport, this may not always necessarily be the case. Indeed, we suggest that the trend towards educating young disabled people and those with SEN in mainstream schools has, in many cases, been accompanied by what might be held to be a series of outcomes that are not only desired by some groups but which were also unintended and unforeseen.

In the final two chapters we turn our attention to the elite level of disability sport. In Chapter 6 we examine the structure and organization of elite level disability sport by focusing, in particular, on the Summer Paralympic Games. We also focus on three intensely debated issues that have become strongly associated with the Paralympics in recent years, namely, the classification of athletes, the inclusion of Paralympic athletes and disability sport events in the Olympic Games, and the use of assistive technology by Paralympians. These issues are then revisited to some extent in Chapter 7 where we examine media coverage of elite disability sport. This chapter explores the changes and degrees of continuity that have characterized the ways and extent to which the international sports media (particularly, newspapers) have reported on the involvement of disabled athletes in the Paralympics and the 2002 Commonwealth Games. On the basis of the evidence provided, the chapter begins to question the largely uncritically held assumption that the growing media coverage of such competitions is a 'positive' development in the evolution of modern elite disability sport, for there is evidence to suggest that, in many ways, such coverage may have done more to reinforce, than challenge, socially constructed stereotypical perceptions of disabled people. Finally, in the Conclusion we reflect briefly upon the key themes that emerge throughout the book and then begin to speculate, somewhat tentatively, upon how these are likely to feature in the future of disability sport.

1   Disability theory and policy

Objectives

This chapter will:

- examine the medical model or personal tragedy theory of disability;
- examine the social model of disability; and
- outline the emergence and development of disability policy.

Introduction

In order to understand something about the key issues which surround the complex relationships between modern sport, disability and society which we examine in this book, it is helpful to have some appreciation of the various theoretical explanations of disability and to explore some key developments in disability policy. This is important for, as we shall explain elsewhere, the ways in which disabled people have been treated historically by other members of the wider society, as well as how disability and the closely related concept of impairment have been conceptualized, are vital pre-requisites for understanding how disability sport has developed and is understood. In this chapter, therefore, we shall briefly examine: (i) some of the major theoretical explanations of disability; and (ii) the emergence and development of disability policy which has been designed to enhance disabled people's experiences and lives in the wider society. Before doing so however, it is not possible to examine in great detail, here, either the history and theoretical explanations of disability or the extent to which disability policy has been successful in achieving the desired objectives. Readers who wish to find out more about these issues might usefully consult any of the important works by some of the key authors within the disability studies field, including Colin Barnes, Geof Mercer, Jenny Morris, Mike Oliver and Tom Shakespeare.

Theories of disability

Disability as a personal tragedy

There is now a large and expanding literature which examines the various contested definitions and theories of disability. It is generally accepted by many authors within the field of disability studies, however, that the existing definitions and theories of disability can be grouped into two broad categories: medical or social. The medical model or personal tragedy theory of disability which dominated thinking about disability for most of the twentieth century, particularly in Western societies, embraces those definitions and perceptions which suggest that disability is an impairment that is owned by an individual and which results in a loss or limitation of function or some other 'defect'. On this view, disability has been traditionally conceptualized in a largely individualized or medicalized way that has its roots in the historical discrimination of disabled people during the rise of industrialism (Barnes, 1997; Barnes and Mercer, 2003; Oliver, 1990). These prevailing views of disability were perhaps most clearly expressed in what has been regarded as the most important definition of disability to be developed during the post-1945 period, namely, the International Classification of Impairments, Disabilities and Handicaps (ICIDH) introduced in 1980 by the World Health Organization (WHO). The WHO definitions of disability, impairment and handicap are often perceived as important in the recent history of disability since they came to be widely used to inform much social and welfare policy and professional practice. One particularly notable example of this was the work conducted by the Office for Population Censuses and Surveys (OPCS) into disabled people's welfare needs in Britain during the late 1980s. In the ICIDH the WHO combined their classification of disease with one that considered disability, impairment and handicap together. These terms were defined by the WHO in the following way:

> Impairment: Any loss or abnormality of, psychological, physiological or anatomical structure or function. (WHO, 1980: 27)

> Disability: Any restriction or lack of ability (resulting from impairment) to perform an activity in the manner or within the range considered normal for a human being. (WHO, 1980: 28)

> Handicap: A disadvantage for a given individual, resulting from an impairment or disability that limits or prevents the fulfilment of a role (depending on age sex, social and cultural factors) for that individual. (WHO, 1980: 29)

Expressing the dominant views of disability which prevailed during much of the twentieth century, the ICIDH definitions clearly suggest that impairment was considered to be a deviation from a bio-medical norm, whilst disability was conceptualized as the consequence of impairment which focuses attention on parts of the body that are not considered to function properly. The ICIDH classification also focused for the most part on what disabled people can and cannot do as a result of an impairment. In this regard, it is clear that the traditional individualized explanation of disability – and, it should be noted, the treatment of disabled people – has typically been informed by medical ideologies of disability in which practitioners (especially medical professionals and educational psychologists) have sought 'solutions' to problems that are believed to be located within the individual without considering the wider societal context in which disabled people live. These 'solutions' were often sought by segregating large numbers of disabled people in separate institutions (for example, hospitals and 'special' schools) on the assumption that this was for their own benefit and to prevent disabled people from being a burden on others in the wider society (Barnes and Mercer, 2003; Goffman, 1961). As Goffman's (1961) seminal study of the experiences of patients in mental hospitals – what he termed asylums – and his closely associated work on stigma (Goffman, 1963) clearly indicates, this process of institutionalization helped stereotype those who were considered 'impaired' as somehow 'different' from other 'normal' members of the wider society. The tendency to define disability in largely medical ways helped stigmatize disabled people as possessing 'undesired differentness' (Goffman, 1963: 5) to those considered non-disabled and helped construct labels which portray disabled people as 'deviant' and 'abnormal'. In this regard, the segregation of disabled people into separate institutions enables more established groups (such as medical professionals and some non-disabled groups) – by means of their relatively more powerful positions – to encourage less powerful groups such as disabled people to internalize and accept an image of themselves that is based on a 'minority of the worst' (Elias and Scotson, 1994). The process of institutionalization also enabled more established groups to encourage disabled people to absorb negative self- and group-images of themselves, whilst reinforcing more positive images of more established groups that are based on a 'minority of the best', that is, on the desirable characteristics (for example, able-bodiedness and 'normality') associated with those who are non-disabled (Elias and Scotson, 1994). Thus, as Nixon (2000: 423) has put it, particularly in Western societies, disabled people have been

> treated as members of a deviant minority group. Deviant status has meant that disabled persons have been relegated to a position outside the mainstream. Minority status has meant that disabled persons as a stereotyped and stigmatised category or group have been accorded degraded status, little power, and few opportunities for economic advancement or success.

A related assumption of the medical definition and explanation of disability, as well as the policies and professional services which it informs, therefore, is that disabled people ought to be 'physically whole' or 'normal' so that they can fit into a predominantly non-disabled society. An obvious example of this taken for granted assumption about the needs of disabled people becomes clear if we think of the ways in which medical professionals are particularly concerned that mobility impaired patients are able to walk however painful or slow that may be, rather than use a quicker and more comfortable medium of travel such as a wheelchair. Within the sporting context, the Great British Paralympian, Dame Tanni Grey-Thompson (2001: 13–14), summarized her experience of how the medical profession sought to manage her experience of spina bifida when a child, when she explained how

> doctors were obsessed with me walking. Their attitude was, I must stay on my feet for as long as possible . . . Everything the doctors did was about keeping me

on my feet when it should have been about finding the best way for me to be mobile.

We shall return to the ways in which concern with able-bodiedness, notions of normality and medicalized understandings of disabled people's lives and experiences have come to be expressed in disability sport when we examine the use of classification systems to organize elite level sport (Chapter 6) as well as the media coverage of disabled athletes participating in the Paralympics (Chapter 7). In the present context, however, it is worth reflecting on how the medicalized or individualized explanations of disability such as those to be found in the ICIDH have been widely criticized for several reasons. First, they are considered to focus exclusively on the personal limitations of disabled people whilst ignoring their other personal and social needs. Second, they present impairment as the sole cause of disability. And third, the ICIDH definitions are said to have further enhanced the already growing power of the medical profession to define what are and are not perceived to be medical problems. In this regard, the definitions of disability, impairment and handicap as used by the WHO are claimed to have encouraged medical professionals to impose their own priorities on the lifestyles of disabled people and to treat them as 'problems' to be 'cured' only through medical intervention and rehabilitative therapy (Barnes, 1998; Oliver, 1990; Shakespeare and Watson, 1997). It can also properly be said that by focusing on the supposed medical nature of impairment and disability the ICIDH-based definitions ignore the ways in which disability (and other sources of social division such as gender and social class) is socially constructed and ignores the complex ways in which perceptions and experiences of disability change and vary from one society to another society and over time (Barnes and Mercer, 2003; Barnes et al., 1999). Nor, for that matter, do the ICIDH definitions convey much about the ways in which disability and impairment have come to be defined as such by groups including the medical profession and other (non-)disabled groups who, because of their generally more powerful positions relative to other, less powerful groups, have a greater ability to define what ought to constitute as 'disability' and 'impairment' for which some kind of remedial action is warranted (Barnes and Mercer, 2003).

The social model of disability

In light of the growing dissatisfaction with the dominant medicalized explanation of disability which prevailed during the twentieth century, from the late 1960s this orthodoxy in thinking and practice began to be widely challenged by several political campaigns led by the disabled people's movement across Europe and North America (Barnes and Mercer, 2003). These campaigns, which were led by disabled activists (especially those who were constrained to live in separate residential care) and organizations led by disabled people, helped challenge the medically-informed assumptions about disability and the perceived status of disabled people as 'second-class citizens' by arguing that it should be understood not as a medical or biological problem but as a social construction (Barnes and Mercer, 2003; Oliver,

1986, 1992; Shakespeare and Watson, 1997). While the political campaigns led by disabled people focused initially on the improvement of welfare services through the work of organizations such as the Union of the Physically Impaired Against Segregation (UPIAS), the emphasis of these campaigns shifted towards placing greater importance on disabled people's rights for 'independent living'. They also began to redirect attention on the need to change the attitudes of people in the wider society towards those considered disabled and specifically:

> the impact of social and environmental barriers, such as inaccessible buildings and transport, discriminatory attitudes and negative cultural stereotypes, in 'disabling' people with impairments. (Barnes and Mercer, 2003: 1)

One outcome of the attempts by the disabled people's movement to challenge the orthodox medicalized view of disability was, therefore, the emergence of what is known as the 'social model' or explanation of disability that 'focuses on the environmental and social barriers which exclude people with perceived impairments from mainstream society' (Barnes, 1998: 78). This explanation of disability has become increasingly accepted by many within the disabled people's movement (such as the UK's Disabled People's Council) – if not to the same degree by others within the wider society – since it rejects the view of disability as being 'caused' by the presence of an impairment but rather as the 'disadvantage or restriction of activity caused by contemporary social organisation which takes little or no account of people who have physical impairments and excludes them from participation in the mainstream of activities' (UPIAS, 1976; cited in Barnes et al., 1999: 28). This alternative explanation acknowledges that, based upon a biomedical definition, some individuals could be deemed to have an impairment but that the complex causes of disability – like all sources of social division – have their roots in the differential and unequal power relations between groups in the wider society.

The emphasis which the social explanation places on the social and environmental constraints that are said to explain the experience of disability in Western societies has helped improve the experiences of disabled people and enable them to take control of their own lives to a greater degree than previously (Barnes and Mercer, 2003; Oliver and Barnes, 2008). The shift towards a social understanding of disability and of the social and environmental constraints which are believed to 'disable' people has also helped the disabled people's movement to bring about significant policy change by governments. As we shall explain in more detail later, in Britain one of the more recent examples of the growing power of the disabled people's movement in bringing about policy change was expressed when the former British Council of Disabled People (BCODP) (now the UK's Disabled People's Council) helped to bring about the introduction of the Disability Discrimination Act in 1995 by a Conservative government who were at the time very reluctant to adopt such an anti-discrimination piece of legislation (Barnes and Mercer, 2003; Oliver and Barnes, 2008). Notwithstanding the degree to which an understanding of the social construction of disability has helped bring about what are perceived to be 'positive' changes in the lives of disabled people, it nevertheless remains the case that many 'disabled people and their families remain among the most socially and economically disadvantaged citizens in Britain' (Crowther, 2007: 791) and elsewhere. It is also clear that the 'economic exclusion of disabled adults is playing a central role in driving child poverty, with one in three children in poverty having a disabled parent' (Crowther, 2007: 792). And at the time of writing, approximately 40 per cent of those who are unemployed in Britain are also disabled (Crowther, 2007). When set against these and other criteria, it becomes clear that insofar as the campaigning of disabled activists and organizations led by and for disabled people may have been successful in breaking down the social constraints on disabled people's lives, there remains some considerable way to go before the social divisions between disabled and non-disabled groups begin to be broken down even further.

The need for a new model of disability

As we explained earlier, explanations of disability have tended to fall into two dichotomous categories – medial or social – with the explanations underpinning the social model of disability being among the most widely accepted. Although there has been growing support for the social model of disability since the 1960s because it 'under-played the importance of impairment in disabled people's lives, in order to develop a strong argument about social structures and processes' (Shakespeare and Watson, 1997: 298), it has nevertheless been criticized by some within the disabled people's movement for failing to provide an understanding of disability which acknowledges the centrality of impairment and experience of disability to disabled people's lives. The perceived over-emphasis on social and environmental explanations of disability is, according to Shakespeare (1996), perhaps understandable and out of fear that an admission of impairment as a medical 'condition' or 'personal tragedy' provides further evidence for the view that disability can only be 'cured' through medical intervention. Regardless of the veracity of these claims, there have been calls by some within the disabled people's movement for a new theory of disability that is not grounded in assumptions about disabled people's lives by those who are non-disabled, but which is informed by disabled people's experiences of disability and recognizes the social and environmental constraints that help structure those experiences (Barnes, 1997; Crow, 1992; Hughes and Paterson, 1997). It is not possible, here, to consider in detail the complex theoretical debates which surround the adequacy of the social model of disability. That has been done elsewhere (e.g. Barnes and Mercer, 2003; Barnes et al., 1999; Hughes and Paterson, 1997; Shakespeare and Watson, 1997). Nevertheless, it is clear that whilst those who advocated the explanations which underpin the social model of disability never attempted to incorporate the individual experience of impairment and disability into their analyses, it could be argued that if we are to begin to explain disabled people's experiences in all areas of social life (including sport) then we need to recognize the many complex interdependencies that exist between their experience of impairment *and* disability. In other words, since disability and impairment are experienced differentially as *interdependent aspects of disabled people's lives* that continuously interplay with each other they cannot, and should not, be easily separated and there is therefore a need to view the lives of disabled people 'in the round'.

Disability as a 'component of health'

In response to the widespread criticism particularly by disabled people and their organizations, as well as academics and medical professionals, that its approach to defining disability ignored the social constraints which underpinned disabled people's experiences, the WHO introduced a revised ICIDH (ICIDH-2) in 2000 (WHO, 2001). The ICIDH-2 took account of the criticisms of the earlier defini-tion of disability and attempted to incorporate both the medical and social models of disability by distinguishing between those limitations to social life that are best dealt with by medical intervention and those that are the cause and subject of social and environmental constraints on disability. In this regard, the ICIDH-2 adopts what has been described as a new 'biopsychosocial' approach to understanding dis-ability. This approach is said to recognize that each aspect of disablement can be explained through a complex interplay of different dimensions – which it terms 'impairments', 'activity limitations' and 'participation restrictions' – of an individ-ual's experience of impairment and their social and physical contexts.

Despite the apparent recognition of the complexities involved in explaining adequately disabled people's experiences of disability and the relationship between disability and impairment, this has not resulted in a substantial shift away – both in policy and practical terms – from the dominant medical understanding of disabil-ity. Indeed, as Barnes and Mercer (2003: 15) have observed:

> There is ample evidence internationally of the continued acceptance of the individual model of disability in policy circles . . . the 'functional limitations' approach is widely incorporated within anti-discrimination legislation (as in the USA and Britain), and it continues to inform surveys of the prevalence of 'disability' within the European Union.

In the second part of this chapter we shall attempt, therefore, to demonstrate how, despite the significant advances that have accompanied the growing recognition of the significance of social constraints to an understanding of disability and reali-ties of disabled people's lives, the ways in which disability and impairment have traditionally been conceptualized in medical terms has tended to characterize much social and welfare policy directed towards disabled people.

The emergence and development of disability policy

Elsewhere in this book we shall demonstrate that whilst disability sport policy has, in many respects, been a marginal policy issue and priority for the British gov-ernment (see Chapters 2 to 5), it is nevertheless clear that broader changes in disability policy and the increasing politicization of the disabled people's move-ment have both helped influence the context within which policies and practices relating to disability sport have emerged and developed. It is important, therefore, to have some appreciation of the wider political and policy context of disability since this provides an important backdrop for understanding aspects not only of disability sport policy, but also of disabled people's experiences of sport and physical activity more broadly.

Pre-1940

As indicated in Table 1.1 which provides a summary of the key landmarks in the early history (pre-1940) of disability policy, the English Poor Law Act passed in 1601 signalled 'the first official recognition of the need for state intervention in the lives of people with perceived impairments' (Barnes, 1997: 17). At this time disabled people were considered to be among the 'deserving poor' and entitled to public assistance, but by the nineteenth century the British government became increasingly concerned that defining poverty as the 'inadequacy or unwillingness to work' (Barnes *et al.*, 1999: 125) encouraged a dependency on public resources. This concern prompted the passage of the Poor Law Amendment Act in 1834 which was introduced to alleviate the financial burden that the government experienced following the introduction of the 1601 Act. The 1834 Act stressed how public welfare assistance led to dependence on the employed taxpayer and emphasized the need for families to take more responsibility for the care of disabled people. As a consequence of the 1834 Act, support from the government was restricted to those who would otherwise have fallen into abject poverty. Those disabled people – of which there were large numbers – that could not, or would not, be cared for by the family were typically located in dedicated institutions. First, asylums for the mentally ill were built, followed by educational establishments for the intellectually impaired, and then for the blind and the deaf. The physical relocation of disabled people away from their families and communities to these institutions, together with a range of professional interventions, were supposedly aimed to help patients cope with normal life and be independent enough not to burden the rest of society (Barnes *et al.*, 1999).

Although it could be argued that the most significant developments in the history of disability policy and, in particular, the political movement of disabled people took place during the 1980s, the origins of these shifts lay in the political activities and campaigning of organizations for the deaf and blind in the late 1800s and early 1900s. In the 1920s, for example, the National League of the Blind and Disabled organized marches of blind workers in Britain and campaigned against charities for blind people, which were perceived as being staffed by 'inefficient, self serving bureaucrats rather than blind people themselves' (Barnes *et al.*, 1999: 159). The campaigns by the National League of the Blind and Disabled, in close co-operation with the Trades Union Congress, led to the Blind Workers Act in 1920. The Blind Workers Act – which was the forerunner of future welfare policies such as the Disabled Persons Act of 1944 – gave financial assistance to, and provided better working conditions for, many blind people who worked in poorly paid industrial environments (Campbell and Oliver, 1996).

Table 1.1 Landmarks in disability policy: pre-1940

Date	Landmark	Description
1601	English Poor Law Act	First intervention of government in the lives of disabled people. Disabled people seen as part of the 'deserving poor' and provided with assistance.
1834	Poor Law Amendment Act	Disabled people seen as a drain on public resources. The Act encouraged families to take more responsibility for their welfare. Only when necessary were disabled people cared for in segregated institutions.
1920	Blind Workers Act	Provided financial assistance for unemployed blind people and blind people in low paid employment. The Act followed a march by blind workers in London protesting against low wages and poor working conditions.

The 1944 Disabled Persons (Employment) Act

As we noted earlier, the origins of the political movement of disabled people lay in their rejection of the institutional care arrangements within the welfare service infrastructure established during the post-1945 period. One example of the grow-ing politicization of the disabled people's movement at this time was expressed in the lobbying activities of the National League of the Blind and Disabled who cam-paigned for the development of policies that were designed to facilitate the access of disabled people to employment and education (see Table 1.2). Of particular sig-nificance in this regard was the Disabled Persons Act that was passed in 1944 to provide 'reasonable access' to employment for disabled people. The Act encour-aged the employment of disabled people by setting up 'a disabled persons' employ-ment register, a nationwide disablement resettlement scheme, a specialized employment placement service and a duty on employers of twenty or more work-ers to employ a 3 per cent quota of registered disabled people' (Barnes *et al.*, 1999: 113). The Disabled Persons Act was expressive of the largely medical ideology of disability referred to earlier which places responsibility for disability on the indi-vidual, and which characterized disabled people as 'useless' workers who should be grateful recipients of government intervention. It is perhaps unsurprising, there-fore, that 'despite all this activity, through the post 1945 period, wages in work-shops for the blind and other disabled workers remained disproportionately low' (Barnes *et al.*, 1999: 159).

The increasing intervention of government in encouraging the development of employment opportunities for disabled people also characterized the kinds of policy that came to be developed in education. The most notable example of education policy that was developed at this time was the introduction of the 1944 Education Act which encouraged local authorities to place disabled children in mainstream (or regular) schools rather than educate them in separate segregated settings. However, as we explain in more detail in Chapter 5, it was not until the 1978 Warnock Report and 1981 Education Act that the political and policy emphasis on

Table 1.2 Landmarks in disability policy: 1944–1969

Date	Landmark	Description
1944	Disabled Persons (Employment) Act	Introduced a series of measures to encourage (but not enforce) mainstream organizations to employ disabled people.
1944	Education Act	Signalled a policy shift toward the education of disabled people in mainstream schools. The Act had limited impact.
1948	Health Services Act and National Assistance Act	Established hospitals and institutions for disabled people that were segregated from mainstream society.

educating young disabled people alongside their non-disabled peers in mainstream schools began to impact on the practice and operations of those schools.

Prior to the beginning of the Second World War, an interdepartmental committee was established by William Beveridge to develop policy that was designed to provide support for those with illness and impairment, which laid the foundations for the development of welfare policy for the rest of the century. The post-war welfare state was developed to coordinate and provide education and health care for both the employed and unemployed, to provide family and childcare support, and to subsidize housing accommodation. The National Health Services Act and the National Assistance Act, both of which were passed in 1948, established a range of care-based hospitals that were intended to provide suitable medical treatment for disabled people by placing them in institutions that were isolated from ordinary hospitals. In this regard, the National Health Services Act and the National Assistance Act enshrined the ideology of caring and furthered disabled people's enforced dependency on others and especially the state. Such was the strength of this political and policy commitment, by the 1960s disabled people were either confined to segregated hospitals where their needs were decided and provided for by medical staff, or they lived in mainstream communities and were expected to live within the constraints of the limited social, medical and economic support that was available.

Much of the legislation that was passed during the 1944–1969 period was instrumental in establishing polices and practices that segregated disabled people and had a significant influence on the ways in which disability sport subsequently emerged and developed (see Chapter 2). It is also the case that, as we shall see next, this prevailing policy direction which encouraged disabled people's dependency on the state and other institutions was further strengthened from the 1970s.

The 1970 Chronically Sick and Disabled Persons Act: a backwards step?

As Barnes and Mercer (1995) have noted, the Conservative government elected in 1970 introduced policies which increased disabled people's dependence on the welfare state and, in that respect, many of their policy priorities were characterized by a strong degree of continuity with those of previous governments (see Table 1.3). For example, in a not dissimilar way to the Acts of 1948, the Chronically Sick and Disabled Persons Act, which was introduced in 1970, was intended to support those who could not work due to their impairment. However, those that were deemed to be 'unfit for work' were provided with state benefits and, as a consequence, became even more reliant on welfare services. According to Swain *et al.* (1993) this policy commitment amounted to a backward step for disabled people, for it was believed that it simply perpetuated disabled people's status as dependent recipients of public services and charity.

At the same time that the Chronically Sick and Disabled Persons Act was passed, disabled people were beginning to challenge more effectively and forcefully the

Table 1.3 Landmarks in disability policy: 1970–1989

Date	Landmark	Description
1970	Chronically Sick and Disabled Persons Act	Encouraged those responsible for public buildings to make reasonable adjustments to enable access by disabled people.
1972	Union of the Physically Impaired Against Segregation formed	Signalled disabled people's discontent with the medical definition of disability and the resulting treatment of disabled people.
1975	United Nations Declaration of the Rights of Disabled Persons	Encouraged disabled people's involvement in policies meant to serve them.
1976	Union of the Physically Impaired Against Segregation publish 'Fundamental Principles of Disability'	Provided the first conceptual distinction between impairment and disability which became a central tenet of the social model of disability.
1978	Report of the Committee of Enquiry into the Education of Handicapped Children and Young People (Warnock Report)	Abolished the categorization of children with 'handicaps' and shifted toward the concept of special educational needs (SEN). Also encouraged the integration of children with SEN into mainstream schools.
1981	Disabled Peoples' International formed	An international umbrella organization established and controlled by disabled people to support a network of national organizations for, and controlled by, disabled people.
1981	United Nations' International Year of Disabled People	Focused attention on highlighting awareness of disabled people's basic human rights.
1981	The British Council of Disabled People formed	A lobbying organization established to provide a coordinated campaign for the rights of disabled people.
1986	Disabled Persons (Services, Representation and Consultation) Act	Emphasized the need to involve disabled people in decisions that affect their lives. It was criticized for being tokenistic.

taken for granted assumptions that were held by those outside the disabled people's movement about disability and the definitions of citizenship that led to their enforced dependency on the state (Barnes *et al.*, 1999). In 1972 disabled people who were said to be discontent with their treatment formed the Union of the Physically Impaired Against Segregation (UPIAS), which published *Fundamentals of Disability* in 1976 and became an extremely influential body in advancing politically the interests of disabled people. The UPIAS believed that disabled people were better placed than professionals to solve the problems that disabled people faced. As we noted earlier, whilst the initial political campaigns led by disabled people focused on the improvement of welfare services and provisions, the work of the UPIAS helped shift the emphasis towards lobbying government and others about the need to enhance the independence of disabled people by changing the attitudes of people in the wider society towards disabled people (Barnes, 1997; Campbell and Oliver, 1996; Swain *et al.*, 1993). In this regard, the policy adopted by the UPIAS was based upon the approaches of the more radical advocacy groups operating in the United States at the same time. In the 1960s, the Independent Living Movement in the United States, for example, sought to achieve greater independence for disabled people, which they measured by the opportunities available for disabled people to make economic and personal decisions rather than the number or range of functional tasks that they could perform. Central to this view of independence was the need to enable disabled people to obtain greater control and running of organizations that were meant to serve them (Oliver, 1990).

This fight for 'rights not care' took place within the context of increasing concern over international human rights and was furthered by the United Nations Declaration of the Rights of Disabled Persons in 1975. The Declaration encouraged the involvement of disabled people in the development of policies that were meant to serve them (Campbell and Oliver, 1996). Whilst prior to the 1975 Declaration there were few organizations that represented and were ran by disabled people, by the end of the 1980s there had been a significant growth in organizations and policies aimed at increasing disabled people's independence. This growth of organizations occurred, or so it is alleged, despite the general disinterest and lack of enthusiasm among government and policy-makers in the newly emerging disabled people's movement (Campbell and Oliver, 1996).

The concern with achieving greater independence and increasing the number and prominence of disabled people in positions of power in lobbying organizations meant to serve them was given added momentum by the formation of Disabled Peoples' International (DPI). DPI was formed in 1981 after delegates at the 1980 World Congress of Rehabilitation International refused to accept a motion to have at least 50 per cent of its executive board represented by disabled people (Barnes and Mercer, 1995). DPI believed that disabled people should be central to the policy-making process within organizations that were supposed to represent and serve disabled people. Over 400 delegates representing 53 countries attended the first World Congress of DPI which is said to have emphasized the significant contribution that disabled people can make to the political policy-making process (Barnes *et al.*, 1999). However, whilst DPI assumed a leadership role in the disabled people's movement, and was granted consultative status with international organizations such as the United Nations, its success in influencing government policy has been limited not least because of the relational impediments which it experienced in trying to develop an effective international organization which was intended to lobby governments on disability rights in a range of countries.

In Britain, one consequence of the impact of the DPI was the formation of the British Council of Disabled People (BCODP) in 1981 which coincided with the International Year of Disabled People. The official activities that took place during the International Year of Disabled People were, however, a source of further irritation to the disability activists since the organizations who were involved were not representative of, or ran by, disabled people (Swain et al., 1993). Accordingly, the dissatisfaction which came to be expressed by groups of disabled activists in Britain encouraged them to set up a national body of organizations in 1981 – the BCODP – run for and by disabled people. The BCODP represented the diverse and increasing number of local self-help and lobbying organizations of disabled people, all of which expected the BCODP to lobby on behalf of their, often tightly defined, interests. Indeed, during the 1980s the BCODP began a series of campaigns that were designed to lobby the government for better transport, benefits and rights and protested against what they believed to be the apparent patronizing approach to disability rights that were said to be perpetuated by high-profile charities such as Children in Need.

The activities of the BCODP were also intended as a response to the prevailing tendency for disabled people's lives to be dominated by non-disabled people, for disabled people to be under-represented in positions of authority, and to have little control over the organizations meant to serve them (Drake, 1994, 1996; Ducket, 1998). In recognition of the greater independence demanded by disabled people, the Disabled Persons Act of 1986 stressed the rights of disabled people to have greater responsibility for their own lives. A central tenet of the Act was greater user input to service delivery where local authorities were required to include representatives of user led organizations in the planning and formation of locally run services for disabled people. Despite this formally stated purpose of the Disabled Persons Act, Barnes et al. (1999: 144) have claimed that there was 'little consultation with user groups' and that, in reality, non-disabled professionals continued to exert a greater degree of influence over disabled people's lives (Barnes et al., 1999; Swain et al., 1993). These criticisms aside, it was nevertheless recognized that the Disabled Persons Act of 1986, together with the Chronically Sick and Disabled Persons Act of 1970 and the appointment in 1975 of a Minister for the Disabled, 'heralded a move toward the treatment of disability as a discrete policy issue rather than as a mere adjunct to other policy issues' (Oliver, 1990: 80).

The gradual interest in disability as a policy issue for government continued to develop in the 1990s. In 1991, for example, the BCODP sponsored the disability activist and university lecturer, Professor Colin Barnes, to write a report entitled *Disabled People in Britain and Discrimination*, which was considered as a comprehensive account of the discrimination faced by disabled people in Britain.

Following its publication, Nick Scott, then Minister for Disabled People, acknowledged for the first time the widespread discrimination against disabled people (Barnes *et al.*, 1999) and by the mid-1990s the Conservative government had, at least in part, accepted the claim that disabled people were being discriminated against in many aspects of their lives and acknowledged the campaigning objectives of disabled people within organizations such as the BCODP. As we noted earlier, one outcome of the more effective campaigning of disabled activities and organizations led by disabled people was the introduction of the Disability Discrimination Act (DDA).

The 1995 Disability Discrimination Act

In 1994 the Conservative government produced a draft DDA that was passed in 1995, and came into force in July 1996, to tackle the discrimination faced by disabled people in society (see Table 1.4). The DDA defines discrimination as:

> treating someone less favourably than someone else, for a reason related to the disabled person's disability – than it treats (or would treat) others to whom that reason does not (or would not) apply; and cannot show that the treatment is justified. (HMSO,1995: s, 20(1), 2.5)

Table 1.4 Landmarks in disability policy: 1990–2001

Date	Landmark	Description
1990	Americans with Disabilities Act (ADA) passed	Aimed to integrate disabled people into mainstream society. Outlawed discrimination in employment, access, transport and local government. Notable success in improving access to buildings. This Act became a benchmark for British disability campaign groups such as BCODP.
1995	Disability Discrimination Act passed	DDA was passed after 15 previous attempts over 13 years to pass a private members bill. Aims for similar basic rights as the ADA but, unlike the ADA, there are no minimum standards and it is criticized by disability activists.
1996	Disability Rights Task Force formed	Conservative government formed the DRTF made up of existing organizations working on behalf of disabled people such as SCOPE and the RNID.
1999	Disability Rights Commission Act passed	The DRC was established under the Labour government to enforce the DDA. The DRC has a much closer relationship with the disability activists through organizations such as the BCODP.
2001	Special Educational Needs and Disability Act passed	An extension of the DDA (1995) to legislate against the discrimination of disabled people in the education sector.

The DDA focused on employment, the provision of goods, facilities and services and the management of land and property. It set out to protect anyone with 'a physical or mental impairment which has a substantial and long term adverse effect upon their ability to carry out normal day to day duties' (HMSO, 1995 organizations, 19(1), (a)5). The Act also stated that it was unlawful for a service provider to discriminate against a disabled person 'by refusing to provide (or deliberately not providing) any service which it provides (or is prepared to provide) to its members of the public' (HMSO, 1995 organizations, 19(1), (a)5). In addition, the Act stipulates that this includes those with sensory, physical and learning impairments but not mental illness, and that those already identified as being disabled under the earlier Disabled Persons Act of 1944 were treated as disabled until 1998 when further assessment took place.

Despite the introduction of the DDA, it was the focus of particular criticism from organizations representing disabled people for its failure to acknowledge a socially constructed approach to disability and the lack of responsibility it placed upon employers to address current inequities within the work place. That there were many areas of public service such as the police and universities that were exempt from the Act also drew particular criticism, as did the rather vague and ambiguous requirements the DDA placed on providers who were required to make 'reasonable adjustments' in their services for disabled people. What constituted 'reasonable adjustments' was especially unclear, and, as Barnes et al. (1999: 115) have noted, 'unlike the sex and race anti-discrimination legislation, discrimination [against disabled people] is only illegal if it is unreasonable'. Finally, although there were several identified weaknesses of the DDA it did represent an 'acknowledgement that disability is on the mainstream political agenda, and a public recognition that disability may be socially created, and not just a personal tragedy' (Walmsley, 1997: 64).

The 1997–2007 Disability Rights Commission and the Equality and Human Rights Commission: enforcing anti-discrimination

Under the Conservative Party the National Disability Council was established to oversee the implementation of the DDA, but following the election of the current Labour government in 1997 the Disability Rights Task Force (DRTF) was created to assess the adequacy of the various components of the Act. The DRTF was quickly renamed the National Disability Task Force and made up of Radar, the Royal National Institute for the Blind, the Royal National Institute for the Deaf, Mencap, MIND and SCOPE, all of whom are organizations 'for disabled people' insofar as they are not run by an elected executive board that is comprised by a majority of disabled people.

The Disability Rights Commission (DRC) was also established as a part of the Disability Rights Commission Act (1999) that was introduced two years after the Labour Party entered office. The DRC was an independent body with the statutory power to enforce the DDA and in May 2002 had 15 Commissioners, two-thirds of whom were disabled and a Secretary of State appointed chairman

(Bert Massie who served on both the National Disability Commission and the National Disability Rights Task Force). Although the DRC was an advisory body it was different from previous non-departmental public bodies with responsibility for disability policy because it had the right to conduct formal investigations, serve non-discrimination notices, act over persistent discrimination, and provide assistance to individuals who had been discriminated against.

One consequence of the activities of the DRC and disability lobbying groups was that that two changes were made to the initial DDA. First, the DRC issued a new Code of Practice which covers Part III of the DDA (Rights to Access – Good Facilities, Services and Premises) by providing further detail on how providers can meet the requirements of the Act. Second, although the education sector was originally omitted from the requirements of the DDA, from 2002, the education authorities and their establishments were required to ensure that disabled people are not discriminated against in their access to, and provision of, educational services. The education sector was brought further into the mainstream of disability policy through the enactment of the Special Education Needs and Disability Act (SENDA) which was passed in 2001 and which requires the education sector to comply with the demands of the DDA. As we explain in Chapter 5, the Act extends the earlier 1978 and 1981 Education Acts and the 1995 Code of Practice which simply encouraged schools and colleges to provide for disabled people in mainstream, rather than segregated, settings.

Following a series of other amendments since the original Act in 1995, an extended Disability Discrimination Act was passed in 2005, which, for example, made it unlawful for private clubs (such as golf clubs and tennis clubs with 25 or more members) to keep disabled people out, just because they have a disability, but in particular places greater emphasis on public bodies' (such as Sport England and local authorities) responsibility to promote equality of opportunity for disabled people. In this context, public organizations as well as those funded by public organizations, are encouraged to take positive steps towards promoting equality of opportunity for disabled people. Within sport this was expressed in the increasing requirement on governing bodies of sport and local authorities to improve disabled people's access to sport, in 2004 Sport England launched *The Equality Standard: A Framework for Sport* (see Chapters 3 and 4).

Following the passing of the DDA 2005 and the passage of SENDA into law, Barbara Roche (Cabinet Office Minister) indicated that a single body would replace the DRC and the other five similar equality-related commissions that currently exist. She suggested that it was not possible to address equality when 'dealing with six separate strands of discrimination including race, gender, sexual orientation, religion, age and disability' (Roche, 2002). While Bert Massie claimed that a single commission 'might work to the advantage of all and be a tremendous opportunity to tackle multi-discrimination' (Massie; cited in Roche, 2002), disabled rights campaigners such as the BCODP were concerned that that the loss of the DRC would impact negatively on their struggle for equality. Notwithstanding these concerns, the Equality and Human Rights Commission (EHRC) was launched in October 2007 to champion 'equality and human rights

Table 1.5 Landmarks in disability policy: 2002–2007

Date	Landmark	Description
2005	Disability Discrimination Act passed	Extended from the 1995 Act, DDA 2005 places greater responsibility on public organizations to provide the same level of service to disabled people as non-disabled people.
2005	Prime Minister's Strategy Unit Report published	'Improving the Life Chances of Disabled People' identified the lack of coordination between government departments on matters relating to disability policy.
2007	Launch of The Equality and Human Rights Commission (and closure of the Disability Rights Commission)	The EHRC was established to improve equality in relation to disability, race, age, sexual orientation, religion or belief as well as human rights.
2007	Establishment of the Office for Disability Issues	Working across government departments, the ODI works to keep disability high on the Equality and Human Rights Commission's agenda and achieve equal rights and choices for disabled people.

for all, working to eliminate discrimination, reduce inequality, protect human rights and to build good relations, ensuring that everyone has a fair chance to participate in society' (EHRC, 2008).

While recognizing the significant contribution of previous Commissions working toward equality (including the DRC, the Equal Opportunities Commission and the Commission for Racial Equality), the EHRC suggests that there is still much to be done, and continuing with the previous commission's work, has taken on responsibility to improve equality in relation to disability, race, age, sexual orientation, religion or belief as well as human rights. Given this broad remit, it is perhaps not surprising that organizations have been set up to support each identified 'issue' of equality. In 2007 – the same year that the EHRC was established – the Office for Disability Issues (ODI) was set up to 'ensure that disability is central to the new Equality and Human Rights Commission' (ODI, 2008). The inauguration of the ODI has also provided a response to the Prime Minister's Strategy Unit report *Improving the Life Chances of Disabled People*, which identified a lack of coordination between government departments in the development and implementation of policy relating to disabled people (Strategy Unit, 2005). In this regard, in partnership with the EHRC the ODI's mission is to support the government's commitment to achieve for disabled people 'the same opportunities and choices as non-disabled people and be respected and included as equal members of society' (Strategy Unit, 2005: 7). To achieve this, the ODI works with six key government departments, namely: the Department for Children, Schools and Families, Department of Health, Department for Business Enterprise and Regulatory Reform, Department for Transport,

Department for Work and Pensions and the Department for Communities and Local Government.

Summary

In this chapter we have sought to examine some of the major theoretical explanations of disability and the emergence and development of disability policy that provide an important backdrop to understanding some key aspects of the relationships between modern sport, disability and society that are considered in the remaining chapters of this book. In particular, the analysis presented in this chapter reveals that the history of disability and the disability policy process has at least four distinctive characteristics. First, there has been a shift from medical, individualized definitions and ideologies of disability to more socially constructed explanations of disability, which place more responsibility for disability on mainstream society. Second, and as a consequence of this shift in understanding, the emphasis in government policy has moved away from segregating disabled people towards encouraging them to take responsibility for their own care and welfare within mainstream society. Third, since the 1970s, disability policy has become increasingly politicized following the greater involvement of disabled activists and the growing – albeit limited – power of the disabled people's movement. Finally, following the lobbying activities of organizations such as BCODP and DRC, and currently implemented through the EHRC and the government departments with whom it works, disability policy is now higher on the government agenda and supported by enforceable legislation.

As will become clear, on the basis of the analysis presented in this chapter, of particular significance to any study of disability sport – in policy and practical terms – is the various competing definitions and explanations of disability that have emerged during the post-1945 period in particular. A related and equally significant point is that while, as we shall explain in later chapters, disability sport remains a largely marginal aspect of sport policy in Britain and elsewhere, broader changes in disability policy and the increasing politicization of the disabled people's movement have both helped influence – albeit indirectly – the context within which disability sport policy, and the way opportunities for disabled people to engage in sport, has emerged and developed. We shall begin to explore some of these issues in Chapter 2 which examines the emergence and development of disability sport.

Revision questions

1   To what extent do the medical and social models provide adequate explanations of disability?
2   To what extent is it possible to develop an explanation of disability that accounts both for disabled people's personal experiences of impairment and the wider social constraints on their lives?

3   Examine the impact that disabled activists and the disabled people's move-
    ment have had on the emergence and development of disability policy in
    your country.
4   What are the similarities and differences between disabled people's experi-
    ences of impairment and disability?
5   How does the analysis presented in this chapter begin to help you make
    sense of the complex relationships between modern sport, disability and
    society?

Key readings

Barnes, C. and Mercer, G. (2003) *Disability*, Cambridge: Policy Press.
Barnes, C., Mercer, G. and Shakespeare, T. (1999) *Exploring Disability: A Sociological Introduction*, Cambridge: Policy Press.
Goffman, E. (1961) *Asylums: Essays on the Social Situation of Mental Patients and Other Inmates*, Now York: Doubleday.
HMSO (2005) *Disability Discrimination Act*, London: HMSO.
Oliver, M. (1996) *Understanding Disability: From Theory to Practice*, London: Macmillan.

Recommended websites

Equality and Human Rights Commission
www.equalityhumanrights.com

Office for Disability Issues
www.officefordisability.gov.uk

World Health Organization's Disability and Rehabilitation Team
www.who.int/disabilities/en

2 The emergence and development of disability sport

Objectives

This chapter will:

- examine the emergence and development of disability sport;
- discuss some of the major changes to the organization and administration of disability sport; and
- examine the need for, and the role of, the English Federation of Disability Sport.

Introduction

In Chapter 1 we explored some of the key theories and concepts that provide an important backcloth for understanding some of the complex relationships between modern sport, disability and other aspects of society. By drawing on these theories and concepts, the purpose of this chapter is to examine the emergence and development of disability sport which, as we shall explain, is a process the roots of which can be traced back to Britain, specifically England, during the 1940s. In doing so, we shall draw on data generated from interviews with several key administrators who have played an important role in the emergence and development of disability sport in England. We also draw on data derived from documentary analyses of government reports, conference summaries and the annual reports of key organizations in the hope of providing an account of the emergence and development of disability sport in England that has a degree of adequacy.

Before doing so however, it is important to note that whilst disabled people have always engaged in a variety of sports and physical activities with, alongside or separate from non-disabled people, sports clubs for deaf people are widely acknowledged to be the first formally known contexts in which modern forms of 'disability sport' took place. For example, following a series of organized sports events and activities for deaf people held in Berlin in 1888, the first World Games for the Deaf were held in 1924 which preceded the establishment, in 1930, of the British Deaf Sports Council (BDSC). The BDSC was originally founded to provide regional and national competitive sports events for deaf people and has since continued to develop interclub sporting competition for deaf people and promoting deaf sport within the world of disability sport. Although deaf people were one of the first impairment groups to have their own sports organization in England, deaf sport has, to some extent, remained peripheral to and relatively independent of developments within both mainstream sport and disability sport (see, for example, DePauw and Gavron, 2005). But let us now examine aspects of the early emergence and development of organizations concerned with the provision of opportunities for disabled people to participate in sport and physical activity.

The origins and early development of disability sport in England

The first formally recognized sports competition specifically for disabled people (with physical impairments) and particularly those with spinal cord injury (SCI) and the war injured, was organized by Sir Ludwig Guttmann, a neurosurgeon at Stoke Mandeville Hospital in England, during the 1940s. Guttmann's initial rationale for encouraging disabled people's participation in sport and physical activity was as a means of physical and psychological therapy. However, he gradually began to encourage those who had been injured during the Second World War to engage in sport and physical activity since he regarded both as important vehicles by which it was possible to promote the rehabilitation of physically disabled people back into civilian life. In this context, Guttmann (1976: 12–13) believed that sport was

> invaluable in restoring the disabled persons' physical fitness i.e.: his (sic) strength, coordination, speed and endurance . . . restoring that passion for playful activity and the desire to experience joy and pleasure in life . . . promoting that psychological equilibrium which enables the disabled to come to terms with his physical defect, to develop activity of mind, self confidence, self dignity, self discipline, competitive spirit, and comradeship, mental attitudes . . . to facilitate and accelerate his social re-integration and integration.

It was on the basis of these ideas about the potential 'value' of sport and physical activities that Guttmann sought to develop opportunities for disabled people to participate in more organized and competitive sports, not only at the recreational level but, as we explain in Chapter 6, at the elite levels of sport too. Indeed, among the many significant contributions made by Guttmann in this regard was the invitation he gave to sports clubs and hospitals to attend Stoke Mandeville – to coincide with the opening of the Olympic Games being held in London – on 28 July 1948 where he organized what came to be known as the Stoke Mandeville Games: the first organized sports competition for wheelchair athletes in England. In light of the perceived success of the Games, the British Paraplegic Sports Society (BPSS) – which later became the British Wheelchair Sports Foundation – was established to provide regular training and competitive opportunities for disabled people (especially wheelchair users and those with SCI) to participate in sport and physical activities. It is not altogether surprising, therefore, that given the role which he played in establishing the Games and the International Stoke Mandeville Games Federation (ISMGF) to organize them, Guttmann has since come to be widely recognized by many within the disability sport movement as playing an instrumental role in the early development of disability sport in England and elsewhere.

Given the rather limited scope of the BPSS, however, the British Sports Association for the Disabled (BSAD) was formed to facilitate the development of sporting opportunities for those disabled people with impairments other than those catered for by the BPSS. As we shall see next, the inauguration of the BSAD came to play a crucial role in the emergence and development of disability sport.

The creation of the British Sports Association for the Disabled

The BSAD was inaugurated on 15 February 1961 by Guttmann at Stoke Mandeville and was promoted as the recognized national body with responsibility for providing, developing and coordinating sport and recreation opportunities for disabled people. As part of this remit BSAD developed and organized sports events (e.g. junior athletic competitions and swimming galas) and served as a governing body on behalf of disability sport organizations (Minister for Sport's Review Group, 1989). In this capacity, BSAD immediately encouraged organizations such as the Central Council of Physical Recreation (CCPR) and the national governing bodies (NGBs) of sport to join its membership and become 'involved in the development and coordination of sport for people with disabilities' (BSAD 1989: 13). It is important to note, however, as Bernard Atha (President of the English Federation of Disability Sport, interview) and Sir Philip Craven (President of the International Paralympic Committee and previous Chairman of the International Wheelchair Basketball Federation) explained during interviews with the authors, BSAD was created by Guttmann primarily to meet the needs of athletes with SCI, for he is alleged to have never felt any great affection for athletes with other kinds of impairments. Nor, for that matter, was Guttmann alleged to have much inclination to open the doors of the BPSS or the BSAD to those other groups of athletes. Indeed, according to Atha, 'although Guttmann was a most remarkable pioneer he was a single minded autocrat and maverick, whose interest was limited to those with spinal cord injury and he would not entertain the involvement of other disabilities which I, as Vice-Chairman of the Sports Council, wished him to do' (interview).

Despite Guttmann's apparent ambivalence towards those with impairments other than SCI, the remit of the BSAD – which was supported by the Sports Council – was nevertheless to act as both a provider of opportunities, as well as a coordinating 'umbrella' agency for all aspects of sport and recreation, for disabled people with all types of impairment. In this regard, during the immediate years since it was established BSAD developed a network of clubs, regional associations with full-time staff to support a regional and national events programme, together with a wide range of training and development initiatives to support local authorities,

national governing bodies and schools. Despite the criticisms from senior administrators that we share in the sections that follow, BSAD's contribution to the
development and delivery of opportunities in sport for disabled people in England,
was widely recognized as the most significant and has never been equalled by
another organization.

By the late 1980s, the activities of BSAD were increasingly recognized as having
a significant influence on the development of disability sport not only in England,
but elsewhere in Britain too. It was also perceived to have been a successful
provider and coordinator of a regional club network and comprehensive national
events programme catering for athletes with a range of physical and sensory
impairment. Simultaneously, however, these largely positive views of BSAD
which prevailed in the late 1980s were accompanied by a series of criticisms of its
activities that, in many respects, were expressions of the on-going conflicts and
tensions between those involved in BSAD and other organizations involved in the
emerging disability sport movement. These criticisms revolved, for the most part,
around the dual roles that BSAD was expected to fulfil and were not entirely
unsurprising since its policies were determined by a board of trustees who held
rather different sets of ambitions for, and expectations of, BSAD. In 1982, for
example, the BSAD board had representatives from seven National Disability
Sport Organizations (NDSOs) and from 10 BSAD regions. Consequently, half of
the board was made up of regional BSAD representatives who were mainly concerned with protecting the interests of its members, whilst the other half were representatives from other disability sport organizations (mainly NDSOs) who sought
to use BSAD for coordinating purposes, and, in particular, to access Sports Council
funds. The dual responsibility for membership (through BSAD's network of clubs)
and national coordination (acting as an umbrella over all the NDSOs) had perhaps
been over-ambitious and misguided. This dual role of serving a membership of disabled people while, at the same time, acting as a development agency was, with the
benefit of hindsight, perhaps untenable and doomed to fail from the outset. It is
important to note, however, that BSAD could not and did not claim exclusive
responsibility for meeting the sporting needs of all disability groups. Indeed, it
could never adequately represent all their interests, but nor could it ignore that
responsibility and invest its limited resources exclusively in its membership services. Nevertheless, BSAD did come to be perceived by some within the world of
disability sport such as Bernard Atha, Derek Casey (ex-Chief Executive of the
Sports Council) and Tim Marshall (Member of the Sports Council) as failing to
coordinate adequately the development of sport for disabled people. This perceived failure became more pronounced as more disability specific organizations
were established and began to impose higher expectations for policy action and
lobbying on BSAD. According to Marshall, 'BSAD's dual role, as a membership
and development agency, may have prevented it taking on a wider developmental
role embracing the needs of CPs, visually impaired people (and others)' (Marshall,
interview).

It was partly as a consequence of the perceived inadequacy of the activities of
BSAD, together with a growing interest in sport among those with non-spinal

cord-related impairments, that numerous sports organizations were established with a specific remit to improve the range and quality of opportunities for disabled people. Some of these disability sport organizations became – and some still are – providers for, and lobbyists on behalf of, disabled people with particular forms of physical, sensory and learning impairment. Cerebral Palsy Sport (CP Sport), for example, was formed in 1968 as a part of the Spastics Society (now SCOPE) to provide opportunities for athletes with cerebral palsy to compete in regional and national competitions (CP Sport, 2003; Minister for Sport's Review Group, 1989). CP Sport was a founder member of the British Paralympic Association and is also a member of Cerebral Palsy International Sport and Recreation Association (CP-ISRA), the international sports organization for people with cerebral palsy that, as we explain in Chapter 6, was a founder member of the International Paralympic Committee.

Further concern about the rather narrow focus of the roles and responsibilities of BSAD also prompted the establishment of other organizations who wished to advance the interests of other disabled people. British Blind Sport (BBS), for example, was one such organization that was established in 1976 'by visually impaired people to enable them to have control of their various sports' (BBS, 2003), and to improve the opportunities for blind athletes to participate in sport and physical activities at recreational and national levels. Moreover, as we explain in Chapter 6, the sparse representation of visually impaired athletes in international disability sport meant that BBS was also developed with the intention of supporting and enhancing the international sports infrastructure for blind athletes. As Marshall has noted, it is perhaps unsurprising that as organizations such as CP-ISRA and the International Blind Sports Association (IBSA) were beginning to be established on the international scale in the late 1970s and early 1980s, athletes and other people with cerebral palsy and visual impairments began to 'create their own organization nationally . . . in order to "map" themselves directly onto/into the international level for their disability' (Marshall, interview). Thus, regardless of whatever BSAD did, or was able to do, for those athletes, the emergence of separate organizations with responsibility for representing the interests of specific impairment groups was perhaps understandable given the diversity of the activities of BSAD.

Another NDSO to emerge during the same period was the British Amputee Sports Association (BASA) which, in 1978, was formed to provide elite sporting events for amputees. In 1990, BASA merged with the British Les Autres Sports Association (BLASA) to form the British Amputee and Les Autres Sports Association (BALASA) to support – at national level – those disabled athletes the needs of whom were not, it was believed, accounted for adequately by BSAD or any other NDSO. In 1980, the United Kingdom Sports Association for People with Mental Handicap (UKSAMPH) was formed to specifically develop sport for people with learning impairments and, similarly, but perhaps not as thoroughly as BSAD did for those with SCI, supported a network of 10 regional English Associations and three home counties associations.

The proliferation of disability sport organizations did not go unnoticed by the Sports Council. In this regard, following his move from Scotland to become Chief

Executive of the Sports Council in England, Derek Casey expressed his surprised at how disparate the different disability sport organizations (DSOs) in England were when he found that, in contrast to his experience of the Scottish Sports Association for the Disabled, there was a clear and distinct lack of consensus among the organizations involved (Casey, interview). He also argued that the coordination of DSOs' activities and priorities were at best negligible, and other DSOs were particularly critical of BSAD. According to Casey, BSAD's financial problems, its weaknesses in some of its regions and the increasing pressure to mainstream its services, contributed to the increasingly difficult position that officers of the BSAD found themselves in. The consequences of the mounting financial constraints under which BSAD were operating was made clear by its then Chief Executive, Dr Bob Price, who explained how 'BSAD had to compete for its funding with national governing bodies of sport' (BSAD, 1985: 19) and did not receive funding from the Sports Council that may have allowed them to play the role that the Sports Council expected of it. These pressures were further compounded by the diverse and complex regional structure of BSAD, for while some of its 10 regional offices employed full-time staff, others were solely reliant on voluntary support which meant that BSAD was unable to coordinate and develop its services effectively across all the regions in which it worked. It was also the case that despite the existence of a national executive and policy to promote its activities nationally, some regions had their own influential executive committees with priorities that were specific to the region within which they worked and that were not always consistent with the formally stated aims of BSAD on a national level. There developed, therefore, a wide variety in the way that BSAD's regions operated, and the quantity and type of work they undertook. Both of these things, it seemed, came to undermine the extent to which BSAD was able to achieve its desired objectives of promoting sport and physical activity for disabled people.

The Isle of Man Think Tank and the creation of BSAD 1987 (Ltd)

Despite its success in establishing a network of clubs and a comprehensive calendar of events, the perceived failure of BSAD to coordinate the activities of other DSOs and the dissatisfaction of DSOs with BSAD, together with the alliance that BSAD had developed with the Sports Council, prompted the Sports Council in 1985 to sponsor the Isle of Man Think Tank which was held on 11–14 December. Organized by the BSAD, and chaired by Bob Price, the purpose of the Think Tank was to 'investigate the current status and future needs of the provision of physical recreation and sport for disabled people in Britain' (BSAD, 1985: 2). The three day meeting focused on discussing why BSAD existed, how BSAD related to the Sports Council and how it related to those DSOs whom it served. The meeting was attended by 56 delegates from 38 organizations representing a broad range of disability sport and mainstream sport organizations. These included the Sports Council, the Central Council for Physical Recreation, the British Olympic Association, the National Coaching Foundation, the Amateur Swimming Association, the English Basketball Association, the British Amateur

Athletics Board, the Physical Education Association, the Disabled Living Foundation, the British Deaf Sports Council, the British Paraplegic Sports Society, the United Kingdom Sports Association for People with Mental Handicap, the British Amputee Sports Association and the Welsh and Scottish Sports Associations for the Disabled. Not surprisingly, Price highlighted the success which BSAD had experienced, for example, in the development of its regional club structure and national events programme as well the challenges faced by BSAD and its partners. In particular, he emphasized that, by 1982, BSAD had a membership of over 450 clubs serving an estimated 40,000 disabled sportspeople. However, the BSAD also had 'a responsibility to a much broader public than its constitutional membership' (BSAD, 1985: 11) which included in its membership seven disability groups (the NDSOs) and 25 other national members, the interests and expectations of whom were somewhat different from those of BSAD. Indeed, it was agreed by delegates at the Think Tank conference that 'it was not appropriate (indeed not possible) for BSAD to do either job effectively, let alone attempt to do both' (BSAD, 1985: 20) and it was concluded that 'many agencies expected too much of BSAD, forgetting that it is a membership agency of limited resources' (BSAD, 1985: 15). In a similar vein, it was also suggested by many of the delegates who represented the participating organizations that 'there had been widespread misconceptions about BSAD's role' at the time and that 'BSAD was not a national governing body and performed for disabled people many of the functions of the Sports Council, the CCPR and the NGBs' (BSAD, 1985: 20). The overwhelming recommendation that emerged from the Think Tank was that 'it would be in the best interests of all concerned for BSAD's development role (and its development staff) to be adopted by the Sports Council itself' (BSAD, 1985: 20) and that BSAD could concentrate on providing events and activities for its membership.

Notwithstanding the apparent political and policy commitment which the Think Tank was seen to provide those within the world of disability sport, the Sports Council largely ignored the recommendations that emerged from it and the initial enthusiasm of government towards disability sport as a policy priority to which it was supposedly committed was at best premature (BSAD, 1985). The reasons for this lack of political and policy response are not entirely clear or formally stated. On the one hand, the lack of any clearly articulated policy response was perhaps surprising given that the wider sport policy agenda being pursued by the Sports Council during the early 1980s was that of increasing involvement amongst key under-participating target groups of which disabled people, it could be suggested, constituted a central part (see Chapter 3). On the other hand, however, it is perhaps understandable since the priorities of the Conservative government focused to a large extent on dealing with the consequences of wider social problems, particularly those which emanated from the riots in some of Britain's inner-cities and football hooliganism (Houlihan and White, 2002). Whatever the underlying reasons were for the failure by the Sports Council to respond to the conclusions drawn by the delegates at the Think Tank conference, the Sports Council continued to fund BSAD – the reasons for which are, once again, unclear – and charged its Chief Executive, Bob Price, with setting up a working party to consider the establishment of a new coordinating umbrella body with responsibility for disability sport. Following a survey of *Sporting Opportunities for Disabled People in Britain* which he conducted in 1987, Price presented the Sports Council with two suggestions. The report suggested that either: (i) BSAD be divided into two bodies, a membership body and a development body; or (ii) BSAD create a new membership body which it would service and that the Sports Council adopt BSAD's development role (BSAD, 1987). The report concluded by offering BSAD's support to the Sports Council for whatever decision was made and hoped that one of the two suggestions would be deemed satisfactory. However, once again, the Sports Council neither accepted nor rejected either of the suggestions contained within the report and it appeared that, in much the same way as it ignored the recommendations of the Think Tank conference, the Sports Council were – to put it at its most charitable – paying lip service to disability sport as a key policy priority. In this regard, on the basis of its lack of formally stated policies and sustained activity regarding disability sport, it might reasonably be concluded that during the mid-1980s the Sports Council were failing to consider disability sport seriously at all and perhaps even saw it as beyond its remit.

Alongside its failure to impact on, in any significant way, the activities of the Sports Council or government more generally, by 1987 the ongoing dissatisfaction with BSAD's policy and practice led to a gradual decline in its membership and a weakening of the credibility of its claim to be the primary advocate on behalf of other DSOs, and its untenable role remained unresolved. In the face of increasing concern that came to be expressed by the DSOs, as well as the Sports Council, BSAD's Executive Board reconstituted itself as BSAD Ltd 1987 and relinquished the coordinating dimension of its role in order to focus on development and membership (BSAD, 1987). Consequently, all seven NDSOs withdrew their membership from BSAD and on 20 June 1987 BSAD became a company limited by guarantee, with the executive comprising of 10 elected delegates from its 10 English regions, representatives from each of the home countries, an elected chairman and two executive directors (BSAD, 1987).

The Minister for Sport's Review Group

As Table 2.1 indicates, by 1989 there was a vast array of disparate organizations concerned with the provision and development of sport for disabled people, seven of which became recognized as the NDSOs. BSAD and the UKSAMPH remained the main development agencies, while the British Paralympic Association (BPA) was the national link to international, European, world and Paralympic competition (see Chapter 6). It was also in 1989 when Colin Moynihan, then Minister for Sport, initiated a government review that was prompted, to a large degree, by the suspicion and discontent aimed at BSAD by the other NDSOs and mainstream governing bodies. The review lasted 18 months and included a survey of 133 governing bodies and 33 disability organizations, meetings with 47 organizations and a conference attended by 106 disabled athletes and 12 coaches. The Review

Table 2.1 Landmarks in disability sport policy: 1930–1989

Date	Landmark	Description
1930	British Deaf Sports Council formed	Providing competitive sporting opportunities for profoundly deaf people.
1948	British Paraplegic Sports Association formed (later renamed British Wheelchair Sports Foundation)	Established following the Stoke Mandeville Games in 1948 to cater for those with spinal injury.
1948	First international disability sport event	Sports clubs for disabled people and hospitals were invited to attend a series of competitive events at Stoke Mandeville.
1961	British Sports Association for the Disabled formed	Inaugurated by Sir Ludwig Guttmann at Stoke Mandeville, BSAD promoted itself as the recognized national body with responsibility for providing, developing and coordinating sport and recreation opportunities for disabled people.
1968	Cerebral Palsy Sport formed	CP Sport was formed as a part of the Spastics Society.
1976	British Blind Sport	British Blind Sport formed to improve the opportunities for blind athletes. BBS became the recognized governing and coordinating body of sport in the UK for blind and visually impaired people, providing opportunities at all levels.
1978	British Amputee Sports Association formed	BASA had a membership of 500 amputees in 1987/88 in the UK, and focused on providing training weekends and competitive events.
1980	United Kingdom Sports Association for the People with Mental Handicap formed	Set up as a coordinating agency of organizations concerned with sport for people with a learning disability. Similar to BSAD, UKSAPMH, was part-funded by the Sports Council, providing training, events and development work.
1982	British Les Autres Sports Association formed	BLASA was formed to cater for all those athletes that were not catered for by the growing number of disability specific organizations.
1985	BSAD hosted the Isle of Man 'Think Tank' on behalf of the Sports Council	A 3 day conference funded by the Sports Council and organized by BSAD to investigate the current provision of physical recreation and sport for disabled people in Britain, and their future needs.
1987	Sports Council's *Everybody Active* project in Sunderland	The project investigated the physical education experiences and sporting opportunities of disabled young people. Results indicated massive structural inequality facing disabled people in sport.
1987	Creation of BSAD 1987 Ltd	BSAD reconstituted itself as BSAD 1987 and relinquished its coordinating role to concentrate on development and membership.
1989	Minister for Sport's Review Group publish *Building on Ability*	Colin Moynihan, then Conservative Minister for Sport, initiated a government review of disability sport.
1989	British Paralympic Association formed	BPA formed to coordinate national squads and events for elite level disability sport.

Group's report, entitled *Building on Ability*, recommended that 'all those involved in sports provision should ensure that a wide range of opportunities are available for disabled people so that they can choose when and how they wish to participate' (Minister for Sport's Review Group, 1989: 6). The report provided a comprehensive account of the activities of the providers of disability sport and other disability organizations, an analysis of the perceived weaknesses in the provision of sport for disabled people, and a series of recommendations for the Sports Council, health authorities, local authorities, DSOs, governing bodies and education and youth services. In particular, the report called on the Sports Council to 'ensure that the needs of disabled people are taken into account in all of its activities' (Minister for Sport's Review Group, 1989: 17) and that it should continue to provide 'financial support towards the costs and should seek to foster closer links between the disability sport organizations' (Minister for Sport's Review Group, 1989: 17).

Although the report acknowledged that there were problems concerning a general lack of awareness, understanding and knowledge of disability sport among mainstream providers of sport, some of its criticisms of the existing provision and structure of disability sport specifically related to the lack of coherence and coordination among disability sport organizations at a national level. In a summary of the activities of the NDSOs the report highlighted the important coordinating and development roles the UKSAPMH and BSAD were perceived to play and emphasized 'without reservation the major contribution BSAD has made to the development of sport for people with disabilities' (Minster for Sport's Review Group, 1989: 9). The report also stated, however, that it would be 'remiss not to report the less favourable perceptions of BSAD at a national level' (Minster for Sport's Review Group, 1989: 9) and, as we noted earlier, it was not surprising to find that the supposed 'wide and deep dissatisfaction with BSAD' (Minister for Sport's Review Group, 1989: 9) featured prominently in its report. Given this situation, the Review Group recommended that BSAD should continue to coordinate centrally the development work it undertook in the regions and should also 'address the reasons for the suspicions which exist about its performance at a national level' (Minister for Sport's Review Group, 1989: 9). An additional – and particularly significant – recommendation of the Review Group was that the various governing bodies of sport and other mainstream agencies should expect to provide disabled people with the same provision and opportunities available to non-disabled people to participate in sport and physical activity (see Chapters 3 and 4). This was the case since it was believed by members of the Review Group that segregated disability sport organizations did not have the requisite resources to do so adequately. Accordingly, the report stated that:

> Governing bodies should accept in principle that they will ultimately assume responsibility for disabled people in their sport and should set a timetable for achieving this. (Minister for Sport's Review Group, 1989: 21)

It could be argued that, until this point in the development of disability sport in England, the Minister for Sport's Review Group's report is perhaps the only official statement that begins to express the working party's view of the then Conservative government's preferred strategic policy direction for disability sport. While it may be regarded by some as one of the most comprehensive reviews of disability sport, Marshall (a member of the Minister's Review Group) claimed in an interview with the authors of this book that the report 'didn't really bite the bullet and go forwards' as many of the recommendations that emerged were not implemented, and, consequently, disability sport continued to lack the coordination that *Building on Ability* had originally called for.

Sports Council policy on sport for people with disabilities

As can be seen from our above analysis and Table 2.2, from the early 1990s the Sports Council came increasingly to play a central role in the disability sport policy process even if, as was the case on several occasions previously, it was reluctant to engage in the process to any significant degree beyond the grant aid provision it made available to DSOs. In 1993, however, the Sports Council published the policy statement *People with Disabilities and Sport: Policy and Current/Planned Action* in which it noted that the need for a strategic approach to the planning and development of sport was well established and that the mainstreaming of disability sport – including the mainstreaming of disabled people and disability sport events (see Chapter 4) – was among its key policy priorities (Sports Council, 1993a). In particular, the Sports Council expressed an alleged commitment to equity, which it defined as 'fairness in sport, equality of access, recognizing inequalities and taking steps to address them' (Sports Council, 1993a: 4). The Sports Council went on to claim that:

> This will require the providers of sport, as a matter of principle, to consult, represent, involve and employ people with disabilities. It is this principle of sports equity that the Sports Council is determined to promote both in its own work and that of its partners. (Sports Council, 1993a: 4)

The overarching aim of the policy was to 'ensure equality of opportunity for people with a disability to take part in sport and recreation at the level of their choice' (Sports Council, 1993a: 7) and seven policy objectives cited as being particularly crucial to the achievement of that aim. These were to:

1   raise the profile of people with disabilities within mainstream sport;
2   ensure that the needs of people with disabilities are taken into account in strategic planning for sport and recreation;
3   provide opportunities for people with disabilities to become actively involved and to reach their full potential at all levels of sport and recreation;
4   improve access to sport and recreation both in terms of facilities and in programme content;
5   encourage British involvement for and by people with disabilities in international sport;

6   make effective use of available resources through partnerships and seek additional finance; and

7   ensure that the structure of sport for people with disabilities is appropriate to demands and needs.

In addition to these seven objectives, the Sports Council recommended in the early 1990s that sport for disabled people was at a stage where 'having developed its own structures, it [the provision of disability sport] should move from a target approach to the mainstream' (Sports Council, 1993a: 5). In other words, echoing the recommendations to be found within the earlier publication, *Building on Ability*, the Sports Council proposed a gradual shift of responsibility for the

Table 2.2 Landmarks in disability sport policy: 1990–2008

Date	Landmark	Description
1990	British Wheelchair Sports Foundation (BWSF) formed	The British Paraplegic Sports Society changed its name to BWSF to extend its provision to all wheelchair users.
1990	British Les Autres and Amputee Sports Association (BALASA) formed	BALASA was formed from a merger of the British Amputee Sports Association and the British Les Autres Sports Association.
1993	Sports Council launch *People with Disabilities and Sport: Policy and Current/ Planned Action*	The policy aimed to ensure equality of opportunity for people with a disability and recommended that greater responsibility was placed on mainstream providers.
1994	Appointment of a National Governing Bodies Disabilities Project Officer	The post was jointly funded by BSAD and the United Kingdom Sports Association for People with a Learning Disability and the Sports Council.
1995	English Sports Association for People with a Learning Disability (ESAPLD) formed	In response to the Sports Councils restructuring, UKSAPMH reorganized itself into ESAPLD and the UKSA. ESAPLD focused on development work and UKSA on coordinating the work of the home countries and the links with international sports organizations.
1995	Sports Council host a *Clear Vision* conference	The first of the 'New Start' Conferences in which the Sports Council chaired a debate on the future of disability sport.
1996	National Disability Sport Conference	A further conference attended by DSOs.
1996	Sports Council's Disability Task Force established	As a result of the 1996 conference a Task Force was established to lead to the mainstreaming of disability sport in England by 2000.
1997	New Start Conference	In June 1997 the National Disability Sports Conference received the Task Force's recommendations and the results of the consultation exercise.
1997	Disability Sport England (DSE) launched	BSAD's name is changed to DSE and its activities focus on membership and events.

1998	The English Federation of Disability Sport formed	The EFDS was established by Sport England as the umbrella agency for the DSOs.
2000	The EFDS launches *Building a Fairer Sporting Society*	The EFDS states its mission to be the united voice of disability sport in England, working with mainstream and disability sports organizations and campaigning for increased choices for disabled people.
2001	Sport England launch Equity Guidelines	A series of guidelines and examples of good practice. Needs of disability sport now subsumed under wider inclusion agenda.
2003	UK Deaf Sport established	Replaces BDSC as governing body for deaf sport.
2004	The EFDS publishes its *Development Framework: Count Me In 2004–2008*	The EFDS renews its commitment to be the united voice of, and to support the mainstreaming of, disability sport.
2005	Disability Sport Events established	Disability Sport England changes name to Disability Sport Events and becomes the events section of the EFDS.
2007	The EFDS Board is reconfigured	The EFDS Board is reconfigured to include NDSOs (BBS, UK Deaf Sport, Wheelpower, Mencap Sport, BALASA), its 9 regional associations and key mainstream organizations such as Sports Coach UK and CCPR.

organization and provision of sport for disabled people away from the NDSOs toward the mainstream sport-specific NGBs and, in the process, highlighted those groups (e.g. NDSOs, facility managers and teachers) whom it considered were, and should be, involved in the policy network of disability sport. Although the Sports Council failed to define clearly the roles and responsibilities of those groups, the emphasis which it placed on mainstreaming and the expectation that NGBs would take on more responsibility for delivering disability sport provided clear evidence of the ways in which government, through the Sports Council, were beginning to adopt an increasingly interventionist approach towards establishing a stronger policy agenda for disability sport. The ways and extent to which mainstreaming – as an increasingly important policy priority – came to impact on the activities of NGBs of sport are examined in Chapter 4. It is worth noting, here, however, that notwithstanding the alleged policy commitment to the principle of mainstreaming, there remained a lack of will and resources among members of the Sports Council to implement the changes that mainstreaming disability sport required, largely because: (i) as an inequality issue in the late 1980s and early 1990s disability was not regarded as a more important policy issue compared to ethnicity and gender; (ii) there was little policy agreement and organizational cohesion among the myriad of DSOs, and, hence, the lobbying of these groups was limited, confused and as a result easily ignored; (iii) the DSOs remained particularly unenthusiastic and apprehensive about the mainstreaming of disability sport since it was perceived to pose a real threat to their activities; and (iv) interest in mainstreaming amongst many of the NGBs of sport was marginal at best.

The renewed interest in disability sport during the early 1990s may be interpreted as an attempt by members of the Sports Council to take more seriously its willingness to address the fragmentation and largely uncoordinated approach to the organization of disability sport, particularly in England. It is perhaps more reasonable to suggest, however, that in light of our foregoing analysis the policy it published in 1993 on sport for disabled people expressed the Sports Council's growing interest in issues of inclusion, equity and equality of opportunity more generally, rather than a particular concern with disability and disability sport per se. Indeed, even though the Sports Council were becoming increasingly involved – if not in a wholly committed way – in the disability sport policy agenda, it was BSAD who continued for the most part to 'provide, develop and coordinate sports and recreation opportunities for people with disability nationally, in partnership with other relevant agencies' (BSAD, 1995: 6) until the late 1990s.

The Sports Council review of disability sport: a new start?

In recognition of the on-going concerns surrounding the coordination and activities of the various DSOs, together with wider political concern about integration and inclusion (see Chapters 1 and 5), in 1995 the Sports Council convened the *Clear Vision* conference on 2–3 December to consider the future structure of sport for disabled people in England. Seventy delegates attended, representing the Sports Council, BSAD regions, and the DSOs. This signalled the start of a series of conferences (which became known as the *New Start* conferences) held by the Sports Council between 1995 and 1998. One of the guiding principles for *New Start* was to improve coordination between the myriad of organizations that claimed to have an interest in disability sport. As one officer of the English Federation of Disability Sport (EFDS) – which was established in 1998 and is to be examined in more detail later – stated, the *New Start* process was 'driven by Sports Council to sort out the mess within the organizational operation of disability sport' (Senior Administrator, interview).

Following the *Clear Vision* conference, the Sports Council convened a *National Disability Sport Conference* in March 1996, one result of which was the establishment of a Task Force to 'lead to the mainstreaming of disability sport in England by the year 2000' (Sports Council Disability Task Force, 1997: 2). The Sports Council's Disability Task Force included key representatives from the Sports Council, the NDSOs and NGBs of sport. The remit of the Task Force was to: (i) advise the Sports Council on matters relating to disability sport; and (ii) to consider and make recommendations as to the future of disability sport within England (Sports Council Disability Task Force, 1997: 9). Amongst other things, the Task Force prepared a series of recommendations the most notable of which was the alleged need for a revised disability sport structure in England, and that disability sport policy be determined by a National Coordinating Committee that could 'sieve for what are local concerns and what is of national significance' (Sports Council Disability Task Force, 1997: 7). The Task Force was, however, clear that the 'new structure should not simply add another tier' (Sports Council

Disability Task Force, 1997: 3) to the existing organizational structure of disability sport, but should safeguard existing work, promote a sport-specific approach, have direct responsibility for disability sport policy, and link local policies and needs with national plans and priorities. They recommended that the National Coordinating Committee be composed of three representatives from a Sports Assembly, two from the Regional Unions and representatives from all of the NDSOs. The Sports Assembly was intended to provide a forum for NGBs responsible for the sport-specific interest in disability sport and for the NDSOs with considerable 'expertise, contacts, networks of participant and resources' (Sports Council Disability Task Force, 1997: 7). The Sports Council sent out these proposed recommendations to, among others, NGBs of sport and NDSOs for wide consultation in preparation for a third conference.

In June 1997 this conference – the *National Disability Sports Conference* – was reconvened to receive the Task Force's recommendations and the results of the consultation exercise. At the Conference, Tim Marshall (as a member of the Task Force and Chair of the Conference) provided an overview of the work of the Disability Task Force, whilst Derek Casey provided the 'bigger picture' in English Sport, and Dermot Collins of the English Sports Council provided the results of the consultation exercise. Collins (1997: 1) suggested in the overall conference report that there was a 'unity of opinion' on the future of disability sport policy, which he suggested was a welcome contrast to earlier attempts to gather support for change. According to Collins (1997: 1) 'the most important outcome of the Conference was the clear mandate received from delegates to proceed with the implementations of the Task Force's recommendations'. According to the Sports Council's report of the 1997 conference, the implications of the Task Force's recommendations had three aspects: (i) the development of Regional forums; (ii) the establishment of a National Development Agency (in essence, a rebranding of the Task Force's National Coordinating Committee); and (iii) the integration of disabled people into the mainstream of English sport (Collins, 1997: 2). In this regard, the Sports Council claimed that a new organization needed to be established to implement these recommendations. The chosen organization – which marginalized still further the activities of the BSAD – became known as the EFDS.

Establishing the English Federation of Disability Sport: conflict, consensus and coercion

The extent to which those involved in the *New Start* process described above agreed with the decision to establish the EFDS is rather contested and subject to much debate. There were three conferences, the first two of which were acrimonious due to the somewhat divergent self-interests and aspirations of the senior officers in attendance but the third, at the King's Fund Centre in London, coordinated by Collins and Casey was described by some as 'staggering . . . totally different . . . there was cooperativeness, and a feeling that "we are all in this together"' (Marshall, interview). Marshall, for example, suggested that 'people at the *New Start* conferences wanted an umbrella organization' to coordinate the activities of all the DSOs, but that clearly 'BSAD was not perceived as being capable of fulfilling that role' (Marshall, interview). Collins (1997: 3) also claimed that 'it marked the first occasion on which a representative national consensus on the future structure and role of disability sport can be seen to have been achieved'. He also claimed that the majority of the participants at the meeting agreed that a new umbrella organization with responsibility for disability sport in England was required to help provide a more secure basis on which to develop more strategic and effective disability sport policy and practice.

Despite the inherent problem with BSAD's role and the dissatisfaction with its performance by the NDSOs, Atha believed that BSAD could be 'reorganized and broadened' to serve as the coordinating development agency if 'it had been prepared to alter its attitude'. However, Gordon Neale (then Chief Executive of BSAD), claimed that BSAD could have been an effective coordinating agency, but by the early 1990s 'people were looking for a change because of history ... opinions were against the old BSAD because they [BSAD] were seen as taking the money out from others [disability sport organizations].' It was also the case that the Sports Council – which later became Sport England – wanted a new, more streamlined disability sport structure in England whilst keeping its own responsibility for this at arm's length. In part, this helped to justify their decision to adopt the development role hitherto played by BSAD and to suggest that there was a need to draw on the expertise which existed within the DSOs. Perhaps even more significant, however, was the fact that at the time the Sports Council was being discouraged from increasing staff numbers due to the financial constraints which it was experiencing (see, for example, Houlihan and White, 2002). They were allowed, however, to fund a body that would carry out development work on its behalf and, in that context, creating the EFDS enabled them to do just that.

The proposal that a new national umbrella organization be formed was, at first sight, met with widespread agreement amongst those who attended the 1997 conference. It should be noted, however, that as an observer at the conference it became increasingly apparent to one of the authors of this book that consensus may only have been reached because of the considerable constraint members of the Sports Council placed on the whole process, particularly in relation to the funding which it promised to make available to the DSOs if they supported their proposal that a new organization be formed. Indeed, a range of concerns were expressed at the conference and reported in Collins's report, which suggested that some attendees were concerned that those who proclaimed their interest in mainstreaming disability sport were doing so reluctantly and were given no choice but to agree to the new Sport England agenda. In particular, the *New Start* process was described by some senior administrators as an 'us and them situation' with NDSOs on the one side, and Sport England on the other. One senior administrator claimed that the NDSOs were significantly constrained to support the creation of the EFDS and 'if you didn't sign up [to the formation of the EFDS] you were going to feel pretty uncomfortable in the future'. Reflecting on the increasing importance and control Sport England came to have over the disability sport policy process, another senior administrator in elite disability sport explained how 'consensus was forced rather than reached . . . people were made to believe that was the only way things were going to go . . . and [thought that] perhaps there is going to be money at the end of it'. Finally, and in addition to these concerns, it was clear that some respondents to the Disability Task Force's consultation exercise and those who attended the 1997 conference expressed particular concern about the extent to which creating a new umbrella organization would simply increase the relational complexities that characterized the existing structures for disability sport. That the key roles and relationship between the NDSOs and the new organization had also not been clarified was also a central source of contention, especially among representatives of the NDSOs (Collins, 1997).

Despite the initial – and, in some cases, on-going – objections from representatives of the NDSOs who attended the conference, a new organization – the EFDS – was eventually established in 1998 after a process which was described by Colin Chaytors (who subsequently became the Chief Executive of the EFDS) as 'torturous'. He also added, however, that notwithstanding the initial reservations of some NDSOs, the EFDS eventually 'came together because the disability sport organizations and the organizations operating within it felt that was the right way to go . . . and eventually everyone had signed up to it' (Chaytors, interview). In the final section of this chapter we shall explore some of the developments that have emerged following the inauguration of the EFDS in 1998.

The English Federation of Disability Sport: 1998–2008

As our analysis thus far has suggested, several complex processes were involved in the establishment of the EFDS in 1998. More specifically, it was suggested that whilst there was a strong degree of consensus amongst representatives of the NDSOs that a new umbrella organization with responsibility for disability sport in England was warranted, this was not without opposition from other NDSOs who felt that the Sports Council were simply interested in developing an independent body to deliver its provision for, and commitment to, disability sport. These concerns came to be expressed even further during the 1990s when, within the context of the on-going uncertainty surrounding the rather ambiguous role of BSAD, it became increasingly apparent that to begin mainstreaming disability sport more effectively there needed to be a more tightly coordinated and integrated organizational structure for disability sport nationally. This was particularly the case because BSAD had clearly failed to generate significant commitment among both NDSOs and NGBs to the process of mainstreaming, even though it was unclear how the establishment of the EFDS would prove to be more effective at overcoming these challenges than BSAD. Nevertheless, in a similar way to the role played by BSAD during the 1980s, the EFDS became the organization recognized by Sport England as the 'umbrella body responsible for coordinating the development of sport and recreation' for disabled people (EFDS, 2000: 8). The EFDS was to act as the umbrella agency for the DSOs and work through 10 regional federations which would coordinate and support the delivery of its national development plan. The EFDS was a company limited by guarantee, had charitable status, could actively fund raise and would receive core funding of over approximately £1.2 million per year from Sport England. Representatives from each of the seven NDSOs and four representatives of the regional federations made up the 11 directors on the Board which managed the affairs of the EFDS, whilst as a consequence of its close relationship with, and significant investment in, the EFDS, Sport England retained observer status on its Board.

In 1998 the EFDS was formally launched with a four-year development plan titled *Building a Fairer Sporting Society* (EFDS, 2000), which was published following a year long consultation involving written responses from 20 individuals from DSOs, 15 from mainstream sports organizations, and 18 from local authorities. In the four-year plan and the consultation on which it was based, it was clearly suggested that a more efficient, coordinated and coherent approach to the organization of disability sport in England was required. Although some progress was made towards the achievement of that goal during the first few years of the EFDS's existence, in its more recent policy, *Count Me In: A Development Framework 2004–2008*, the Chief Executive of the EFDS, Colin Chaytors, claimed that 'there is still a need for a powerful, united voice for disability sport in England and for increased working between everyone involved in the development and delivery of disability sport in this country' (EFDS, 2004: 7). Indeed, reflecting on its work since 1998, Chaytors has recently suggested that under his leadership he has attempted to ensure that the EFDS fulfils this role by positioning the EFDS 'as an organization that predominately works with key organizations and partners that provide or govern sport and leisure activities in England' (Chaytors, interview). Chaytors views the role of the EFDS not, it should be noted, as delivering activities or programmes since it does not have the capacity to do that; rather, for Chaytors, by drawing on the expertise and resources available within his organization, the central purpose of the EFDS is to 'support, enable and advise those organizations that have the responsibility for the provision of activity or opportunity' (Chaytors, interview). To help achieve this aim, the EFDS now has six formally stated objectives:

- environment: to develop and enhance the inclusion of disabled people in community based sport and physical activity opportunities;
- sport: to develop sporting pathways for disabled people;
- training: to improve skills, knowledge and understanding of the community to effectively deliver sport for disabled people;
- education: to improve the quality and quantity of PE and school sport for young disabled people in special and mainstream education;
- empowerment: to empower disabled people to take a full and active role within sport; and
- media (information, promotion, lobbying): to increase awareness and understanding of sport for disabled people. (EFDS, 2004: 20)

But to what extent has the EFDS been able to achieve these objectives? Has it, in fact, provided the 'united voice' for disability sport that was expected of it? And has it been able to improve the relationships between, and coordination of, the various other organizations with responsibility for disability sport in England? We shall explore some of these issues in the remaining pages of this chapter.

The relationship between the EFDS and Sport England

For reasons explained earlier, the EFDS is perceived to have a very close working relationship with Sport England (and, of course, other organizations, too, such as the Youth Sport Trust and Sports Coach UK), not least because Sport England played a significant role in the 'creation of the EFDS' (Atha, interview) and because the EFDS are perceived to be 'doing the work of Sport England' (Atha, interview) in relation to disability sport provision in England. As we noted earlier, the encouragement which Sport England gave to the creation of a separate organization with responsibility for disability sport in England was interpreted by some as further evidence of the lip-service it paid – and continues to pay – to disability sport as a central policy concern. It was believed by some of those who supported the development of the EFDS and who hold senior positions within the organization (e.g. Atha and Chaytors), however, that the close relationship which the EFDS had with Sport England would enable its members to lobby central government much more effectively than previous DSOs. In order to achieve this, the EFDS was required to develop effective collaborative links with the existing NDSOs who were centrally involved in the provision of disability sport in England, since they, too, were also considered to have a role to play in the future of disability sport. However, since its formation, the relationship between the EFDS and some NDSOs (who may have a place on the Board of Directors of the EFDS) has been at times hostile and fractious and this has come to undermine significantly the extent to which the EFDS has been able to achieve its formally stated objectives. Such a view was brought out in an interview with one senior administrator who suggested that the EFDS 'don't have any real impact upon the policy at all' and 'try to inflict their policy on us (NDSOs)'. This was also the view of John Chatsworthy who, at the time, was a BBS representative on the EFDS Board. In particular, he described how during EFDS Board Meetings 'some individuals (were) starting to run away with the idea that they [the EFDS] can steamroller their policies into any plan without consultation' (BBS, 2002: 2) of other Board members. In this regard, representatives of some NDSOs considered the EFDS as an unnecessary and unhelpful addition to the myriad of disability sport organizations which, rather than improving the organizational infrastructure for disability sport, actually had the effect of increasing further the complexity of the ways in which disability sport is delivered in England.

A further consequence – at least in part – of the development of the EFDS was that the role of some NDSOs in England changed, and in some cases quite substantially. In 1997, for example, the BSAD was renamed and reorganized to become Disability Sport England (DSE) partly, it should be noted, to be consistent with the restructuring within the Sports Council, but also to focus more exclusively upon their membership and events programme. DSE originally had to obtain funding for all of their events and since Sport England provided funding to disability sport through the EFDS, it was alleged that 'other disability groups had to jump through hoops to access a part of the funding set aside for events' (Neale, interview). It was also suggested that prior to the establishment of the EFDS the NDSOs were working more effectively together with governing bodies to develop a coordinated events programme, and that many of the activities and initiatives that the EFDS has developed – such as the *Inclusive Fitness Initiative* which aims to 'enable disabled people's access to fitness equipment' (EFDS, 2001: 8) – are not sustainable given the already limited resources available to the NDSOs (Neale, interview). Although the EFDS receives grant aid from the Sport England Lottery Fund to develop programmes such as the *Inclusive Fitness Initiative* that helps address its commitment towards mainstreaming, the monies that are made available to the EFDS have – not surprisingly – led those working within other DSOs to suggest that this prioritization of funding has come to limit significantly the funding which may be obtained from Sport England by other DSOs to develop their activities. The Chair of CP Sport, Christine Cruice, for example, has argued that since the establishment of the EFDS the financial support available to the remaining DSOs has been particularly threatened and that CP Sport, in particular, has been especially vulnerable because SCOPE no longer considers CP Sport as a part of its priorities (CP Sport, 2002). In a not dissimilar way, the Chair of UK Deaf Sport, Craig Crowley, also recently expressed particular concern over the mounting financial constraints on DSOs as a consequence of their changing relationships with the EFDS since its inauguration. More specifically, reflecting on the impact that the formation of the EFDS has had on the provision of deaf sport in England, Crowley claimed that 'there has been strong focus on channelling resources to the Olympics and Paralympics, but the Deaflympics has not been awarded equity as a stand alone event' (UK Deaf Sport, 2008).

It is certainly the case that since the establishment of the EFDS other DSOs have experienced – at times, considerable – financial difficulties as the funding priorities of Sport England for disability sport has tended to focus disproportionately on the EFDS. But the consequence of this has not just simply been the tendency for organizations to respond to the financial constraints which they were experiencing by renaming themselves in the hope of obtaining a greater share of the limited funds that are available for disability sport activity. In some cases DSOs have actively sought to redefine their activities as a consequence of their changing relationship with the EFDS and Sport England during the late 1990s and the early years of the twenty-first century. In 2005, for example, the then Chief Executive of Disability Sport England, Gordon Neale, attempted to realign his organization into what he saw as a more strategic and favourable position with the EFDS by reorganizing the activities of DSE. In particular, it was decided that Disability Sport England would become Disability Sport Events with the objective of becoming the recognized national events agency that explicitly works in partnership with mainstream governing bodies of sport on behalf of the EFDS. This decision to subsume Disability Sport Events 'within EFDS as its events arm' (Chaytors, interview) was crucial to ensure the future existence of DSE, for there was 'serious concern that if not made a part of EFDS, DSE's substantive events programme would disappear' (Chaytors, interview). To help preserve the identity of DSE and safeguard its future existence and role within the EFDS, Chaytors explained that within a partnership or service level agreement DSE would host and stage the event, but the mainstream governing body would be expected to 'have it as a key part of their competition structure, supported and endorsed and part of their development programme'. The decision to subsume DSE's activities within the EFDS should not, in Chaytors' view, 'be seen as an opportunity for mainstream bodies to get out of their responsibilities' (Chaytors, interview) towards the mainstreaming of disability sport.

Since DSE has assumed responsibility for coordinating disability sport events in England, the operations of the EFDS have also changed with its attention shifting from the activities of individual DSOs towards raising awareness of the sporting needs of disabled people among mainstream sports partner organizations such as NGBs and County Sport Partnerships. In this respect, in January 2006 the EFDS launched its *Count Me In* scheme that is designed to provide resources and advice to help its partners meet the disability-specific objectives of the Equality Standard (Sport England, 2004). Later that year the EFDS hosted a *Count Me In* conference which included a presentation by Sue Campbell (now Chair of the Youth Sport Trust and UK Sport). During the Conference Campbell emphasized the need to improve the coordination of sport for disabled people and to 'put in place a much stronger, better structure for disability sport' by developing clearer pathways between grassroots and elite levels of participation (Campbell, 2006). Although it is not yet clear what, if any, impact this recognition by Campbell as a representative of one of the more powerful sporting organizations may have on the future provision of and policy direction for disability sport, it was perhaps significant that calls for better governance of, and a more coordinated organizational structure for, disabled people to compete in sport came not from the EFDS, but from a mainstream organization in the form of UK Sport. At the time of writing, and whilst the evidence is at best patchy, this may – we emphasize *may* – mean that, following decades of hesitancy and the adoption of an arm's length approach towards disability sport policy, there is perhaps now a growing political and policy commitment by government to disability sport. It may, of course, also point towards the continued failure of the EFDS and other organizations to provide a clear policy direction for disability sport and to help improve the organizational effectiveness and infrastructure that is available for disabled people to participate in sport. Another possibility is that despite the policy commitment by the EFDS to the process of mainstreaming disability sport, in practice this is much harder to achieve and is dependent to a large degree on the willingness of mainstream NGBs of sport and other providers to help facilitate that process. These are issues that we shall return to in Chapters 3 and 4.

Summary

In this chapter we have attempted to examine briefly aspects of the emergence and development of disability sport from its origins in England during the 1940s. In doing so it has become clear that, since the 1960s and the establishment of the BSAD in particular, the number and range of organizations with a responsibility for delivering disability sport has increased quite substantially. Despite the rather complex and *ad hoc* development of these organizations which, at times, has meant that their roles and responsibilities have tended to overlap with those of other organizations and helped limit the extent to which they have achieved their desired objectives, there now exists a wider range of sports, that are provided more regularly and in a wider variety of contexts, for disabled people with a range of impairments. It can also be properly said, however, that notwithstanding the significant contribution which it makes to the provision of disability sport, in many respects the formation of the EFDS represents something of a missed opportunity to improve the organizational structure of sport for disabled people. More particularly, although the inauguration of the EFDS in 1998 marked a significant moment in the development of disability sport, it appears to have increased, rather than helped improve, the fragmented, complex and cumbersome nature of the organization of disability sport that has emerged during the course of the last half a century or so.

It might with equal validity be noted that disability sport has rarely been the focus of any sustained or clearly defined political and policy commitment in Britain. This was certainly the case until the early 1990s when government – through non-departmental public bodies such as Sport England – came to play an increasingly interventionist role in setting the disability sport policy agenda. Whilst government has, to varying degrees, retained a preference for adopting a largely hands-off approach to the delivery of its disability sport policy goals by leaving the responsibility for doing so to organizations such as the EFDS and NDSOs, its commitment towards the process of mainstreaming disability sport has nevertheless become increasingly important over the decade or so. In the next chapter we shall examine how the process of mainstreaming has come to impact differentially on the provision of disability sport activities by local authorities, before going on to examine, in Chapters 4 and 5, respectively, the ways in which NGBs of sport and mainstream (regular) schools have responded to the growing expectation that they should meet the needs of disabled people in their activities.

Revision questions

1   Discuss the contribution made by Sir Ludwig Guttmann and other organizations who played a central role in the emergence and development of disability sport.

2   To what extent has the government in your country influenced the development of disability sport?

3   How would you explain the roles played by disability sport organizations in the organization and administration of contemporary disability sport?

4   How would you summarize the roles and responsibilities of the EFDS – or your national equivalent – in the provision of disability sport?
5   What practical insights may be derived from the analysis presented in this chapter for those working for a disability sport organization and a mainstream sport organization?

Key readings

English Federation of Disability Sport (2004) *EFDS Development Framework: Count Me In 2004–2008*, Crewe: EFDS.

Guttmann, L. (1976) *Textbook of Sport for the Disabled*, Oxford: HM and M Publishers.

Minister for Sport's Review Group (1989) *Building on Ability: Sport for People with Disabilities*, Leeds: HMSO/Department of Education.

Sports Council (1993a) *People with Disabilities and Sport: Policy and Current/Planned Action*, London: Sports Council.

Thomas, N. (2008) 'Sport and disability', in B. Houlihan (ed.) *Sport and Society: A Student Introduction*, 2nd edn, London: Sage.

Recommended websites

Disability Sport Events
www.disabilitysport.org.uk

English Federation of Disability Sport
www.efds.net

Sport England
www.sportengland.org

3 Local authorities and disability sport development

Objectives

This chapter will:

- examine the development of sport policy and its impact on local authority disability sports development in Britain;
- examine the role of local authorities in the provision of disability sport; and
- explore current provision of disability sport in three local authorities.

Introduction

The previous chapter examined the emergence and development of disability sport in Britain and focused, in particular, on the significant role played by the British Sports Association for the Disabled (BSAD), the English Federation of Disability Sport (EFDS), and various disability sport organizations (DSOs) in the provision of sport for disabled people. In addition to these organizations, local authorities are also among a number of other key providers of opportunities for disabled people to engage in sport and physical activity. It is particularly notable, however, that whilst the important role of local authorities in providing facilities and promoting involvement in sport among so-called under-participating groups (especially young people, older people and ethnic minority groups) has been widely acknowledged (e.g. Houlihan and White, 2002), we currently know very little about how local authorities seek to meet the needs of disabled people in this regard. The central objective of this chapter is, therefore, to begin to address this hiatus by providing a brief overview of the development of sport policy and its impact on local authority disability sports development in Britain. Since it is not possible to examine all of the complexities involved in the changing organization and delivery of disability sport provision at local authority level, we shall begin to explore the role played by local authorities in the delivery of recreational sporting opportunities for disabled people by drawing on three local authority case studies. These case studies are intended to provide a 'snapshot' of current locally delivered disability sports development and to demonstrate the existence of widespread differential practice in the local provision of sport for disabled people.

The 1960s–1980s: facility building, target groups and Compulsory Competitive Tendering

Perhaps the first – but particularly crucial – point worthy of note is that in order to understand something about how disability sport development is currently organized by local authorities in Britain, we need to know something of how it has come to be like that over time. We also need to know something about the changing political and policy priorities given not only to the role of local authorities in implementing national sport policy, but to the emphasis given to disability sport as an aspect of local authority sport policy and provision more generally.

As Houlihan and White (2002) skilfully explain in their text, *The Politics of Sports Development*, government involvement in the organization and administration of sport in Britain can be traced back to the early twentieth century. They add, however, that one of the most important organizational developments that came to play a central role in sport policy and sports development activity in Britain was when, in 1957, the Central Council of Physical Recreation (CCPR) – an independent voluntary body representing a wide range of governing bodies in the promotion, improvement and development of sport – commissioned Sir John Wolfenden to serve as Chair of a Committee to examine the state and status of sport in the UK. In this regard, Wolfenden helped raise the political profile of sport in Britain and played a crucial role in providing 'the context within which public involvement in sport was to be considered for the next generation' (Houlihan and White, 2002: 18). More particularly, it was the publication of the Wolfenden Report in 1960 which came to have a significant impact on the future development of sport policy and, hence, sports development work, in Britain. Among the main recommendations of the report was, first, that there was a need to reverse what was identified as a

> manifest break between, on the one hand, the participation in recreational physical activities which is normal for boys and girls at school, and, on the other hand, their participation in similar (though not necessarily identical) activities some years later when they are more adult. (CCPR, 1960: 25)

Although Wolfenden did not say much about the participation of disabled people, the identification of this so-called 'Wolfenden Gap' became a key policy issue that has remained a more-or-less central aspect of sport policy and development work over the last 40 years or so. A second main recommendation of the report was that a new body be created to be responsible primarily for the distribution of governmental grants to sporting organizations, such as the CCPR and governing bodies of sport, and the promotion of sport as a whole. This body, it was recommended, should remain 'independent' from government to preserve the so-called 'non-political' nature of sport. Whilst the then Conservative government failed to respond to the proposal by Wolfenden that a new umbrella organization be formed to develop sport, this body – established in 1965 – became known as the Advisory Sports Council (ASC) following the election of a Labour government in 1964.

The ASC eventually received 'Royal Charter' status in 1972 following the re-election of the Conservative Party two years previously, and became known as the Sports Council at a time when sport was becoming increasingly recognized as an accepted area of government policy.

Although there had been some development of leisure centres and swimming pools in the 1960s, one of the main priorities of the newly formed Sports Council was to increase the facilities in which the population could participate in sport and physical activity as part of the wider commitment to providing 'Sport For All'. Indeed, it was 'the period from the early 1970s to the early 1980s (that) was to transform the opportunities for participating in sport' (Houlihan and White, 2002: 21) and in which the emphasis in sport policy was characterized by a rapid expansion in the development of sport and leisure centres in local authorities funded primarily by the Sports Council and other public organizations. Thus, through the grant aid which they received from the Sports Council, local authorities came increasingly to be seen as significant providers of opportunities and facilities to participate in sport and physical activity. Indeed, between 1971 and 1981 the Sports Council helped local authorities to 'achieve the construction of over 500 new swimming pools and almost 450 new indoor sports centres' (Houlihan and White, 2002: 21).

The emphasis which the Sports Council and local authorities placed on facility building was strongly associated with increasing levels of participation among the general population from the 1970s. It was recognized, however, that the reported increases in participation had a differential impact on different social groups, with disabled people and other so-called under-participating groups (e.g. the unemployed and black and ethnic minority groups) not experiencing the same rises in participation as other sectors of the population. In light of the persistence of inequalities in participation, during the early 1980s 'there were clear signs of a shift away from facility provision . . . to a strategy of concentrating resources on particular sports or sections of the community' (Houlihan and White, 2002: 33), which to some extent included disabled people. To begin to address the inequity in provision and opportunity experienced by disabled people as well as women, black and ethnic minorities, young people, the elderly, and the unemployed, local authorities began delivering a series of projects which epitomized the 'Sport For All' ethic that, in addition to the activities of the emerging DSOs (see Chapter 2), placed local authorities at the heart of local sport provision for disabled people.

The Sports Council operationalized its commitment to 'Sport For All' and its policy on mass participation with two major initiatives. First, through the Manpower Services Commission – which was established by the government in 1974 to help coordinate and manage the country's employment and training services – the Sports Council set up the *Action Sport* programme in 1982 and began to provide local authorities in various inner city areas with £1 million per year between 1982 and 1985. A central objective of the 15 *Action Sport* programmes – which were run in Birmingham and London in response to the inner-city riots of 1981 – was to develop, in partnership with other interested agencies, sustainable, consumer-driven opportunities for low participant groups (particularly the unemployed). The significant diversity in the populations of each authority was expressed in the diversity and type of programmes offered by groups of sports development officers who were recruited by local authorities to implement them. Many local authorities recognized the contribution that sports development could make to their local communities and subsequently provided further funding for the programmes which they then sought to tailor towards the needs of groups within their region.

The emphasis which the Sports Council placed on the need to enhance mass participation, particularly among low participant groups within the *Action Sport* programme, was expressed further in its publication *Sport in the Community: The Next Ten Years* (Sports Council, 1982). In this document the central role that local authorities were perceived to play in enhancing participation was clearly recognized when it suggested that:

> most sport is played locally, and so the development of mass participation depends critically on local initiatives. This will require local authorities and education authorities, local sports clubs, other local voluntary groups and local commercial interest to work both separately and in partnership. (Sports Council, 1982: 35)

The position which the Sports Council took on the role to be played by local authorities in sports development, together with its other strategic policy aims for sport was, however, largely ignored by government and the NGBs of sport. Despite such political reticence, the prevailing perceptions regarding the value of local authorities in the delivery of policy goals related to mass participation and 'Sport For All' was once again expressed when, in 1984, the Sports Council launched 15 National Demonstration Projects (NDPs) to identify strategies to ameliorate the barriers to participation for a range of under-represented groups. In particular, the formally stated purposes of the NDPs was to: (i) improve participation through outreach development in the community; (ii) enhance opportunities for particular target groups such as women and disabled people to participate in sport; and (iii) develop school sport, in partnership with the education authorities (Sports Council Research Unit, 1991). Although disabled people were once again of marginal interest to many of the NDPs, the findings of the *Everybody Active* project (an NDP) which focused on the experiences of young disabled people aged 11–24 years old, did generate valuable lessons that contributed to the *Action Sport* programmes and which helped shape the context within which sport policy and development for specific identified target groups would be considered in the next two decades or so (Stafford, 1989). Indeed, in relation to the development of sport for disabled people, the recommendations of the NDPs (Sports Council Research Unit, 1991) were later expressed in the objectives contained within *Building a Fairer Sporting Society* which, as we noted in the previous chapter, was published by the EFDS in 2004 (EFDS, 2004). Of greater significance for present purposes, however, was that despite the rhetorical commitment amongst members of the Sports Council to enhancing 'Sport For All', the participation of disabled people was largely ignored during the early 1980s, even though it was recognized that failing 'to tackle the needs of (this group) would put the Council in breach of its Royal Charter' (Sports Council, 1982: 7).

The lack of policy focus on the sports participation of disabled people within local authority areas in favour of other supposedly under participating groups was also to be found in the Sports Council's 1988 follow-up strategy, *Sport in the Community – Into the Nineties*. Building on the target group approach which it took in *Sport in the Community: The Next Ten Years* and the NDPs, in this strategy the Sports Council once again focused on specific under-participating groups, particularly women and young people, but paid very little attention to the sport development needs of disabled people. In fact, during the 1980s the role which local authorities were perceived to play in the promotion for sport for disabled people was only really explicitly recognized and promoted in the Minister for Sport's Review Group's report, *Building on Ability*, which, as we explained in Chapter 2, summarized the findings of a large wide-ranging review of the organization and provision of sport for disabled people in Britain. On the basis of its findings, the Minister's Review Group reported that there was considerable variation in the ways in which disability sport was delivered and prioritized within the sports development services offered between local authorities across Britain. Some local authorities, it argued, 'pursue their obligations with diligence, imagination and generosity', whilst others were regarded as doing 'little more than pay lip-service to the needs of disabled people' (Minister for Sport's Review Group, 1989: 23). Despite the differential practice which existed between local authorities during the 1980s, the Review Group nevertheless emphasized that as well as providing facilities within which disability sport development takes place, 'at a local level, the main providers of sporting opportunities are the local authorities, sports clubs, and disability sports clubs such as those affiliated to BSAD' (Minister for Sport's Review Group, 1989: 10). Within this context, local authorities were clearly seen by the Review Group as playing a central role in the provision of sporting opportunities and facilities for disabled people, and, insofar as that was the case, the Review Group made a series of recommendations to the Sports Council regarding the need to firmly embed local authority disability sport provision in its future policies and strategies. One of its main recommendations was that local authorities 'should assume responsibility for ensuring the provision and coordination of sport for people with disabilities at a local level' (Minister for Sport's Review Group, 1989: 10). It was not only the delivery of sports services by local authorities to disabled people in local communities that was seen as important, for the Review Group also recommended the sporting needs of disabled people should be central to, and clearly articulated in, the wider policies and priorities of local councils. In particular, it was recommended that 'as part of their wider policy towards disabled people, local authorities should include a statement on sport setting out their agreed aims and policies' (Minister for Sport's Review Group, 1989: 23) for the sport development needs of disabled people. The Review Group also made a series of recommendations designed to increase the sports participation of disabled people in local communities which included the need for local authorities to improve access to buildings, to consider offering concessionary rates to disabled people, to introduce disability awareness training programmes for sports centre staff, and seek to develop partnerships between the private and voluntary sectors (Minister for Sport's Review Group, 1989).

Those working within sports development more generally during the late 1980s and early 1990s were, then, seen by the Review Group as vital to facilitating not only the promotion of sport for disabled people, but also in helping to achieve the wider commitment to mainstreaming that was beginning to be established on the disability sport policy agenda. This emerging policy commitment – which is explained in more detail in the next chapter – and the calls on the Sports Council by the Minister's Review Group to enhance local authority sports provision for disabled people, was, however, accompanied by a potential threat; namely, the introduction of Compulsory Competitive Tendering (CCT) in the late 1980s.

Despite the lack of any real interest in sport development policy – particularly that of the Sports Council – by the Conservative government during the 1980s, it suggested that there was a clear need to streamline the organizational structure of sport in Britain, reduce levels of bureaucracy, and increase the efficiency of those bodies' responsibility for the organization and delivery of sport (including local authorities). It was also concerned that many local authorities at the time were particularly inefficient financially and that there was, as a consequence, a need to control more closely local government spending (Coalter, 2007; Houlihan and White, 2002). One of ways the Conservative government attempted to do this was through the introduction of CCT. CCT was originally introduced in the Local Government Planning and Land Act in 1980 and was extended in the Local Government Act of 1988 to include a wider variety of service provision, including the management of sport and leisure facilities such as pools, leisure centres, golf courses and tennis courts (Henry, 2001). The Act meant that local government services could be put out to 'tender' for private administration and whilst the tendering of sport and leisure services through CCT eventually began in the early 1990s, 'sports development was still peripheral to most strategies' (Houlihan and White, 2002: 44) when they were put out to tender.

Even though many contracts for the right to deliver local services were won in-house by local authorities, it was recognized that the introduction of CCT and the considerable structural change this would bring about at the local authority level would 'have their impact on sport' (Sports Council, 1988: 7). Amongst the concerns that were expressed about the impact that CCT would have on local authorities was the potential threat this posed for those sport development programmes which focused on specific target groups such as disabled people. In particular, it was suggested that the 'target group approach' favoured by the Sports Council where specific attention was given to those groups whose sports participation was considered low and required additional support but which generated a poor return on investment, would be difficult to provide for in the newly privatized leisure industry (Elvin, 1993). In relation to the specific impact that CCT would have on the sports development opportunities available to disabled people in local authorities, the Minister for Sport's Review Group expressed particular concern about 'the possible effects [of CCT] on access to facilities by disabled groups and individuals' and recommended that 'local authorities seek to ensure that adequate provision for disabled people and groups is made and maintained' (Minister for Sport's Review Group, 1989: 26). In a not dissimilar way, BSAD made clear its concern about the constraints that CCT would have on disabled people's participation in local authority sport when, in 1990, it published *Compulsory Competitive Tendering: Policy Guidelines for Leisure Management: To Safeguard Provision for People with Disabilities* (BSAD, 1990). The central purpose of the document was to provide local authorities with 'guidelines for the provision of sport and leisure for people with disabilities' (BSAD, 1990: 1). In it BSAD also encouraged local authorities to include its suggestions in their strategy documents to help prevent the possibility that disabled people's experiences of, and opportunities for, participating in sport was not further threatened by the structural changes to sport and leisure services that were brought about by CCT. As Jackson (2008: 33) has noted, during the late 1980s 'the emerging sports development arena whose main function was to reach . . . previously neglected sporting communities' such as disabled people 'was a clear casualty of (the) focus on bottom-line financial calculations' which characterized the process underpinning CCT. Indeed, despite the attempts of organizations such as BSAD, it was clear that CCT had compromised the extent to which the provision of disability sport by local authorities and the broader policy objective of mainstreaming could be achieved (Sports Council, 1993a).

The early 1990s to 1997: from addressing inequity to school and elite sport

As we have explained above, the period between the 1960s and 1980s was characterized by a significant growth in the contribution of local authorities to the organization and administration of disability sport, even though this was curtailed somewhat by the introduction by CCT and 'a marked lack of sustained political interest and direction in sport' (Houlihan and White, 2002: 52) which continued in the early 1990s. It was also around this time when, building on the work of the *Action Sport* programmes and NDPs that were developed during the 1980s, the Sports Council published a series of policy 'Frameworks for Action' for young people, women, black and ethnic minorities, and disabled people in which it was developing the concept of sports equity. The Sports Council (1993b: 4) defined the concept of sports equity as being

> about fairness in sport, equality of access, recognizing inequalities and taking steps to address them. It is about changing the structure and culture of sport to ensure that it becomes equally accessible to everyone in society, whatever their age, race, gender or level of ability.

As Houlihan and White (2002: 63) have noted, the introduction of sports equity as a central feature of each of the Frameworks for Action 'represented a shift in thinking from the target group approach that had been popular in sports development work in the 1980s'. For the first time it also placed responsibility for addressing inequity on governing bodies, local authorities and other traditional providers of sport. In this context, the Sports Council began to place considerably more emphasis on the ways in which the principles of equity should be embedded across all levels of the sports development continuum. It also focused particular attention on the need to break down not only the individual and social constraints to sports participation, but significantly those aspects of the structure and culture of sport that also come to limit the involvement of under-participating groups such as disabled people. The policy for disabled people (Sports Council 1993a) placed particular emphasis on the ways in which the Sports Council would work with NGBs and DSOs at a local level to promote participation and equity for disabled people. However, for reasons we explained in Chapter 2, the position statement the Sports Council developed in relation to disabled people did not generate as much impact as those which related to other issues of equity, particularly gender equity and specifically the rights and experiences of women, which had a significant impact on international sport policy following the publication of the Brighton Declaration (1994). It is also important to note that the general principle of sports equity which underpinned the Sports Council's series of policy statements 'stimulated little comment at the time' (Houlihan and White, 2002: 63) by government and 'had limited impact on the sports development community' (Houlihan and White, 2002: 64). According to Houlihan and White (2002: 64) the marginal impact that these equity policies had on those working in sports development, particularly in some local authorities, can be related to

> the weak influence of the (Sports) Council at the time, and partly because the ideas they contained did not fit with the immediate priorities and concerns of governing bodies or Conservative-controlled local authorities. Those local authorities that were Labour-controlled considered themselves well ahead of the Sports Council on equity issues, regarding the Council as a conservative and somewhat inequitable institution itself in both its membership and operations.

It was also clear that whilst the principles underpinning the notion of equity would 'prove significant over the medium term to longer term' (Houlihan and White, 2002: 63), the marginal impact which the Sports Council's recommendations on equity initially had at government level can be related to the general lack of interest in sport by the Thatcher government. However, following the replacement of Margaret Thatcher by John Major as leader of the Conservative Party in 1990, and Major's subsequent success at the 1992 general election, the political salience of sport increased substantially such that sport policy and sports development policy, in particular, 'was about to enter a period of sustained increase in public investment in sport, but also one of sustained governmental interest and debate about the role of sport in society' (Houlihan and White, 2002: 52–3). The processes that were involved in the greater state involvement in sport policy and the implications this had for local authorities have been examined in some detail elsewhere (e.g. Coalter, 2007; Houlihan, 2002; Houlihan and White, 2002) and cannot be repeated here. Nevertheless, it is clear that – at the risk of some considerable over-simplification – the growing political salience of sport and sport development policy can be related to several interrelated processes:

- Major and many members of his cabinet were sports enthusiasts and began to bring this enthusiasm to the sport policies and strategies of government.
- The creation of the Department of National Heritage (DNH) in 1992 brought sport as an important government priority to cabinet level status for the first time.
- The development in 1994 of a National Lottery from which sport (through, for example, sport organizations and local authorities) – as one of a number of 'good causes' – was to receive substantial amounts of money; and
- The publication of *Sport: Raising the Game* – the first sport policy to be published by a British government for 20 years.

Within the context of local authority disability sport the publication of *Sport: Raising the Game* (DNH, 1995) was of particular significance, for it marginalized considerably the role of local government and made little reference to mass participation ('Sport For All') or to local authorities who are the key vehicles of its promotion. The explicit policy emphasis was not on mass participation or enhancing the involvement of specific groups such as disabled people, as had been the case previously, but on school sport and elite performance, with a more efficient and streamlined structure for the organization of sport in the United Kingdom also being emphasized as a key priority (DNH, 1995; Green, 2008; Houlihan and White, 2002). That local authorities and the concept of 'Sport For All' were largely ignored in *Sport: Raising the Game* was particularly important and not insignificant, for as we noted earlier it is in the context of local authority leisure provision (such as leisure centres, private health clubs and gyms) that many disabled people may participate in sport and physical activity, both in segregated and integrated settings. The failure to integrate this provision into the wider sport development policy priorities of government may, therefore, have come to threaten the extent to which those within disability sport were able to maintain and enhance levels of participation and the quality of disabled people's experiences of sport at local authority level. In part, as Houlihan (2002) has noted, this omission can be interpreted as an expression of the government's view that the facility infrastructure for mass participation and, hence, the achievement of 'Sport For All' objectives, was not in place and that responsibility for these and, with it, the involvement of disabled people in local authority sport, was a matter that could be left to local government. In addition, the little attention that was paid to 'the contribution of local government, which spends over £800 million each year on sport, was a reflection of the Conservative government's longstanding antipathy towards local authorities' (Houlihan, 2002: 196).

The focus of much of the funds that were made available to sport through the National Lottery was also disproportionately skewed towards the achievement of these dual policy objectives. Furthermore, as Houlihan and White (2002) have noted, although local authorities were heavily constrained to develop funding strategies to access approximately 40 per cent of Lottery money allocated to them and were encouraged by the Sports Council to think more strategically about sport and recreation, 'there was little incentive for local authorities to respond as bids for Lottery funding based on analysis of need and levels of participation, or on goals such as the reduction of deprivation or community regeneration, were explicitly prohibited' (Houlihan and White, 2002: 73). It is not unsurprising, therefore, that during the mid-1990s the sports development needs of disabled people in local authorities was, as best, pushed to the margins of sports development policy – if not in the practices of local authorities – as state involvement in setting the national sport policy agenda began to increase quite substantially As we shall see next, however, local authorities would soon be seen as important providers to the delivery of government policy goals, particularly in relation to mass participation and social inclusion.

Local authorities and disability sport since 1997

It was within the developing policy context described above that the Labour government (elected in 1997) first published *A Sporting Future for All* (DCMS, 2000) and the *Government's Plan for Sport* (DCMS, 2001). Then, in conjunction with the Strategy Unit which reports directly to the Cabinet Office and the Prime Minister, *Game Plan* was published in 2002 (DCMS/Strategy Unit, 2002). As Green (2008: 97) has noted, whilst Labour's *A Sporting Future for All* and *Sport: Raising the Game* from the previous Conservative government 'are from different sides of the political spectrum, they demonstrated a striking note of unity on the twin emphases of school (youth) sport and elite development'. Of particular relevance to this examination of disability sport, however, was that in addition to the retained emphasis on school and elite sport, there was a renewed commitment by the government to the promotion of 'Sport For All' and to the role of local authorities (particularly those in areas of high deprivation) in achieving this objective. In particular, local authorities were said to be 'key providers of sport and recreation and play a central role in the delivery of sport in and for the community' and government claimed to recognize 'the need to support Local Authorities in building up sports and leisure services which serve the needs of . . . people' (DCMS, 2001: 21). Labour also expressed a commitment to developing local authority facilities and working with other private commercial leisure facilities as just one means by which to develop mass participation in sport and physical activity and to ensure that local residents 'have easy access to high quality and affordable facilities' (DCMS, 2000: 36).

The renewed emphasis on 'Sport For All' and the role of local authorities as the main agents in delivering mass participation goals and policy implementation clearly demarcated the sports development policies of the Labour government from those of its predecessors. However, one of the policies that was central to the New Labour government's manifesto and which distinguished its policy from that of the previous Conservative government, was the policy emphasis which it came to place on social inclusion. Along with social exclusion, social inclusion has come increasingly to dominate the policy agendas of many Western governments, and especially those in Europe. In Britain, social inclusion became a cornerstone of social policy following the election of the Labour government in May 1997. Upon entering office, the Labour Party established the Social Exclusion Unit (SEU) to examine how it could achieve its social inclusion and welfare policy objectives, both of which it saw as achievable only through 'joined up government', that is, through cross-departmental strategies leading to 'the construction of a comprehensive policy response to a complex and multi-dimensional problem' (Houlihan and White, 2002: 84). The SEU subsequently established the PAT 10 Working Group to report on the potential contribution that the arts and sport might make to the promotion of greater social inclusion and the broader requirements of best value. The findings of the PAT 10 report have been outlined in greater detail elsewhere (e.g. Coalter, 2007; Collins and Kay, 2003; DCMS, 1999; Houlihan and White, 2002; Long et al., 2002). It is apparent, however, that together with the review of the England National Lottery Strategy in 1998, the PAT 10 report provided the foundation for a focus on social inclusion in future sport policy. For example, in A Sporting Future for All, it was claimed that 'Sport can make a unique contribution to tackling social exclusion in our society' (DCMS, 2000: 39) and local authorities (together, for example, with schools and local sports clubs) were identified as playing a crucial role in developing 'creative and innovative ways of using sport to help re-engage people [such as disabled people] and to equip them with the skills and confidence to re-join the mainstream of society' (DCMS, 2000: 39). That local authorities are considered by the Labour government to play a central role in developing and managing 'inter-agency working and partnerships for the delivery of both sports development objectives and broader community regeneration benefits' (Houlihan and White, 2002: 111) was reinforced further in Sport England's (2006) recent publications entitled Sport Playing Its Part. In this collection of publications Sport England point to the ways in which sport and key agents of its promotions such as local authorities aid the delivery of the desired community-, health- and environmental-outcomes, as well as meeting the needs of those considered vulnerable to social exclusion such as disabled people.

The aforementioned views regarding the supposed social benefits of sport are, of course, not new. They have been repeatedly articulated in policy statements and other semi-official pronouncements since the 1960s. Nevertheless, the growing expectation from the mid-1990s that sport-related policy interventions can achieve a vast array of desired social objectives is merely one expression of the ways in which government ministers in Britain – as elsewhere – have become increasingly interventionist in setting the sport policy agenda (Green, 2008; Green and Houlihan, 2006), one of the more recent examples of which is the ways in which the government outlined its political and policy priorities in Game Plan (DCMS/Strategy Unit, 2002).

As well as being a core policy priority of A Sporting Future for All and the Government's Plan for Sport, social inclusion is a central theme that runs through aspects of Game Plan. Game Plan featured a list of benefits that participation in sport and physical activities is alleged to have in the promotion of social inclusion of particular social groups, including disabled people. Of particular significance in the present context was that *Game Plan* devoted a chapter to local delivery of sport policies and recognized that if participation in general, and specifically amongst under-represented groups such as disabled people, was to increase in the future, then it was at the local rather than national level that particular attention needed to be focused (DCMS/Strategy Unit, 2002: 183). At the time of its publication, it was suggested in *Game Plan* that 31 per cent of Sport England grants were distributed to local authorities and that 80 per cent of government funding for sport was delivered by local authorities through leisure departments and the funding of physical education and sport by local education authorities (DCMS/Strategy Unit, 2002: 183). Despite the funds which are available for those working in local authority sports development, it was also acknowledged that:

> Sport and physical activity are not always seen as a priority at a local level . . . As a result, sport and leisure expenditure is often the first to suffer if resources are reduced. A significant proportion of budgets is spent on the management and maintenance of facilities (rather than the strategic development of sport and recreation). (DCMS/Strategy Unit, 2002: 183)

Particular criticism was also expressed in *Game Plan* regarding the sports provision that is available in most local authorities and especially of the roles played by local authorities in enhancing participation amongst under-represented groups such as disabled people. It was also suggested that there existed a wide variation in the levels of investment in sport and recreation across different local authorities and that there needed to be, amongst other things, clearer sporting priorities and objectives that focused on the needs of local communities; better strategic planning for sport; wider consideration of the options for policy implementation; and practical steps to improve services and bring about a 'joined up' approach to the delivery of sport and physical activity to local residents (DCMS/Strategy Unit, 2002: 184). One way in which it was proposed that local authorities might be encouraged to place sports provision more centrally within their services was indicated by a similar desire to develop performance indicators at a local level. After eighteen years out of office, 'New Labour' instigated a reinvigorated effort to 'modernize' government organizations and the public sector generally, including those working within sports development (Coalter, 2007). In this regard, sports organizations, and those working within sports development, are now being increasingly expected to provide detailed data regarding the monitoring and evaluation of strategies, not least to demonstrate the impact their services are having on the achievement of desired social outcomes (Coalter, 2007). Thus, a particular policy priority of *Game Plan* is that 'there should be a non-directive approach to local provision, with more use of performance framework tools such as public health focused targets and local PSAs (Public Service Agreements)' (DCMS/Strategy Unit, 2002: 162), which are now very much part of the day-to-day reality of the operations of sports development work in local authorities.

As the above summary of some important inclusion policy developments indicates, one consequence of the growing involvement of government in sport-policy-making has been that sport policy priorities have shifted away from the development of sport and achievement of sport-related objectives, towards the use of sport to achieve other desired social objectives. It is also the case that – whilst a myriad of 'disadvantaged groups' such as disabled people are identified in much of the New Labour political rhetoric regarding social inclusion – it is young people and school-aged children who are the principal target group of sport-related interventions where proactive responses to a range of social problems and the achievement of social policy goals are emphasized (Green, 2006; Houlihan and Green, 2006). At the local level the role of local authorities in contributing to the achievement of these objectives and sports development provision per se should not be underestimated. However, those working in local authorities are nevertheless becoming increasingly constrained to maintain their sports development priorities within the context of 'conflicting pressures through being expected to contribute to the government's social inclusion objectives' (Houlihan and White, 2002: 107). These conflicting pressures are, in turn, being generated within a context of a rapidly changing social and political policy climate where, in the battle for public funding, those working in disability sports development have to compete with representatives of many other public services that might generally be perceived to have a more pressing claim for a greater share of public funds (for example, health and education) and are being constrained increasingly to move beyond simply extolling the intrinsic benefits of sports participation towards providing a more persuasive justification to develop disability sport for broader social objectives. Although there exists very little systematically collected and published data on disability sports development – which is a point that we cannot stress too strongly – it may be that, as in other areas of sports development work, one consequence of the rapidly changing sport and public policy context has been that local authority disability sport provision has become increasingly diverse and that the nature of, and opportunities for, disabled people to participate in sport varies substantially from one local authority to another. In some cases local authorities have, as part of the need to become more 'socially inclusive', conducted audits, developed disability sport plans and policies, and established a comprehensive range of programmes across a variety of sports and activities for recreational users as well as competitive athletes. In other local communities the sports opportunities available for disabled people and the commitment and/or ability of those working in local authorities to develop disability sport is considerably less developed, with many variations in policy and practice existing in-between these two poles.

In light of the lack of available evidence which examines the activities and role played by local authorities in the delivery of recreational sporting opportunities for disabled people, the case studies that follow begin to provide just a 'snapshot' of current locally delivered disability sports development. The three case studies of local authorities – Barrow Borough Council, Nottinghamshire County Council and Kent County Council – cannot be regarded as representative of local authorities in England, but were nevertheless purposively selected to demonstrate the existence of differential practice in the local provision of sport for disabled people

Barrow Borough Council

Barrow Borough Council in the Borough of Barrow-in-Furness is located in a remote part of south western Cumbria on the Furness Peninsula in the north-west of England and is to the north of Morecambe Bay which is set against the Lake District National Park. Barrow-in-Furness developed rapidly in the mid-nineteenth century around its iron, steel and shipbuilding industries. Although the town still relies heavily on submarine and ship-building, the closure of the steelworks located there in 1985, together with substantial job losses which resulted from the declining local shipbuilding in the early 1990s, was strongly associated with a rapid and sustained economic decline in the area. In 2007, the population of Barrow-in-Furness was estimated to be 71,980, and with the exception of the Barrow Island Ward which has 2,606 residents, the remaining 12 electoral wards which comprise the area are said to have approximately 5,500 local residents (Barrow Borough Council, 2008a). Overall, Barrow is ranked as the thirty-second most deprived area in England according to the 2007 indices of multiple deprivation (Barrow Borough Council, 2008b) which is a Super Output Area (SOA) level measure of multiple deprivation that relates to income deprivation, employment deprivation, health deprivation and disability, education, skills and training deprivation, barriers to housing and services, living environment deprivation and crime (Office of the Deputy Prime Minister, 2006). In terms of the ethnic composition of the region, 98 per cent of residents in Barrow are self-defined as White British (Office for National Statistics (ONS), 2008a).

Despite its relatively high levels of economic and social deprivation, Barrow Borough Council claims to be committed to the development of sport and 'aims to encourage, promote and support opportunities for sport and physical activity for people with a disability in the Barrow Borough area' (Barrow Borough Sports Council, 2006). The Borough Council has a Disability Sports and Leisure Forum and District Disability Association and also operates five sports facilities and 19 sports clubs which are available for disabled people. Since 2003 the Borough Council has employed a sports equity officer to help facilitate and coordinate sports development opportunities for disabled people and this has meant that 'some of the barriers to participation – such as a lack of information about what is available – have begun to be addressed' (Steventon, 2004: 34).

In 2004, an audit of sports opportunities for children and adults with a disability in Cumbria was conducted by Cumbria Sports Partnership (Steventon, 2004). Despite the emphasis that Barrow Borough Sports Council places on the development of sport for disabled people, the audit highlighted that there were gaps in the provision of disability sport in the local community. These identified gaps in provision were said to be strongly related to the financial constraints experienced by the Borough Council, the limited number of staff which it employs, and the number of volunteers required to organize disability sport events (Steventon, 2004). The audit also highlighted that many young disabled people and disabled adults were unable to access mainstream sport and leisure provisions (particularly local authority leisure centres), and of the 144 sports clubs that responded to the audit, only 15 deemed themselves to be welcoming and inclusive to disabled people (Steventon, 2004: 36). In its conclusion Steventon (2004: 37) claimed that 'children and adults with a disability in Barrow cannot access quality sports opportunities in the way that children and adults without a disability can' and that, 'exclusion from the sports clubs, and specialist Sports College also means exclusion from progression routes to competitive opportunities'.

In light of these findings, the Barrow and District Disability Sports and Leisure Forum was established in 2005 with the aim of removing 'the barriers which prevent people with disabilities from accessing sports and leisure opportunities in the Borough' (Barrow Borough Sports Council, 2006). To help achieve this aim, the Borough Council established the *Barrow Disability Physical Activity Development Project* and produced a four year development plan (2005–2009) to help facilitate the mainstreaming of disability sport events and disabled athletes in its activities (Barrow Community Regeneration Company, 2005). The objectives of the plan are to:

- to increase the number of local sport and leisure organizations providing accessible and progressive sport, leisure and physical activity opportunities for people with disabilities;
- to increase the provision and range of sporting and physical activity opportunities and improve access to exciting opportunities;
- to increase awareness of the project and promote opportunities;
- to increase disabled participation through sport and physical activity; and
- to improve partnership working, linking closely with both traditional and non-traditional sporting partners. (Barrow Community Regeneration Company, 2005: 1)

In addition to its *Disability Physical Activity Development Project*, Barrow Borough Sports Council sought to increase its mainstream sports development activities for disabled people by producing the *2006–2011 Sport and Physical Activity Strategy* in which it recommended that 'clubs need to improve opportunities for disabled people to get involved and focus on specific sports in addition to having access to disability sports clubs' (Barrow Borough Sports Council, 2006: 14). The *Disability Physical Activity* project is managed by the Barrow and District Disability Sports and Leisure Forum which consists of local, regional and national organizations that have an interest in meeting the aims of the project. Among the many and diverse range of activities provided by the Borough Council that are designed to improve opportunities in sport for disabled people in Barrow is the *Disability Sports Club 7* project, which was established in 2004 as a weekly multi-sport club for 5–25-year-olds at the Hoops Basketball Centre and the Barrow and District Table Tennis Centre (Steventon, 2004). The purpose of *Club 7* is to help enhance the physical, social, moral and cultural skills of disabled and non-disabled students in order to enhance their quality of life and contribution to society. Participants in the *Club 7* project are given the opportunity to take part, improve skill and develop interests in a range of sports with other disabled people and, where and when appropriate, are offered opportunities to participate alongside non-disabled people within mainstream sports clubs. In addition, a Disability Sports Fair was organized by Barrow Borough Council in 2005 initially as a one-off event but such was the perceived success of the project this has since turned into an annual event where clubs, schools and leisure providers from across the area provide a day of information, assistance and taster sessions of accessible sports for all ages. A Hoops Multi Skills session delivered at the local Hoops Basketball Centre by disability sport development workers is also available free of charge for young disabled people and their families to attend, as are locally delivered weekend trampoline clubs for autistic young people (Barrow Borough Sports Council, 2008). Finally, in partnership with the Youth Sport Trust (YST), Barrow County Council run a *TOP Sportsability* programme which provides training, resources cards and equipment in five games – boccia, goalball, polybat, table cricket and table hockey – that have been adapted to meet the needs of specific groups of disabled people and can be played by disabled and non-disabled people. The YST provides teachers with training on each sport, how to use the resource cards, and how they may use the sports to help facilitate the inclusion of young disabled people in sport and physical activity as part of the sports activities delivered by schools in the local area.

The provision of sport for disabled people in Barrow tends to follow a rather traditional model of disability sports development where the focus is on local delivery of 'segregated' activities and awareness raising for mainstream sports clubs and facilities. However, while Barrow Borough Sports Council appear committed to providing sports opportunities for disabled people which enhance and complement those offered by mainstream local providers (such as schools and sports centres) and are beginning to work with national organizations such as the YST, the commitment of mainstream clubs is limited and segregated disability sport provision is considered to be 'patchy' (Steventon, 2004: 37). While the objectives of Barrow's *Disability Physical Activity* project provide a broad range of ambitious targets reflective of the sporting needs of disabled people and the key role local authorities are considered to play, the extent to which they have been achieved is, as yet, unclear. Moreover, the precise ways and extent to which Barrow's sports development activities impact on the sports participation and experiences of disabled people in the region is unknown but this is something that, clearly, will require further research by those working within sports development in the region if they are willing and able to develop their activities for disabled residents.

Nottinghamshire County Council

According to the latest available census data, the population of Nottinghamshire is estimated to be 748,510, and with the exception of Mansfield which had 98,200 residents, the remaining local authority districts that comprise the area have between 105,300 (Rushcliffe) and 111,400 (Ashfield) residents which account for between 14 per cent and 15 per cent of the regional population (Nottinghamshire County Council, 2005a). The 2007 indices of multiple deprivation scores reveal that there are 30 Nottinghamshire SOAs in the most deprived 10 per cent of England and 110 in the most deprived 25 per cent. There are, however, considerable variations between the levels of deprivation between the local authority districts, with the highest levels of deprivation being concentrated in Mansfield and Nottingham, with the lowest levels being concentrated in the Rushcliffe and Broxtowe authorities (Nottinghamshire County Council, 2005a). The ethnic composition of the various authorities under the auspices of Nottinghamshire County Council is similarly variable, with the proportion of residents who consider themselves White British ranging from 98 per cent in the Ashfield local authority to 96 per cent in Newark and Sherwood and Mansfield (ONS, 2008b, c, d). In Nottingham, where the proportion of White British residents is significantly lower than in other authorities in the region (81 per cent), approximately 3 per cent of local residents were self-defined as being of Pakistani origin, 3 per cent as Black or Black British Caribbean origin, and a further 2 per cent as Asian or Asian British Indian (ONS, 2008e).

Nottinghamshire County Council has a long established history in the development of local authority disability sports development not least because of the close relationship that some of its residents helped establish with key national and international disability sport organizations such as CP Sport and CP-ISRA. In 1988, CP Sport moved its offices from London to Nottingham where world class competitions in the intervening years between the Paralympics were held. In 1989, 1993, 1997 and 2001 national disability sport officers, together with Nottingham's own local authority officers and staff and from Nottingham Trent University's sport department, organized and ran the Robin Hood CP World Games. More specifically, Colin Rains who worked at the time for Nottinghamshire County Council and was the CP World Games Director and CP Sport's President, and Doug Williamson, a Lecturer at Nottingham Trent University for over 20 years, have made a significant contribution to the development of disability sport in the area by encouraging the local authority and its officers, as well as the university's students, to take a lead in the development and delivery of recreational as well as competitive sporting opportunities for disabled people. This long established commitment to local authority led disability sports development is also evident in the activity of its present Sports Development Unit. The Sport Development Unit has a Sport Disability team which provides a range of services and is currently supported by a principal officer, five sports development officers and two administrative assistants. The unit publishes a regular newsletter which contains details of, for example, previous and forthcoming local sporting events (such as fixtures lists for Nottinghamshire's disabled cricket team), details of national events (such as the Open Wheelchair Tennis Championship held at the City of Nottingham Tennis Centre), and articles which provide disabled residents with information on local disability sport projects, club developments and opportunities to participate in sport in the local area.

In terms of the sporting activities it provides for disabled people in the local community, Nottinghamshire County Council's Sport Development Unit currently runs the Nottinghamshire School of Sport which is open to disabled people aged 8 years old and above. The School of Sport is presented as a sports week to encourage local disabled people to participate in athletics, boccia, football, swimming, cricket, tennis, wheelchair basketball, archery, wheelchair badminton, powerchair football and wheelchair rugby. The aim of the project is designed to help participants develop a range of personal skills and especially those which help to enhance their independence from others and develop self-confidence. Young disabled people are also encouraged to participate in Nottinghamshire County Council's annual Youth Games – a mass participation event for young people living in the area – where they are able to become involved in sports such as boccia, athletics, football and zone hockey (Nottinghamshire County Council, 2008).

In what might be an unusual local authority run project, in 2002, Nottinghamshire County Council's Sports Development Unit established the *Sports Direct* project to help break down barriers faced by disabled people seeking employment in the sports industry. The project offers 'training and work placements to people with disabilities to help them achieve qualifications in sports coaching and sports development' (Nottinghamshire County Council, 2006: 8), particularly in sports such as football, cricket, athletics, boccia and swimming. The participants are also required to take courses in more generic coaching subjects such as child protection and first aid and have work placements with qualified mentors in sports clubs or leisure centres. The project is delivered by the Sports Development Unit in partnership with organizations such as local colleges, the Nottingham Disability Football Focus Group, Nottinghamshire Coach Development Group, the English Federation of Disability Sport, Sports Leaders UK, Nottingham Equality in Sport Partnership, Yes 2 Work, District Sports Development Officers and governing bodies of sport to help offer participants relevant sports-related work placements at leisure centres and local colleges and assist in their search and preparation for employment. Of the 89 participants who joined the project between 2004–2006, '40 have attended a Level 1 coaching course with 28 achieving the award, 7 have been signed on to a level 2 course, with 2 achieving their awards . . . 43 beneficiaries have completed the project and have either gone into further education or have found employment' (Nottinghamshire County Council, 2006: 8). According to Nottinghamshire County Council, a direct result of its *Sports Direct* project is that currently 'Nottinghamshire has a significantly higher proportion of coaches with a disability (7 per cent) than the National figure (2 per cent)' (Nottinghamshire County Council, 2007b: 16).

A further project deigned to enhance the participation and experiences of sport and physical activity among young disabled people is through the *Inside Out* project that was developed in 2003 by Nottinghamshire's Inclusive Physical Education and Sport group to support disabled pupils' access to PE and school sport inside and outside the curriculum (Nottinghamshire County Council, 2005a). The project is funded by Nottinghamshire County Council to offer support to mainstream schools with the objective to deliver inclusive PE and sport opportunities for disabled pupils and those with formally identified special educational needs (Nottinghamshire County Council, 2005a). As a part of the project, support packages are made available by local authority 'sport-disability officers' to schools, providing information on things such as how to run inclusive sports festivals and adapt mainstream sports equipment for disabled people, as well as providing information on how to access the expertise of qualified disabled sport coaches in the local community.

Until 2007, Nottinghamshire's *Inside Out* project Officer was Carol Halpin who claimed that the project has been hugely successful and between 2003 and 2007 has 'raised disability awareness in schools with 11,104 pupils, delivered inclusive activities to 1035 pupils, provided training for 511 school staff and coaches, given one off advice and support to 331 school staff and 61 parents, held workshops and provided Disability Awareness in Sport training for 89 young sport leaders from schools' (Nottinghamshire County Council, 2007b: 9). Halpin goes on to suggest that – as a part of the project – festivals which are led by sports officers and supported by Ambassadors (elite disabled athletes) and sports leaders from secondary schools have been particularly successful in helping to provide training to teachers and support to disabled pupils within mainstream schools. The festivals allow the opportunity for pupils with disabilities from different mainstream schools to meet, and for them and their teachers to share ideas and experiences of inclusive PE. Halpin has recognized, however, that some schools are unsure whether it is appropriate – given the overriding aims of the project – to 'single out' and arrange sporting festivals specifically for disabled pupils, as a means of achieving inclusion (Nottinghamshire County Council, 2007b: 9).

Reflecting the recommendations expressed in the Minister's Review of Disability (1989) and government recognition of the crucial role that local authorities have to play, this brief snap-shot provides a clear indication of Nottinghamshire's commitment to the delivery of mass participation opportunities for disabled people. While it is important to emphasize that the above is merely an illustration of the amount and broad range of sports development activities that Nottinghamshire is delivering, it would be fair to suggest that these activities typically focus on providing support to mainstream providers (e.g. mainstream schools and sports clubs) but also delivery of disability sport events, supporting disabled people's employment in sport, and recognizing the significant need for training and education of coaches and teachers. It is also clear that Nottinghamshire works closely with some key mainstream sports organizations (such as the Youth Sport Trust) and some regional and national governing bodies of sport (such as the Football Association (FA), and Nottinghamshire's Table Tennis Association) as well as disability sport organizations (such as the EFDS and CP Sport). For example, Nottinghamshire is providing opportunities in disability football for local players which are supported by and a part of the FA's broader development strategy (FA,

2006). While such partnerships support the authority, as well as the partner organization to achieve their own respective objectives in relation to disability sport
development, the range and focus of activities is determined by Nottinghamshire,
not by Sport England, the EFDS, the FA or any other national agency. In this
regard, while providing a crucial role in local delivery that has developed substantially over recent years, due to the range of constraints that influence local authority policy described earlier and the absence of a coherent national strategy for
disability sport, it seems likely that provision of sport for disabled people at a local
level will vary from one authority to another. While we would not want to suggest
this is necessarily wrong – indeed a local authority's role is to respond to its residents' needs – as the two case studies already indicate, the lack of a clearly defined
disability sport policy focus is likely to lead to the provision of differential patterns
of provision and opportunity for disabled people to participate in sport and physical activity locally.

Kent County Council

The county of Kent has a diverse population distribution and community profile;
it has areas of rural and urban living – parts of which are affluent, others of which
are more deprived economically and socially – and has a large white population
with pockets of black and minority ethnic communities. The publication of the
mid-year 2006 population estimates published by the ONS in 2007 indicated that,
excluding the Medway Council area, Kent County Council remains the largest
non-metropolitan local authority in England with a resident population of
1,382,900 people; a 0.7 per cent increase between 2005 and 2006 (Kent County
Council, 2007a). Sevenoaks District is the fastest growing local authority in the
area, whilst Dartford Borough is currently the smallest local authority in Kent
County Council. Of the 12 local authorities within the area, Dover and Shepway
currently have a declining population (Kent County Council, 2007a). The district
rankings of deprivation – as measured by the 2007 indices of multiple deprivation
– illustrate the extreme variations in socio-economic status of local authorities
across Kent. The district of Thanet, for example, is within the top 20 per cent most
deprived SOAs in England; the Sevenoaks and Tonbridge and Malling districts
are, by contrast, within the least 20 per cent deprived areas in England (Kent
County Council, 2008). In 2005, the largest ethnic group in the Kent County
Council (KCC) area was White British (94.7 per cent), though the proportion of
local residents of Black Minority Ethnic (BME) origin (5.3 per cent) has increased
by 76.3 per cent between 2001 and 2005 (Kent County Council, 2007b).
Currently, those of Indian origin represent the largest BME group in Kent (1.2 per
cent), with the majority living in the Gravesham region which, together with
Dartford, account for just over 25 per cent of the county's BME population. The
largest population increases among BME groups were observed amongst those
local residents who defined themselves as Black African (Kent County Council,
2007b).

Kent County Council has a reputation for being amongst the most active providers of sports development for disabled people at the local level in England. In addition to the Kent Sports Development Unit which provides a central role in the development of sporting opportunities for local residents, other providers who play a role in the County Council's disability sport provision include the Kent County Forum for Sport, Kent Association of Leisure Officers, Kent Association of Sports Development Officers, local authority sports development teams, a network of county governing bodies, sports specific development officers and various disability bodies such as the EFDS.

At the time of writing the Kent Sports Development Unit has a specialist, full-time officer responsible for the development and coordination of sports opportunities for disabled people in the county. The post of Kent Sports Development Manager for Disabled People is funded by Kent County Council's Sports Development Unit to support the work of partners in the delivery of, and training to support, opportunities in sport for disabled people. The post was established in 1993 by a partnership between Kent County Council Sports Development Unit, Dartford and Gravesham Area Social Services, the Sports Council and Queen Elizabeth's Foundation for Disabled People, with representatives from each agency on a steering committee to advise and support the office in post. In 1996 the post was incorporated within the Kent Sports Development Unit with the intention of providing a central strategic and organizational base for the development of disability sport in the local community. In particular, this organizational structure was purposively developed to help facilitate the dissemination of information, networking and partnership building to help provide disability sport events, activities, training and a range of opportunities to local disabled people to engage in sport and physical activity. An additional – and increasingly important – aspect of the existing organizational infrastructure for disability sport is the Kent Disability Sports Advisory Group which was created in 2003 as a means of providing support and advice to Kent's Sports Development Manager for Disabled People and to discuss and formulate ideas on disability sports development in Kent. The advisory group also acts as a support mechanism to the disability sports associate officers and other sports development workers working across the county. The group currently consists of the County Manager, the Kent *Rural Disability Sportslink's* project officer, associate officers and the Gravesham *Disability Sportslink* project staff representative. The group meets regularly to exchange 'good practice' and to discuss policy and practice regarding matters such as event management, child protection and risk assessment (Kent Sports Development Unit, 2008).

Following the publication of its first *Strategy for Disability Sport* in 1996, Kent County Council's Sport Development Unit published the *Kent Disability Sports Strategy 2004–2008* to provide a framework to develop, expand and establish sporting and recreational opportunities to all disabled people in Kent. Notably, the strategy states 'that this disability sports strategy should be seen as a module to accompany and elaborate on the Strategic Framework for Sport in Kent 2003–2008' (Kent County Council, 2004: 1). That local authority disability sport is considered to be an extension of the County Council's existing mainstream sports development activity is reflected in the strategic recommendations that features in its *Disability Sports Strategy 2004–2008*. It is claimed, for example, that one of the aims of the strategy is 'to work with each of the 13 local authority sports development officers/teams and Kent Active Sports Partnership to secure disability sports development targets as part of their overall programme' (Kent County Council, 2004: 15). A second, related aim, is to 'develop partnerships with sports specific governing bodies, voluntary, public, private and commercial sector organizations across Kent' (Kent County Council, 2004: 15).

Among the many and varied sports activities organized for disabled people in Kent is the *Rural Disability Sportslink* project that was initiated in 2000 as one of 15 national projects funded by Sport England's *Active Communities* programme. The central objective of the project was to help increase disabled people's access to, and participation in, the outdoor rural environment of Kent. This, it is said, is achieved through the development of sports facilities and activities in the countryside with the following sports and recreational activities cited as particular priorities:

- cycling – promoting the sport, providing bikes and trails for disabled people;
- walking – guided walks for blind people;
- climbing – volunteer training, advice to managers of facilities and indoor climbing walls;
- riding – increasing access to riding clubs and stables;
- archery – taster events, club development, equipment loan schemes; and
- country events – for promoting natural parks to young disabled people. (Kent County Council, 2004: 14)

Following its review in 2003, the Kent *Rural Disability Sportslink* project was considered a major success in promoting sporting opportunities and experiences amongst disabled people, with the following said to be amongst the key achievements of the project:

- 7 taster sessions organized in a variety of sports;
- 130 disabled people had tried out new sports and recreational activities;
- 14 specific education and training courses had been organized;
- 154 people had become qualified leaders, instructors or coaches;
- 18 disabled people had become sports leaders or attended specific sports related training;
- 18 new sports and recreational clubs and opportunities had been established;
- 182 young disabled people have been involved in the Pedalability school programme; and
- £80,368 has been attracted for further development of the project. (Kent County Council, 2004: 14)

Building on the perceived success of this project, the Kent *Outdoor Pursuits Disability* project was initiated in 2005 and funded by Sport England's *Active England* programme, the aim of which was to increase access to the outdoor environment and encourage recreational physical activity in the countryside. More specifically, this involves trained staff working with disabled people on a one-to-one basis to break down barriers to participation in outdoor sports so that people of all abilities can take part alongside family and friends. According to Kent County Council, in 2005 alone the project encouraged 3,500 people to participate in at least one outdoor pursuit (Kent Sports Development Unit, 2008). This one-to-one approach was partly inspired by Gravesham's *Disability Sportslink* project – a partnership between Gravesham Borough Council and Kent Sports Development Unit – which employed staff to provide direct and personal support to disabled people, so that they could try sports and activities at established clubs or, where demand existed, establish new sports clubs and sessions.

Brief mention should also be made of two other disability sport programmes that are also provided as part of the local authority sports development services to local residents in Kent, namely, the *Kent Disability Sports Associate Officer Scheme* and the *Inclusive Fitness Initiative* (IFI). The Associate Officer Scheme was originally set up in 1995 as a means to register, acknowledge and support the voluntary contribution made by individual coaches and administrators in Kent to sport for disabled people. Focusing on volunteers in powerlifting, boccia, wheelchair basketball and athletics, those coaches and administrators awarded 'associate' status were provided with an annual honorarium and basic expenses in return for the experiences and expertise in meeting the needs of disabled athletes which they shared with the County's Sport Development Unit. Such has been the perceived success of the scheme and it now includes 'associates' in football, rugby union, swimming, netball, archery, cycling, and new-age curling, and has been regarded as a pioneering programme which represents 'good practice' in local authority disability sport development. The second programme is the IFI – a National Lottery Funded project led by the EFDS – which assists fitness facilities in becoming more accessible to disabled and non-disabled people. Fitness facilities that have been awarded IFI status have staff trained in working with disabled people and equipment that has been tested by, and considered suitable for, the majority of disabled people who participate in disability sport development. By 2007, four sport and fitness centres in Kent had been given IFI status and in two of the facilities – Pent Valley Fitness Site and Julie Rose Stadium Ashford – disabled people made up over 15 per cent of its users (Kent Sports Development Unit, 2008).

In addition to the selected sports development projects provided by Kent County Council, there are a wide range of sport-related services offered directly to disabled people and to mainstream and disability sport organizations. At the time of writing, the unit offers, for example, in partnership with other organizations such as the EFDS, CP Sport, the Tennis Foundation and the YST, training for PE teachers, training in boccia, a comprehensive internet-based database on accessible sports specific clubs, have-a-go wheelchair tennis taster sessions, inter-school goal ball competitions, multi-sport disability school games (for nine mainstream and 21 special schools), county-wide competitive events and pathways to national competition (Kent Sports Development Unit, 2008).

It appears from this brief overview that the range and extent of sports development activity and provision for disabled people in Kent is more developed and wide-ranging than the other two local authorities. The county council's activities range from organizing and delivering events for disabled people, to supporting disability sports clubs and increasing the opportunities for disabled people to engage in sports and use mainstream facilities that currently exist for non-disabled people. It is also apparent that working with mainstream providers to enhance the sporting opportunities and experiences for disabled people is a key priority which seems to be integrated firmly into the mainstream activities of the Sports Development Unit in Kent. The same can also be said for the relationships which Kent County Council has begun to establish with some national governing bodies. In addition, the funding and policy commitment which it gives to ensuring that the activities of its disability sports development officers are tightly integrated into those of other colleagues within the Sports Development Unit is also a particularly striking feature of this local authority's provision of disability sport.

Summary

As we noted earlier, it can properly be said that together with the activities of various DSOs, organizations such as the EFDS and some governing bodies of sport, local authorities are among a number of key – if not the main – providers of opportunities for disabled people to participate in sport and physical activities of various kinds. We have also drawn attention, however, to the fact that despite the increasing importance that has come to be placed on the role of local authorities in the provision of sports development since the late 1990s in particular, historically, disability sport has been loosely integrated into the sports development activities of some local authorities. It is also fair to claim from this brief analysis that there is some similarity in each of the local authorities' main aims in relation to disability sport development. However, as our three case studies have begun to indicate, there exists differential policy and practice between individual local authorities and that, as a consequence, the sporting experiences and opportunities available to disabled people may vary considerably – perhaps very considerably – from one local authority to another. There is, for example, considerable variety in the range and number of sports clubs and competitions available to disabled people in each authority. Accordingly, whilst keeping in mind the limited data that are available on local authority disability sports development, there is reason to believe that despite the emphasis which has come increasingly to be placed increasingly on the mass participation and social inclusion agendas at local authority level, there does not appear at present any coherent policy – or, indeed, anything approaching it – designed to enhance either the mainstream or segregated sports development provision for disabled people between local authority areas.

Revision questions

1   To what extent have national sport policy and development priorities impacted on those of local authorities? Illustrate your answer with reference to an example of a mainstream and disability sport policy or strategy.
2   Examine the reasons why local authorities are believed to play an increasingly important role in policy implementation for sports development since the late 1990s.
3   How might we explain the existence of differential policy and practice for disabled people within and between local authorities?
4   Using a local authority case study of your choice, examine the sports development policies and strategies that are intended to enhance the sporting opportunities and experiences for disabled people.
5   To what extent has the growing expectation that local authority sports development officers focus more on the use of sport to achieve non-sporting objectives (such as the promotion of social inclusion) impacted on the sporting opportunities and experiences of disabled people?

Key readings

Department for Culture, Media and Sport (DCMS) (1999) *Policy Action Team 10 (Arts and Sport): A Report to the Social Exclusion Unit*, London: DCMS.
Department for Culture, Media and Sport (DCMS)/Strategy Unit (2002) *Game Plan: A Strategy for Delivering Government's Sport and Physical Activity Objectives*, London: DCMS/Strategy Unit.
Houlihan, B. and White, A. (2002) *The Politics of Sports Development: Development of Sport or Development Through Sport?*, London: Routledge.
Sports Council (1993a) *People with Disabilities and Sport: Policy and Current/Planned Action*, London: Sports Council.
Sports Council Research Unit (1991) *National Demonstration Projects: Major Lessons and Issues for Sports Development*, London: The Sports Council.

Recommended websites

Barrow Sports Council
www.barrowsportscouncil.org.uk

Kent County Council
www.kentsport.org.uk

Nottinghamshire County Council
www.nottinghamshire.gov.uk

4 Mainstreaming disability sport

A case study of four sports

Objectives

This chapter will:

- discuss the contested and often contradictory meaning of the principle of mainstreaming in disability sport policy and practice;
- examine the emergence and development of mainstreaming as a policy issue in mainstream and disability sport; and
- examine how the principle of mainstreaming has come to impact on the policy and practice of the national governing bodies of four professional sports.

Introduction

As we have explained in the previous chapters of this book, since the mid-1980s increasing emphasis has come to be placed on the process of mainstreaming within the context of disability sport. In Chapter 2, for example, we noted that the aims of the British Sports Association for the Disabled (BSAD), debates at BSAD's 'Think Tank' in 1985, the recommendations of the Minister for Sport's Review Group in 1989, the Sports Council's policy on people with a disability in 1993, the *New Start* conferences between 1995 and 1997 and Sport England's Equity Guidelines, all focused on shifting the responsibility for disability sport away from disability sport organizations (DSOs) towards mainstream providers such as national governing bodies (NGBs) of sport and local authorities. However, of the various policy statements and conference reports which referred to the alleged need to enhance the mainstreaming of disability sport in the 1980s and early 1990s, the Minister for Sport's Review Group's report *Building on Ability* was perhaps the most significant in helping to increase the salience of mainstreaming in disability and mainstream sport. As part of the review, the group conducted a large-scale survey of disability sport in Britain and on the basis of its findings concluded that 'some (NGBs) see little relevance in their own activities for people with disabilities either now or in the future' (Minister for Sport's Review Group, 1989: 18). To tackle this, the report provided the most detailed published account of how NGBs should, in the eyes of the Review Group, mainstream disability sport.

In particular, the Review Group recommended – albeit rather ambiguously in places – that governing bodies should:

- include the needs of people with disabilities in their coach training;
- nominate a senior officer to take responsibility for [disability sport] events;
- actively encourage disabled athletes to take part in events and competitions they organize, either in direct competition with able bodied athletes or in parallel events;
- work with disability sport organizations to modify their award schemes to cater for people with disabilities;
- involve disabled people in both their decision making and administrative structures; and
- see the promotion of participation amongst people with disabilities as an integral part of their function and encourage clubs to be more welcoming. (Minister for Sport's Review Group, 1989: 19–21)

More specifically, for the Minister's Review Group, a governing body would be considered to be mainstreaming successfully if it: (i) has responsibility for the provision and coordination of its sport for disabled people; (ii) has implemented policies which provide disabled people with equitable club, event and coaching opportunities; (iii) has in place decision making processes which involve disabled people and works effectively with disability sport organizations; and (iv) has values of mainstreaming that demonstrate a belief in retaining responsibility for servicing the needs of disabled people as a part of its general duties. The EFDS have also claimed more recently that mainstreaming is about NGBs taking on responsibility for the coordination and provision of opportunities for disabled people (EFDS, 2000). The EFDS suggests that DSOs (e.g. British Blind Sport) provide an important source of expertise and assistance to support policies and programmes designed to facilitate the mainstreaming of disability sport but believe that it is the responsibility of mainstream governing bodies to provide opportunities for disabled people to participate in sport as a participant, coach, administrator, official, or spectator. Thus, the EFDS consider the mainstream governing bodies to be the lead organization with DSOs providing assistance, support and technical expertise (EFDS, 2000). In its recent policy, *Count Me In* (EFDS, 2004), and in response to an extensive consultation exercise which took place prior to its publication, it stated – rather ambiguously – how it conceptualized mainstreaming. In this context, mainstreaming for the EFDS refers to the process of integrating 'disability sport with non-disabled sport' even though it recognizes that 'in some cases this may not be possible but it could be done even if they [NGBs] have a separate group but it is set up within the non-disabled structure so that disabled people still have the same structure and benefits' (EFDS, 2004: 21). Finally, as we noted in Chapter 3, according to Sport England the central purpose of the EFDS is to 'drive the work of others' (Chaytors, interview) in relation to mainstreaming and the equity planning process provides a useful tool with which to do it. To support mainstreaming of disability sport and to address the inequity in the opportunities provided for disabled people by governing bodies, in 2000 Sport England published *Making English Sport Inclusive: Equity Guidelines for Governing Bodies* (Sport England, 2000). This policy statement provided 'general guidance on planning for inclusion and gives specific advice in relation to the following groups: ethnic minority communities, people with disabilities [and] women' (Sport England, 2000: 3).

Although the process of mainstreaming has been central to much of the policy rhetoric of organizations such as the British Association of Sports for the Disabled (BSAD), the EFDS and Sport England, it is clear that there is currently no universally accepted definition and understanding either of what mainstreaming is in theory and, perhaps more importantly, how the assumptions which surround mainstreaming are implemented in practice. Within this context, the central objective of this chapter is to examine how the principle of mainstreaming has come to impact on the policy and practice of the national governing bodies of four professional sports: football, swimming, tennis and wheelchair basketball. In particular, we shall draw on a range of survey and interview data as well as documentary evidence in order to explore: (i) the role of each of the governing bodies in providing and coordinating sport for disabled people; (ii) the main policies and activities of each governing body and the relationships it has established with other organizations to facilitate the mainstreaming of disabled people and disability sport in its activities; (iii) the particular perceptions of key personnel within each governing body towards mainstreaming disability sport in their organization; and (iv) the progress each governing body has made towards the mainstreaming of disability sport by using the Minister for Sport's Review Group's recommendations outlined earlier.

The English Football Association

Roles and responsibilities in football for disabled people

Since its inauguration in 1863, the English Football Association (FA) has become one – if not the – largest and most powerful governing bodies of sport in England. There are currently approximately 7 million participants, 37,500 affiliated clubs, 500,000 volunteers, 2,000 competitions and 30,000 qualified coaches under its jurisdiction (FA, 2001). Its claimed mission is to 'use the power of football to build a better future' and its aim is to 'lead the successful development of football in England by working in partnership with key agencies to provide quality footballing opportunities for all' (FA, 2001: 5). However, despite its substantial income, football for disabled people has, until the last decade or so, not been a priority for the FA. Football in general is also not a priority sport for UK Sport and it is not unsurprising that football for disabled people has not benefited from the funding made available to governing bodies of sport from UK Sport, which from April 2006 assumed responsibility for performance-related support of elite Paralympic (and Olympic) athletes in England. To this end, the UK operates three programmes (World Class Podium, World Class Development and World Class Talent) as part of a World Class Performance Pathway, through which (via their respective governing bodies), talented athletes (in selected sports) enjoy the benefits of 'coaching, training and competition support, medical and scientific services and access to the best facilities that the UK has to offer' (UK Sport, 2008), and a financial contribution towards living and sporting costs. As we will highlight later in this chapter UK Sport's support of talented athletes in sports other than football contributed to some governing bodies' nascent interest in the mainstreaming of disability sport.

In light of the general lack of enthusiasm in football for disabled people amongst some members of the FA and UK Sport, responsibility for the development of disability football until the late 1990s was left to some DSOs such the English Sports Association for People with a Learning Disability, Cerebral Palsy Sport, the British Deaf Sports Council and the British Amputee and Les Autres Sports Association. Indeed, these organizations have played a crucial role in the provision and development of football for specific groups of disabled people and have assumed responsibility for selecting and training national football teams for their respective disability groups without support from the FA. Since the late 1990s, however, the FA began to work closely with the EFDS – mainly due to the interests and commitment of a few key officers within each organization – to discuss the delivery of grassroots programmes and the development and promotion of regional opportunities for disabled people to participate in football (Thomas, 2004). As we shall see next, the FA's recent expressed commitment to the development of disability football has focused on both club football and the development of its various national teams for disabled people.

History and policies

As we noted earlier, prior to 1998, despite seeking support from the FA, DSOs developed football-related activities almost entirely independently of the FA which recognized it had limited involvement in disability football. In particular, the FA claimed that this was due 'to the plethora of organizations representing disabled people' making it 'difficult to produce a coherent all embracing strategy for disabled football' (FA, 2007). Eventually, following a period of sustained lobbying by BSAD, UKSAPLD, CP Sport and BALASA, and a series of meetings in 1995 between these DSOs and Robin Russell (then FA Director of Education), the FA published *Coaching Players with Learning Disabilities* (FA, n.d). Although in it the FA provided basic advice on how to coach disabled people, this was not followed by any further policy commitment to develop football for disabled people from the FA who claimed that, without better coordination among the DSOs, it was difficult to produce a 'coherent all embracing strategy for disability football' (FA, 2007). However, in July 1999, the coaches of the England learning disability football teams – who were volunteers normally working with disability sport organizations – asked the FA for support to attend the European Championships. This occurred at a similar time when: (i) the EFDS was established; (ii) Adam Crozier became Chief Executive of the FA; (iii) Jeff Davis (who was previously an officer for BSAD and had considerable experience of disability football) joined the FA; and (iv) the FA's Football Development Committee was established. The FA agreed to support the learning disability football team at the European Championships by funding a technical advisor, manager, coach and physiotherapist. With the formation of the Football Development Committee and the establishment of the EFDS in 1998 as the umbrella organization for the seven NDSOs (see Chapter 2), the FA claimed that with regard to its relationship with DSOs and its understanding of the policy objectives within disability sport development, for the first time, 'lines of communications became clear' (FA, 2007).

Following its decision to help the England learning disability football teams attend the 1999 European Championships, the FA then agreed to a request from the EFDS to match-fund the *One 2 One Ability Counts* football development programme, which provided funding opportunities for Football in the Community sections of professional clubs and FA Charter Standard accredited clubs to offer regular training sessions to disabled players at a local level. Established in 1999, the *One 2 One* programme was implemented by the FA in partnership with the EFDS and was described by Adam Crozier, then Chief Executive of the FA, as 'a great success' that 'promoted a model [of partnership in disability sport] that could be used by other governing bodies' (Crozier, 2002: 10). This partnership model facilitated the support of 54 participating clubs that were involved in the programme by 2005.

Building upon the perceived success of the *One 2 One* programme, in 2001 the FA produced a *Football Development Strategy 2001–2006* that, in consultation with the EFDS, contained a significant section devoted to the development of disability football and incorporated the *One 2 One* programme. The strategy stated that the FA aimed to lead the 'successful development of football in England [and] to become the world's leading governing body in the development of Disability Football' (FA, 2001: 35). The FA also recognized that it was necessary to break down more effectively the barriers facing groups such as disabled people to play, coach, manage, referee and watch football than had been the case hitherto. Underpinning this expressed commitment by the FA to adopt a more central role in the development of football for disabled people, it published a National Equity plan the objective of which was to 'remove the barriers or discrimination that may prevent opportunities for all' (FA, 2001: 27) and to achieve greater equity and social inclusion for groups such as disabled people. In particular, the FA expressed its commitment to embed the needs of disabled football players into its general duties when it suggested that it would:

- establish a Football Association Disability Working Party (which includes the EFDS);
- establish County Disability Coaching Centres;
- produce, develop and agree a disability player pathway model/talent identification for males/females;
- work with the EFDS and Youth Sports Trust and the Local Education Authorities to ensure every special school or Unit (within mainstream) delivers Soccability; and
- support six national disability squads – provide a technical advisor, kit, and medical support to each squad. (FA, 2001)

Building on the alleged commitments it made to mainstream disability football within its development strategy, the FA subsequently published *Football for Disabled People* (FA, 2004) and to coordinate its implementation, appointed Jeff Davis to the position of National Development Officer for disability football in 2004. The FA also formed a Disability Advisory Group (DAG), to help meet the requirements of the FA's Ethics and Sports Equity Department, the purpose of which was to promote the access of disabled people to football.

Despite this growing but gradual interest in football for disabled people and the particular financial constraints under which it claimed to work, the FA committed £1.2 million – which is considerably less than that which it devotes to football played by non-disabled people – between 2004 and 2006 to help develop disability football from the grass roots to elite level (FA, 2004). Funding was targeted to ensure the *Ability Counts* club is the 'hub' for disability football activity, providing both regular playing and training opportunities, which is supported by the links between the club and the respective County Football Association (FA, 2004). However, whilst County FAs were encouraged to produce and implement a County Disability Plan to establish a network of inclusive clubs around the country, the effectiveness of this structure and the overall commitment to disability sport – at least initially – remained variable, in large part due to the need for staff development among the FA's football coaches (Davis, interview).

Building on its previous policy statements, in 2006 the FA published *Football for Disabled People: Strategy Update* (FA, 2006) which highlights some of the alleged progress made by the FA in mainstreaming disability sport. The update emphasizes that the FA now supports international disability squads for players with different kinds of impairment, including those athletes who are blind, partially sighted, deaf and hearing impaired, have cerebral palsy and learning difficulties, as well as amputees. The teams all receive official England kit, a physio, a fully-trained technical advisor, and money towards travel costs for attending European and World Championships, whilst England 'caps' are awarded to all players who play in a major tournament. According to the FA's Jeff Davis, the central aim of the initiatives that inform the strategic direction of *Football for Disabled People: Strategy Update* 'is to see every football player (and we mean every football player) in the country have the possibility to play organized football and realize their maximum potential' (FA, 2007). Among the many claimed successes of the strategy which are cited by the FA include, for example, how in 2005–2006 the FA encouraged 50 teams to take part in the *One 2 One* programme; delivered training in disability football to 365 teachers in mainstream and special schools; established local and regional disability football structures; a skills award scheme; and a coach education programme. Perhaps one of the more notable achievements – and key to the strategy's success in helping to facilitate disability football within the FA's activities – has been the establishment of disability working groups within 45 County Football Associations to coordinate and implement local activities and opportunities. Through its disability working group, Wiltshire FA, for example, now provide coaching in special schools and special needs units, events, festivals and tournaments, and delivers the *One 2 One* scheme through Swindon Town

Football Club's Football in the Community Scheme. Staffordshire FA is another county FA that has recognized its leadership role in developing football for disabled people and it now has its own full-time disability coach who works with special schools, adult day centres, runs coaching for disabled players courses and has developed in partnership with Stoke City Football Club an FA Disability Centre of Excellence (Staffordshire Football Association, 2008). The purpose of the centre is to help coaches identify and develop talented disabled players and it offers trials to any disabled player. Those players who are selected train once a week and play against other centres in the region such as those in Birmingham and Nottingham. The centre which is based at Stoke City FC employs a director, administrator, physiotherapist and coaches to support each of the two age groups; under 14s and under 17s (Staffordshire Football Association, 2008).

In its document *Ethics and Sports Equity* (FA, 2008), the Football Association outlines its work in relation to tackling inequity generally but also summarizes its achievements in the development of disability football since 2005. The FA illustrates its increasing commitment to disability football development, by highlighting the support given to the six national disability football teams, its hosting of the European Blind Football Championships, the development of a Level 1 Coaching Disabled Footballers' Course, its 15 Centres of Excellence (for Disability Football). It also highlights the work of its County Football Associations, claiming that 'by the third quarter of this year, 7,500 disabled players had attended festivals, 950 attended coaching centres, 42 Soccability courses, 20 Soccability clubs, 600 male and 100 female coaches have attended the coaching disabled footballers course this year' (FA, 2008). Much disability football development has been driven by a partnership model in which the County Football Associations have worked with the local authorities and professional football clubs. For example, Liverpool County FA has worked with Everton FC and Liverpool City Council to develop a Disability Centre of Excellence in partnership with Merseyside Sports that won the FA Football Development Award for best practice in Disability Football (FA, 2008).

The FA has recently invested over £250,000 in disability football and has an established National Disability Working Party 'bringing together key organisations/expertise to devise and implement the strategy for disability football' (FA, 2008), but states that it 'will be investing £600,000 over the next three years . . . which will not only continue to support the elite national squads, but develop a grassroots infrastructure that will create pan-disability coaching centres around the country' (FA, 2008).

Perceptions of mainstreaming

As indicated in the introduction to this chapter, despite the overwhelming presence of mainstreaming as the central policy objective within disability sport development, there is no universal definition of what it means and how key administrators' ideologies and assumptions may be influenced by practice. In this regard, it is important to establish for each of the sports considered here key administrators' perceptions on the role of governing bodies (of mainstream sport) and DSOs in the process of mainstreaming. According to Davis, 'DSOs should be a part of the system designed to provide opportunities to their members' but maintains that the FA, as a mainstream governing body, be the lead agency for the development of football for disabled people. Thus, Davis considers the FA (as the governing body of football) to be the agency that has (and should have) responsibility for the development and provision of football for disabled people. Davis recognizes, however, that 'they [the FA] need to do a lot more work before disability provision becomes part of the normal programme' (Davis, interview), that is, a central part of the mainstream activities of the FA. He is also of the view that DSOs, and specifically the EFDS, have an important role in disability football, for in his opinion, the FA 'have the football knowledge' but 'many of the FA's officers have never worked with disabled people' (Davis, interview) and this is what the EFDS can offer the FA to achieve its objectives for developing disability football.

Speaking of the relationships the FA has established with the EFDS and the progress it has made towards mainstreaming football for disabled people, Chaytors (Chief Executive of the EFDS, interview) has suggested that the 'FA have been incredibly supportive of EFDS' and 'have now mainstreamed their disability football programme and have allocated an increasing fund to elite and development squads'. According to Chaytors, the initial policy and priorities of the FA between 2003 and 2005 was, however, on just the 'elite five disability teams and less on the grassroots programme'. Since then the EFDS are said to have 'encouraged the FA to improve opportunities and provision at local and regional level' for disabled footballers since the rather narrow approach that the FA had adopted towards its provision of football for disabled people was thought to 'be unsustainable' (Chaytors, interview). Notwithstanding the increasing importance that the FA is believed to have placed on mainstreaming disability football within its core activities, and whilst it now has an established disability working party, Chaytors suggests that the FA is too dependant on the influence of Davis. While recognizing his significant contribution to the development of disability football, Chaytors suggests that in order to 'achieve mainstreaming' the FA 'need to get to the stage where it is more than one lone individual [Davis] putting the case forward for disabled football' (Chaytors, interview). Chaytors indicates here that until the needs of disabled people are considered by *all* of its staff and each and every part of the FA's core business, then disability football will remain marginal and potentially vulnerable to changes in the priorities of those other than Davis.

Summary: football

Despite its relatively recent commitment to mainstreaming disability football the FA has met almost all of the Minister's Review Group's recommendations for mainstreaming disability sport into the activities of governing bodies. The FA now includes the needs of disabled football players in its coaching and player development opportunities, has a National Development Officer who has taken on responsibility for disability football, and established a support pathway of opportunity from local to regional and national levels. Moreover, while the FA originally intended to work with the EFDS who developed the national football development *One 2 One* programme, since 2003/04 the FA decided to develop and implement its disability football strategy without support from the EFDS, because it had the resources to do so. In other words, whilst the FA welcomed the EFDS's support in, for example, identifying potential young players, the FA had the infrastructure of coaches, trainers and clubs to implement its strategy without the EFDS. It is important to note, however, that the initial shift in the FA's disability football development priorities was less to do with a policy commitment instigated by key decision makers within the FA's senior management or the lobbying efforts by DSOs, than it was the result of: (i) funding provided by a commercial telecommunication company (British Telecom); (ii) the personal friendship of key individuals in the EFDS and the FA (Crozier and Chaytors); and (iii) the commitment to disability football on the part of one FA officer (Davis). Indeed, despite the commitment it now gives to the development of football for disabled people and the progress it has made towards meeting the needs of disabled people, it could be argued that the FA has nevertheless until recently tended to pay lip-service to the mainstreaming of disability football within its policy and practice.

British Swimming

Roles and responsibilities in swimming for disabled people

In a similar manner to many other governing bodies of sport, the twin policy objectives of British Swimming (BS) are to ensure that everyone has an opportunity to learn to swim and reach his or her own goal and to increase the likelihood that elite level swimmers will achieve gold medals at the Olympics. (BS is the NGB for swimming; responsible for international competition, and with the three home countries as its members, i.e. ASA is its English member.) Between 2006 and 2009, as a sport which can access funds from UK Sport due to its medal winning potential, disability swimming will receive £5,713,200 from the Lottery for its World Class Performance Plan (UK Sport, 2006). The National Performance Director of Disability Swimming, Tim Reddish, stated that BS welcomed further investment into disability sport and would use the additional funding towards 'building a comprehensive programme focused on identified athletes they believe have the potential to win medals at both the 2008 and 2012 Paralympic Games' (UK Sport, 2006).

While the Sports Council and the Amateur Swimming Association (ASA) were involved in the development of disability swimming from the 1960s, it was not until 1997 that the ASA decided to assume full responsibility as the governing body of disability swimming, the reasons for which we explore later. Supported by Sport England, BS is now the governing body of disability swimming even though DSOs, and particularly Disability Sport Events (DSE), remain major providers of national swimming events. Traditionally, BS has had limited contact with the EFDS and a fractious relationship with other DSOs, and has tended to rely upon its own volunteers and individual disabled swimmers for advice and support in matters relating to disability swimming rather than on DSOs (Thomas, 2004).

History and policies

The involvement of BS in the coordination of swimming for disabled people has a long history and can be traced back to the establishment in 1969 of an informal coordinating group for swimming and disabled people (BSAD, 1985). In 1974 the ASA appointed an officer to develop swimming for disabled people and, in 1976, due to the interests of the ASA and the activity of DSOs such as BSAD, a National Coordinating Committee on Swimming for People with a Disability was established.

Since these early developments there has been a growth in competitive swimming events for disabled people not least because of the popularity of swimming in special schools and the activities of DSOs. According to David Sparkes (Chief Executive of British Swimming), however, it was the introduction of national events led by BSAD that heralded the beginning of well-organized, high performance and high profile swimming events for disabled people. Sparkes suggests that together with the improving profile of national and international events, by the late 1990s aspiring disabled swimmers were shifting 'away from disability specific groups', preferring to seek support from 'traditional [mainstream] swimming clubs', as they wanted access to the best coaches and to train with non-disabled swimmers (Sparkes, interview).

In August 2002 the ASA published a *Disability Development Plan (2002–2006)* in which it sought to demonstrate the ASA's commitment to take responsibility for the development and delivery of disability swimming. A series of objectives to facilitate the mainstreaming of disability swimming were included within the plan and these focused, in particular, on the alleged need to 'improve competitive opportunities, talent identification, opportunities for coaches, teachers and officials, club structures, and the promotion of disability swimming' (ASA, 2002: 62). The plan also stated that 'each ASA district should have its own classification team', all disabled swimmers should be 'registered on the ASA swimmers' database', and 'all coaches and teachers should have disability swimming as a part of their continual professional development' (ASA, 2002: 63–6).

During discussions at the *New Start* conferences (held between 1995 and 1997) on the future of disability sport in the UK (see Chapter 2), it became clear to Sparkes that the DSOs were playing the 'governing' lead role that national governing bodies of sport ought to play. Sparkes believed that there was a 'plethora of disability specific organizations with a plethora of agendas' and that 'if disability sport was ever to mature and grow up it would only do so through governing body interference' (Sparkes, interview). Sparkes recommended to the ASA's Great Britain and England Committees that the ASA should 'proactively get involved' in the development and delivery of opportunities in disability swimming. As a consequence, in 1997, the Swimming Committee considered the implications of taking responsibility for disability swimming (ASFGB/ASA, 1997) and on 8 November 1997, with Sparkes's support, a GB Disability Swimming Committee was established (ASFGB/ASA, 1997).

The ASA's relationship with both the EFDS and some DSOs such as DSE (previously British Sports Association for the Disabled) and CP Sport has been strained since the DSOs have not provided (to BS) collectively 'a united front' and 'tend to work in isolation from [each other]' (Sparkes, interview). While sympathetic to their position and recognizing that organizations such as CP Sport and Disability Sport Events 'may see us [British Swimming] as taking over their role', Sparkes is clear that running events for those 'who aspire to go to the Paralympics' is 'central to British Swimming's role' (Sparkes, interview). While Gordon Neale (Director of DSE) agreed that the coordination of disability sport in general has been poor, with regard to swimming he suggested that BSAD's programme of regional and national swimming events for clubs and schools has had a 'profound and positive influence on the swimming programme [for disabled people] in this country', and suggests that governing bodies such as BS will for a long time need the expertise and experience of the DSOs. While continuing to work with DSOs and in particular DSE, BS further expressed its commitment to disability swimming with the publication of *Swimming's Strategic Plan 2005–2009* (BS, 2004a: 3) which re-emphasized the commitment of BS to disability swimming by stating that 'Swimming remains focused on the achievement of success at the Olympic and Paralympic level' and that 'a specified aim by 2009 is to have 50 disability swimmers ranked in the top 20 world rankings' for their events. In its recent *Vision for Swimming: The Next Ten Years*, BS reasserted its alleged commitment to 'ensuring that the sport is accessible to all, regardless of age, gender, creed, ethnic origin, economic position, disability or level of ability' (BS, 2004b: 3). Notwithstanding this stated commitment, BS remains reliant on DSE in the provision of events for competitive events, and to this end in 2005 a Service Level Agreement between DSE, the EFDS and BS was developed to facilitate clearer pathways for competitive disabled swimmers. Sparkes commented on this agreement by claiming that

> the ASA and British Swimming have traditionally worked closely with DSE and EFDS to ensure that we are a world leader in disability sports provision. The new partnership has cemented that relationship and means swimmers benefit from a competition structure that allows them to progress from regional meets through to national championships and onto British squads. (EFDS, 2007)

Sparkes goes on to suggest that 'by working together we hope to develop a world-class meet to attract world-class competitors and give our athletes the best possible preparation in the run-up to London 2012 [and that] it will also allow us to equip staff and volunteers with the necessary expertise in order to host the best possible Paralympics and provide a lasting legacy from the Games' (EFDS, 2007). Neale added: 'the close working relationship that has developed over the years with

British Swimming is exemplified here [by the launch of the SLA]' and hopes that this will 'confirm to other National Governing Bodies of Sport that we [DSE] are here to assist them [NGBs] as a service support mechanism for including disabled people within their sport, and developing positive player pathways together' (EFDS, 2007). This close working relationship between BS and DSE in the delivery of events is one that is said to improve the range and coherence between opportunities for disabled swimmers but also benefits both organizations. It could be argued, however, that so long as DSE remain the providers of elite competitive events, governing bodies such as British Swimming, for example, may never fully take on responsibility for disability sport.

British Swimming has made significant steps towards mainstreaming swimming for disabled people and is keen to promote itself as a governing body that is taking responsibility for the provision and coordination of swimming for disabled people. While it is difficult to identify the precise motives for British Swimming's shift towards taking greater responsibility for disability sport, it appears that the pressure exerted by DSOs, the Sports Council and Sport England on the ASA and British Swimming to take responsibility for disability swimming was, at least to some extent, important. However, it is also the case that the lack of consensus and coordination bedevilling disability sport at a time when funding was available from UK Sport's World Class programmes provided the ASA with an opportunity to take a greater responsibility for disability swimming as part of its remit. It was a decision influenced by opportunism more than government or interest group pressure, and provided a further expression of the particularly limited influence of Sport England and the EFDS on developing policy for disability swimming.

Perceptions of mainstreaming

The ASA and, more recently, BS, have produced a series of statements within various policy related reports (ASA, 1997, 2002; BS, 2004a, b) all of which are designed to enhance its provision of disability swimming. These policies, together with changes to event rules and improvement in club and coaching structures, begin to indicate some commitment to mainstreaming disabled swimmers and disability swimming events throughout all the organization's activities. It is anticipated that there will be Disability Liaison Officers in all counties by 2009 to help provide knowledge about competition opportunities and support to local swimming clubs' capacity to include disabled people. Furthermore, indicating its commitment to embed the needs of disabled swimmers into its core activities, all BS officers, rather than just its Disability Officer, provide advice and information on swimming for disabled people.

Sparkes believes that the whilst the ASA and BS have traditionally 'not done enough' to develop and provide opportunities in swimming for disabled people, its role now is to provide 'training, coaches, competition, doping control, support structures, kit, transport . . . whatever is needed' (Sparkes, interview). He suggests that the DSOs can provide 'additional competitive opportunities specific to disability groups, but that DSOs' role is to 'augment and complement our [BS's] policies'. In this regard, Sparkes argues that the EFDS should play an important 'role in introducing children to swimming' but emphasizes that – despite their role in development and the provision of competitive events – responsibility for developing swimming for disabled people should remain that of BS rather than something which falls under the jurisdiction of a generic DSO such as the EFDS (Sparkes, interview). More specifically, whilst Sparkes recognized the success of some separate DSOs in delivering events, he suggested that 'ultimately the successful sports will be those sports that are sports rather than disability specific sports' (Sparkes, interview). In that sense, it is clear here that, in Sparkes's view governing bodies such as BS are the appropriate governors of, and providers for, disability sport, and organizations such as CP Sport (as disability specific sports organizations) can, and should, only play a supportive role.

Our above analysis would appear to suggest that BS have begun to take the mainstreaming of disability swimming as a more or less central aspect of its policy and practice seriously and have been cited by Sport England as an example of good practice. In particular, Sport England have claimed that the 'ASA has taken a full responsibility for the integration of Paralympic swimmers within its World Class Performance Plans' (Sport England, 2000: 33). Chaytors also acknowledges the progress of British Swimming, which he says 'now has a very good structure for disability swimming, with its own high performance director, development teams across the country and a huge network of clubs, a number of which are disability friendly' (Chaytors, interview). Chaytors is also of the view that whilst BS does 'a lot of work in providing training for coaches, officials and administrators', opportunities for disabled people to participate in swimming are not as widespread as they could be and as indicated earlier competitive events are significantly supported by DSE. In that sense, Chaytors suggests that for BS there 'is still much to do' (Chaytors, interview).

Summary: swimming

In a similar way to the English FA which we examined earlier, BS has met many of the Minister for Sport's Review Group's recommendations regarding the mainstreaming of disability sport. In addition to the number of swimming officers dedicated to disability swimming, BS also has disability-specific policies and runs events in order to enhance the promotion and provision of swimming opportunities for disabled people. For example, British Swimming's competition rules encourage the inclusion of disabled swimmers into mainstream as well as DSO events, with the DSO events considered as a complement and an alternative to those provided by BS. However, while BS involves disabled people within its own decision making processes and has recently – through a Service Level Agreement – nurtured a stronger partnership with DSE, it does not seem to work effectively with all DSOs. Indeed, some key personnel in disability sport (such as Neale of DSE) remain concerned that disabled swimmers at the grassroots level will continue to need the support of DSOs and others (such as Atha, President of the

EFDS) do not believe that governing bodies such as BS will meet their formally stated objectives which are designed to facilitate the mainstreaming of disability sport. It is also clear that while there is a general consensus amongst key administrators that disabled people should have access to both mainstream and disability swimming events and opportunities, there remains considerable debate over which is the most appropriate organization capable of delivering these services.

Tennis Foundation

Roles and responsibilities in tennis for disabled people

The Lawn Tennis Association (LTA) is the governing body of tennis in England and in its 2006 annual report it reported revenues of £47.2m, with much of its main income being derived from a surplus of £25.5m generated by its most prestigious event, the Wimbledon Championships. In addition to these monies, the LTA receives additional government funding through its Whole Sport Plan initiatives. However, whilst the LTA is responsible for the development of tennis in England, it is the Development Committee of the Tennis Foundation (TF) – which is an autonomous partner to the LTA and was known as the British Tennis Foundation (BTF) until October 2007 – that makes decisions relating to the development of disability tennis in England. The TF is the official registered tennis charity that works closely with the LTA, the national governing body for the game of tennis in Great Britain. Sue Wolstenholme (former Director of the British Tennis Foundation and former Chairman of the ITF Wheelchair Tennis Medical Commission) represented the British Tennis Foundation's Development Committee and reported BTF's disability tennis work to the LTA. The LTA is the main funding partner of the BTF and in 2005 it donated £3.75m to help fund the activities of the development of disability tennis under the auspices of the BTF (LTA, 2006).

The TF is currently responsible for the implementation of the World Class Performance Plans (described earlier in this chapter) for disability tennis, and for activities between 2006 and 2009, as a Paralympic priority sport, wheelchair tennis received £669,000 National Lottery monies. The TF currently employs among its staff a Head of National Disability Tennis and a Head of Education and Disability Development and its main focus has been the development of opportunities for wheelchair tennis, deaf tennis and learning disability tennis.

History and policies

Wheelchair tennis was first played in the United States of America during the 1970s but it was not until 1983 that it was played in Great Britain. In 1992 wheelchair tennis became a Paralympic sport, and is now played in over 50 countries by over 6,000 wheelchair tennis players. In England, it was the LTA Trust that provided the initial leadership in wheelchair tennis. The LTA Trust was established in 1988 as a charity to provide and support opportunities for young people and disabled people to play tennis, and changed its name to the BTF in 1997 and then, in 2007, to the TF. While the TF is also concerned with coach education, schools tennis, indoor tennis, fundraising and sponsorship in general, tennis for disabled people forms a major focus of the TF's work. The role of the EFDS in tennis development is simply to encourage participation through its regional structures. For example, the EFDS's regional officers may support the TF in identifying potential players or coaches and promoting to disabled people and local disability sports clubs, coaching courses, taster days and competitions. It was not until relatively recently however that tennis emerged as an area of development within disability sport.

During the 1990s, there was considerable debate amongst a number of DSOs over who should be the lead agency for the development of tennis for disabled people. In particular, BSAD, who encouraged mainstream agencies such as the LTA to take on responsibility for disability sport, had done little in the way of running disability tennis events or improving disabled people's access to tennis clubs. In that context, the TF decided to work very closely with the sports-specific disability organizations, and, in particular, the National Wheelchair Tennis Association, UK Sport Association for People with Learning Disabilities, UK Deaf Sport and British Deaf Tennis Association. These DSOs had already established clubs and events but welcomed the support of a governing body with access to the resources, infrastructure, and expertise, to coordinate across a range of impairments, the development of disability tennis. In January 2001 the BTF published their *Programme of Tennis for People with Disabilities* (BTF, 2001), which provided an outline of the DSOs with whom the BTF work and the national and regional structures and events in wheelchair, deaf and learning disability tennis. It also provides an indication of the wide range of activities and programmes organized by the BTF, including: assessment weekends, weekend camps for beginners, a festival of tennis for deaf players, LTA coaching courses for deaf and wheelchair players, and the provision of national championships.

Although the National Wheelchair Tennis Association (NWTA) and the British Deaf Tennis Association (BDTA) had been running national events and developing opportunities for disabled people to play tennis with the cooperation of the LTA, following the *New Start* process the BTF took a lead role in the development of tennis for disabled people. Whilst the NWTA and the BDTA were established to take specific responsibility for the development of tennis for wheelchair and deaf athletes, respectively, the British Wheelchair Sports Foundation and British Deaf Sports Council (of which the NWTA and BDTA were members) were unable and unwilling to assume the sports development role that was required to coordinate effectively disability tennis. Both organizations also believed that the BTF was the most appropriate agency to coordinate and provide tennis opportunities from local club coaching to national and international events. In collaboration with its partners (such as NWTA and BDTA), the current range and number of coaching and training events and competitions provided and supported by the TF is vast and expanding. For example, there are various regular camps for specific groups such as female wheelchair players, introductory tennis sessions in spinal injury units, and advice and support by qualified and experienced coaches at

Wheelpower's Junior Games (Wheelpower is the new name for the British Wheelchair Sports Foundation; for more details see Chapter 2). As Wolstenholme (interview) has noted, there is now 'a full programme for performance wheelchair tennis players, with a worldwide circuit of tournaments throughout the year' and, as part of this, sports science support is coming to play a major role within the TF's programme that is run by a Performance Director, Performance Coordinator, and four National Coaches. Deaf tennis players also enjoy the benefit of two dedicated national coaches, international competitions run on a four-year cycle, including the Deaflympics (the equivalent of the Paralympics) and warm weather training sessions in La Manga. An annual national tournament for learning disability players is also organized and, as part of the role of the new Education Manager for the TF, there is now a commitment to introduce tennis to many more special needs schools.

In relation to deaf tennis the TF currently works with UK Deaf Sport, British Deaf Sports Council and the British Deaf Tennis Association, particularly in relation to international matters. As deaf sport is not included in the Paralympics, there are no World Class Performance Plans available to support deaf tennis in England. Therefore, the TF funds its own competitions and development activities. In addition and indicating the significant role played by the TF, Lynn Parker, the TF's Disability Tennis Manager – who has acted as tournament director for numerous British Deaf Tennis Association championships – because of her significant experience and involvement in deaf tennis, is on the board of UK Deaf Sport. The decision taken by the BTF to focus initially on wheelchair and deaf tennis was because there already existed: (i) a demand by wheelchair and deaf players; (ii) recognized national associations for deaf and wheelchair tennis; and (iii) an international competition structure for which NWTA and BDTA provide the link, but has since made significant developments in tennis for those with learning difficulties.

It is worth noting that for wheelchair and deaf tennis players as well as tennis players with learning disabilities, the TF has developed organizational structures that demonstrate the central role it plays in providing and coordinating tennis at all levels. For example, it shows clearly the important function of its own tennis clubs in providing opportunities locally, but also its status as the governing body responsible for linking international agencies such as the British Paralympic Association and the International Wheelchair Tennis Association. According to Wolstenholme, there have been some major improvements in disability sport in general, and in the development of, and opportunities in, tennis for disabled people especially (Wolstenholme, interview).

Perceptions of mainstreaming

As indicated in the case studies of football and swimming, given the ambiguity of, and variable commitment to, disability sport, it is important to explore key administrators' perceptions of mainstreaming and roles they believe that DSOs and governing bodies of sport should play in this process. In this regard, Wolstenholme is clear that the TF's role is to ensure that disabled people have access to a full range of tennis opportunities: 'to introduce disabled people to tennis and to ensure that if they want to progress or want to compete, the pathways are there for them' (Wolstenholme, interview).

To facilitate this role, the TF works closely with the NWTA, Wheelpower, UK Deaf Sport, BDTA, Special Olympics, BPA and UK Sport and helps to ensure that at 'come and try' or festival days run by other organizations, tennis is represented so that anyone who is interested can be guided towards a tennis club or centre for further opportunities to participate in disability tennis. Wolstenholme emphasizes the importance that the TF also attaches to its consultation with disabled tennis players. According to Wolstenholme, committees within the NWTA and BDTA are predominantly made up of disabled tennis players and insists that the TF must continue to consult and be guided by the wishes and needs of disabled players, insisting that decisions on matters relating to disability tennis should lie with the disabled tennis players, not the disability sport organizations that may purport to represent them. She also contends that – with the support of NWTA and BDTA – under the auspices of the TF, tennis for disabled people is effectively coordinated, adequately resourced and able to benefit from and influence the policies and programmes of the LTA. However, while Wolstenholme believes that the TF is the appropriate lead agency in disability tennis she recognizes the success of some organizations, that have existed separately from a mainstream governing body (e.g. the Great Britain Wheelchair Basketball Association).

In relation to the TF's relationship with other DSOs, Wolstenholme suggest that they have an important role to play in the identification of potential players, but admits that their contact with the EFDS in particular has been limited. In Wolstenholme's view the 'EFDS was set up after New Start with a view to getting more people into disability sport' and 'to work more with governing bodies but, they've had a very difficult task and really . . . very little has been achieved in the way of mainstreaming since [the EFDS's establishment in 1998]'. Wolstenholme maintains that while there has been some confusion over the role that the EFDS is believed to play in mainstreaming, 'EFDS could do a really good job of locating and attracting disabled people into sport, one of the jobs that governing bodies find the most difficult, as it is very hard to find out where many disabled people are'. Chaytors (Chief Executive of the EFDS) suggests that the EFDS has

> always had a good relationship with tennis, working with the LTA and the Tennis Foundation, but it is very much on specific impairments [i.e. wheelchair, deaf and learning disability] . . . they are doing some great work but they could be doing a lot more . . . with other impairment groups where they're hardly doing anything . . . and one of our roles is to encourage and influence or embarrass them to do more.

It appears therefore that while the TF is acknowledged by organizations such as the EFDS as providing a good example of 'how to' mainstream disability sport, it is also clear that in Chaytor's view at least, that there are other development activities and impairment groups (other than wheelchair, deaf and learning disability) that the TF need to turn their attention to before they can claim to have mainstreamed tennis for disabled people.

It is clear, however, that despite the obvious commitment of the TF to the mainstreaming of disabled tennis players and disability tennis activities into the LTA, the LTA has failed to take seriously its responsibilities for disability tennis; prefers to adopt a largely hands-off approach to mainstreaming; and appears to have little interest in developing the sport as part of its activities. Indeed, despite the TF's capacity to focus on disability tennis separate from the wider concerns of the LTA, there is no evidence to suggest that Sport England or the EFDS's commitment towards disability tennis has had much impact on the development of tennis for disabled people within the LTA more broadly.

Summary: tennis

As we noted earlier, the TF is a separate organization that was created by the LTA to take primary responsibility for organizing tennis for disabled people in England. Through the TF the governing body has provided a comprehensive programme of development activities, coaching clinics and events which provide a pathway from beginner to excellence. The relationship between the TF and the disability tennis organizations (e.g. BDTA and NWTA) appears to be productive and complementary. The TF's role with the EFDS and DSE is almost non-existent, since the TF do not perceive they need the support of generic disability sports organizations, other than to identify potential players and promote various TF events and development activities.

Unlike our case studies of football and swimming, at first sight it would appear that our case study of tennis provides what may be seen as one of the best demonstrations of a sport whose organizing body – the TF – has begun to successfully mainstream disability sport and, in so doing, has met all of the recommendations identified by the Minister for Sport's Review Group. The TF appear to have a long-term commitment to disability tennis and involve disability tennis organizations and disabled tennis players (but not so much with generic disability sport organizations such as the EFDS) in its decision making processes. It could be argued, however, that disability tennis has not been mainstreamed at all, for it is the LTA not the TF that is the mainstream governing body of tennis, and for reasons explained earlier, the LTA appears to have little interest in developing tennis for disabled people as part of its activities.

Great Britain Wheelchair Basketball Association

Roles and responsibilities in wheelchair basketball for disabled people

Founded in 1936 the English Basketball Association (now known as England Basketball) is an organization of member clubs and players who elect an executive board of directors to act as the mainstream governing body for ambulant/running basketball in England. The formally stated purpose of England Basketball (EB) is to: (i) govern and enhance the sport of basketball in England; (ii) encourage and enable people to participate in basketball regardless of their ability, age, gender, status, disability or ethnic background; and (iii) lift the performance and quality of basketball throughout England (EB, 2008). In 2001 the EBA launched its Equal Opportunities policy which claimed it is 'responsible for ensuring that all those who wish to participate in the sport of basketball are treated on an equal basis . . . irrespective of age, gender, marital status, ethnic origin, disability or religious persuasion' (EBA, 2001: 1). However, in its 2002 development plan EB didn't identify any objectives or policies specifically directed at disabled players who are not eligible or interested in wheelchair basketball (EBA, 2002), which as we will examine in more detail shortly, was governed by a separate governing body: the Great Britain Wheelchair Basketball Association. Thus, at this juncture, the EBA demonstrated no tangible evidence of their commitment to developing basketball for disabled people.

However, since its 2002 policy the EB has begun to provide assistance in the development of opportunities for disabled people through its regional officers, and as a result, in 2006, with the support of the DSOs, EB achieved the Preliminary Level of the *Equality Standard: A Framework for Sport*. The *Equality Standard* was launched in 2004 as a collaborative response from the four home country Sports Councils and UK Sport and supported by the CCPR, Women's Sport Foundation and the EFDS to the recommendations of the Government Plan for Sport (DCMS, 2001). The standard provides a framework for assisting NGBs to widen access and promote participation in sport and physical activity from so-called under-represented groups such as disabled people. The standard aims to assist sports organizations in meeting their legislative obligations and drive them to demonstrate not just good practice in equality, but in all aspects of their governance. In this regard, the Chief Executive of EB, Keith Mair, claims that: 'England Basketball and Sport England, in consultation with our [England Basketball's] equity partners, are striving to ensure that our sport is inclusive' and employs its own equity officer to implement its action plan. Indeed in an update report (EB, 2006), EB states that: 'Extensive work has been undertaken to establish strong links with equity organisations and to identify the barriers that may discourage participation. England Basketball will continue to work to increase participation and to progress through the Equality Standard levels' (EB, 2006). However, with specific regard to wheelchair basketball, EB have made it clear that the Great Britain Wheelchair Basketball Association (GBWBA) is responsible for 'the organization and development of wheelchair basketball played in Britain and for international pathways is affiliated to the International Wheelchair Basketball Federation' (EBA, 2001: 1a). Indeed, the Great Britain Wheelchair Basketball Association is the only organization recognized by Sport England as a governing body of basketball for disabled people. In that sense, while it may be a pragmatic response to the circumstances specific to wheelchair basketball, Sport England's support for GBWBA – as the appropriate governing body for wheelchair basketball – appears to contradict the stated policy objectives by the Minister's Review Group (1989), Sports Council (1993, 2000) and the EFDS (2004), for the mainstreaming of disability sport.

History and policies

In contrast to the three case studies presented thus far, the organizational structure of wheelchair basketball for disabled people is rather different, for the GBWBA first emerged and has since remained independent of the mainstream governing body (EB). We examine the development of wheelchair basketball as part of the origins of disability sport in Chapters 2 and 6, but in the present context it is worth noting that in 1955 a touring team named the US Pan Am Jets first brought wheelchair basketball to the UK when they took part in the first international competition held at Stoke Mandeville. Wheelchair polo was the first sport to be introduced in 1946 at Stoke Mandeville by Sir Ludwig Guttmann (Strohkendle, 1996) and in 1947 polo was replaced by netball, which Strohkendle described as a distant cousin of wheelchair basketball. According to Strohkendle, wheelchair basketball was first played in the USA when war injured soldiers adapted the running game to a game on four wheels. While the International Stoke Mandeville Games were soon described as the 'Mecca' for disability sport (Strohkendle, 1996: 17), in the 1952 Games the highly skilled American side were surprised to have to play what was more like 'netball in a car park' (Strohkendle, 1996: 17); indeed, Craven claims that in Britain between 1948 and 1954 wheelchair basketball first developed as 'netball and then it became basketball in 1955' (Craven, interview).

While commentators such as Strohkendle and Sir Philip Craven (International Paralympic Committee President and ex-Chairman of GBWBA) pay particular credit to Sir Ludwig Guttmann's influence on both the creation and development of wheelchair basketball (see Chapter 2), unlike other disability sports that were developed in and since the 1940s, wheelchair basketball 'was created by disabled people and run by wheelchair basketball players' (Craven, interview). A simple classification system, in which athletes are scored on a point system according to their functional ability in basketball – examined in more detail in Chapter 6 – encourages athletes with paraplegia, spina bifida, amputees, brittle bones, cerebral palsy and multiple sclerosis, as well as non-disabled people to play.

The Great Britain Wheelchair Basketball League was formed in the late 1960s and was closely followed by the inauguration of the GBWBA (GBWBA, 2002). Similar to other wheelchair sports associations, GBWBA was affiliated to the British Paraplegic Sports Society (later to become the British Wheelchair Sports Foundation and then Wheelpower) and was established:

(i) To promote community participation in healthy recreation in particular by the provision of facilities for the playing of wheelchair basketball in Great Britain; and
(ii) To relieve those persons who have a severe permanent physical disability of one or both lower extremities who are resident in Great Britain or eligible to play for Great Britain by encouraging and promoting the sport of wheelchair basketball with the object of improving conditions of life and to assist in their integration into society. (GBWBA, 2007: 1)

There have been Paralympic basketball events for wheelchair athletes since 1960 and events for athletes with a learning disability since 2000. The funding GBWBA receives as part of its World Class Performance Plan supports three officers including a Performance Director, a National Coach, and a Sports Science officer. The GBWBA also employ (through the EB administration) a full-time National Development Officer working specifically on the development of wheelchair basketball. Originally the Great Britain Wheelchair Basketball League was not affiliated to the International Stoke Mandeville Games Federation because the League was part of the British Paraplegic Sports Society (which became British Wheelchair Sports Foundation and now Wheelpower). However, the GBWBA is now responsible for administering its own national league, cup competitions and tournaments and is still a member of the British Wheelchair Sports Foundation even though, in Craven's opinion, that is because 'they [Wheelpower] want us, rather than we need them' (Craven, interview). As discussed in Chapter 2, Wheelpower is the national organization for wheelchair sport in the UK which seeks to promote and develop opportunities for disabled men, women and young people to participate in recreational and competitive wheelchair sport. It also acts as the umbrella body for 17 different wheelchair sports associations of which GBWBA is one. The role of the GBWBA is:

- to act as the sole controller and governing body of the game of wheelchair basketball;
- to represent the view of the Association [GBWBA] at international wheelchair basketball meetings;
- to be the sole arbiter of all questions pertaining to wheelchair basketball;
- to be actively involved in any discussions of laws, rules and notes pertaining to wheelchair basketball by making representations to the International Wheelchair Basketball Federation;
- to make direct links with the running basketball association (EBA) in the home countries where the Association (GBWBA) is represented;
- to provide players for the Great Britain representative sides;
- to organize and govern competitions within the boundaries of the Association;
- to raise funds and invite contributions from any person or persons whatsoever by way of subscriptions, donations as otherwise provided that the Association shall not undertake any permanent trading activities in raising funds for its charitable objects; and
- to do all such lawful things as shall further the objects of the Association. (GBWBA, 2002: 1)

Although GBWBA was established initially as a 'rehabilitation and recreational activity for spinal cord injured patients', over the last half a decade or so, it has developed into a competitive sport with 65 teams in 10 divisions of a National Wheelchair Basketball League (GBWBA, 2008: 1). As indicated earlier GBWBA's classification system allows anyone 'who can conceivably play wheelchair basketball to do so', and notably in relation to this examination of mainstreaming, able bodied players are 'eligible to play in all divisions in the National, Women's and Junior Leagues' (GBWBA, 2008: 1). In this regard therefore, it is perhaps ironic that while 'mainstreaming policy' typically encourages national governing bodies of mainstream sport to adopt disability sport, in this particular case study of wheelchair basketball, the recognized and supported governing body (GBWBA) is separate from the mainstream organization (EB), and, moreover in what could be described as an example of 'reverse integration', non-disabled people are being provided with sporting opportunities with and by disabled people. Indeed, it is clear from GBWBA's constitution and practice that the game of wheelchair basketball is run by disabled people

The Executive Committee of the GBWBA, which is made up predominantly of wheelchair basketball players, 'decides on policy and what is good for the game' (Craven, interview). However, Craven recalls how, in the 1980s, the GBWBA 'were forced [by UK Sport] to partner EBA in order to access government funding' (Craven, interview). Similar pressure was exerted by Sport England in 1997 when member organizations of the EBA (including the GBWBA) were invited to a meeting to discuss their development plans. Craven recalls how the Chief Executive of the EBA recognized the benefit of GBWBA submitting its own World Class Performance Plans and recommended that GBWBA 'should continue to develop its relationship with EBA as the EBA 'might be able to learn something' about how to run a governing body of sport (Craven, interview). The GBWBA were subsequently awarded a World Class Performance grant but for Craven what was arguably more significant was the decision by UK Sport 'to award the money to the Great Britain Wheelchair Basketball Association – *the governing body of the sport in Great Britain*' (Craven, interview; emphases in the original). A clear illustration of the autonomy that GBWBA enjoys is provided by the continued funding arrangement for wheelchair basketball's national teams, in which the funding from UK Sport for the World Class Performance Plans are administered through the Great Britain Wheelchair Association, rather than England Basketball.

Perceptions of mainstreaming

EB believes that responsibility for the development of disabled players' competitions, coaching and international representation, lies with both the mainstream governing bodies and disability sport governing bodies such as GBWBA and consider the DSO's role as giving advice to disabled people regarding specialist sporting skills, rather than taking responsibility for the development of wheelchair basketball (Thomas, 2004). It is interesting to note that the EB recognize that 'mainstream bodies are not doing enough' and that 'disabled people should be more in control of organizations meant to serve them' (Thomas, 2004: 253). However, despite the commitment made in their equal opportunities statement in 2006, there is little indication that attempts are being made by EB to: (i) make the running game more accessible to disabled people; and (ii) involve disabled people in the decision making processes relating to the development of the running game. It appears, therefore, that while EB is content that GBWBA is the most suitable agency for developing wheelchair basketball, it appears to have had little interest in developing basketball for other groups of disabled athletes. Reasons for the apparent lack of commitment to disability sport on the part of EB is not clear. That said, EB's ambivalence is likely to have been influenced by: (i) EB's reliance on GBWBA as the governing body of the wheelchair game; (ii) the limited development of basketball for ambulant disabled players; (iii) the lack of coherent lobbying by the DSOs for better opportunities in basketball; and (iv) the typically marginal status of disability sport as a priority for governing bodies generally. In addition, a further reason for the limited development of ambulant basketball may be the conflicting views between members of the GBWBA and EB on key issues relating to the development of disability sport. For example, contrary to the view of GBWBA, EB indicated – in a survey of the attitudes of governing bodies toward mainstreaming – that the Paralympic events should be integrated into the Olympics (Thomas, 2004). While the issues surrounding integration in elite sport and, in particular, the Paralympics are examined more fully in Chapter 6, it is worth noting here that GBWBA and EB's perceptions of mainstreaming may have significantly impacted upon EBs interest and commitment to develop basketball for disabled people.

In relation to perceptions of mainstreaming and the role of governing bodies, Craven (of GBWBA) claims that the most appropriate governance 'model' for wheelchair basketball, is to have – as they do now – a separate autonomous body recognized as the governing body for that sport. In Craven's view GBWBA has policies, practices, and an infrastructure that allows it to effectively govern the wheelchair game without the support of EB, or DSOs such as the EFDS. He does not believe that the GBWBA needs an organization such as the EFDS and, therefore, does not have a 'close' relationship with them. Reflecting upon the perceived success of the GBWBA, and considering the development of other disability sports, Craven also suggests that it may be in the interests of DSOs (such as DSE) to retain control of some sports (such as swimming), as it enables the DSOs to better secure their own future and to control more effectively the development of their sport.

Summary: basketball

The policies, policy-making processes, values and general administrative arrangements within wheelchair basketball are substantially different to those in our other case studies. Wheelchair basketball has its own governing body, and while the GBWBA has developed relationships with EB and DSOs such as the EFDS to serve its own purposes, it is as autonomous and self-reliant as any sports-specific governing body. The GBWBA is, however, only concerned with wheelchair players and the mainstream governing body (EB) has been generally inactive in taking responsibility for the development of basketball for other impairment groups such as the deaf and people with learning disabilities. With regard to the Minister for Sport's

Review Group's recommendations for mainstreaming, it is perhaps fair to suggest that none of these have been met, and yet perhaps ironically, Sport England, the EFDS, EB and GBWBA are all satisfied that roles, responsibilities and organizational relationships are suitable and appropriate for the sport. While the key personnel (such as Craven) in wheelchair basketball have similar perceptions of the most appropriate forms of policy and practice in relation to mainstreaming, these perceptions contradict the general principles of mainstreaming as set out by the Minister for Sport's Review Group as well as the policies of Sport England and the EFDS.

Summary

As we noted in Chapter 2, over the last 40 years or so a wide range of DSOs have emerged to develop particular sports for particular groups of disabled people. Typically, many DSOs have offered opportunities for disabled people to participate in sport in isolation, and often without support, from mainstream governing bodies of sport. However, in light of increased government funding, intervention and the publication of various policy statements such as those provided by the Minister for Sport's Review Group (1989), in recent years mainstream governing bodies of sport have begun to consider – albeit inconsistently and in rather varied ways – issues related to its provision of sport for disabled people. Partly prompted by, for example, Sport England's *Guidelines for Governing Bodies* (Sport England, 2000) and the *Sport Equality Charter* (2004), governing bodies such as British Swimming have, to varying degrees, begun to consider the provision of its sport for disabled people. However, we have also noted that mainstreaming is only a recent area of policy interest for most governing bodies and with the exception of BS, many of these organizations have typically demonstrated limited commitment towards mainstreaming disability sport or have, at best, played only a peripheral but supportive role to the DSOs. Research undertaken by Thomas (2004) confirms the limited commitment of NGBs to the inclusion of disabled people in their sport. The reasons for the recent interest of some mainstream governing bodies in the development of disability sport are complex but would appear to be more strongly associated with the external funding opportunities that are becoming increasingly available, and the strong personal relationships between and committed individuals within DSOs and NGBs, than a consequence of continual pressure exerted by the government or the lobbying activities of various disability sport organizations.

It is also clear from the four case studies presented in this chapter that the role played by the EFDS in relation to mainstreaming and with governing bodies of sport is inconsistent and highly variable. While the EFDS was initially central to the mainstreaming of football, for example, it has played no substantive part in the mainstreaming of tennis. Sport England's relationships with governing bodies is equally inconsistent; indeed, despite its mainstreaming agenda Sport England is supportive of the GBWBA yet unwilling to support the creation of a similar sport-specific disability sport organization for tennis or swimming. Thus, whilst mainstreaming has become a central tenet of disability sport policy and its supposed benefits widely extolled by the EFDS, the DSOs, NGBs and Sport England, the DSOs consistently refuse to relinquish their responsibility for disability sport and most NGBs are reluctant to absorb disability sport into their general duties. At the time of writing, therefore, an appropriately cautious and not altogether profound conclusion may be that the ways and extent to which the mainstreaming of disability sport occurs within individual sports is dependent to a large extent on the various networks of power relationships that exist within and between the governing bodies of sport, as well as the resources available (including finance and staffing) and historical engagement in disability sport by the organizations involved.

Revision questions

1 How might you account for the contested and often contradictory meaning of the principle of mainstreaming in disability sport policy and practice?
2 Using a sporting case study of your choice, discuss the ways and extent to which governing bodies of sport have attempted to mainstream disability sport.
3 Examine the reasons why there appears to have been no uniform approach towards the mainstreaming of disability sport among governing bodies of sport.
4 What opportunities and challenges does mainstreaming disability sport have for those working in governing bodies of sport?
5 If you were employed by a governing body of sport, what issues need to be considered if you were expected to facilitate the mainstreaming of disability sport in your organization?

Key readings

English Federation of Disability Sport (2004) *EFDS Development Framework: Count Me In 2004–2008*, Crewe: EFDS.
Football Association, The (2004) *Football for Disabled People*, London: The Football Association.
Minister for Sport's Review Group (1989) *Building on Ability: Sport for People with Disabilities*, Leeds: HMSO.
Sport England (2004) *The Equality Standard: A Framework for Sport*, London: Sport England.
Strohkendle, H. (1996) *The 50th Anniversary of Wheelchair Basketball*, New York: Waxman.

Recommended websites

British Swimming
www.britishswimming.org

The Football Association
www.thefa.com

The Great Britain Wheelchair Basketball Association
www.gbwba.org.uk

The Tennis Foundation
www.tf.org.uk

5 Disability, physical education and school sport

Objectives

This chapter will:

- outline the emergence of policy related to the inclusion of disabled pupils and those with special educational needs in mainstream (or regular) schools;
- examine the differential outcomes of educating disabled pupils and those with special educational needs in physical education and school sport; and
- argue that the process of inclusion does not seem to have generated the desired impact on improving pupils' experiences.

Introduction

In the previous chapters of this book we have examined how the use of a range of sporting and physical activities to promote the greater social inclusion of disabled people in sport and in the wider society more generally has come increasingly to dominate the policy agenda of many Western governments, and especially those in Europe. The central objective of this chapter is to examine the increasing use of physical education (PE) and school sport as vehicles of social policy targeted at promoting the inclusion of young disabled people and those with special educational needs (SEN) in mainstream (or regular) schools.

Inclusion policy in education and physical education

Before we examine these issues, it is important to note that the recent and increasing emphasis which has come to be placed on issues of inclusion in policy related to PE and school sport has emerged out of the broader educational and sport policy priorities of governments. It has also been historically associated with the ideas surrounding mainstreaming (Chapter 4), regular education, least restrictive environment and normalization. Indeed, although it is a process the roots of which can be traced back to the mid-1800s, it was during the post-1945 period and since the mid-1990s, in particular, that the inclusion of young disabled people and those with SEN alongside their age-peers in mainstream settings has increasingly become a key cornerstone of government legislation and policy in many countries. Indeed, as we have seen in previous chapters of this book, there is now hardly any form of government social policy that does not contain at least some reference to issues of 'equal opportunity', 'equity' and 'inclusion'. In educational policy, the Salamanca Statement on inclusive education, for example, reflected the ostensible commitment by governments world-wide to providing a more inclusive education system and 'equalizing opportunities' for all pupils in mainstream education (United Nations Educational, Scientific and Cultural Organization (UNESCO), 1994). A survey of government legislation relating to SEN in 52 countries following the publication of the Salamanca Statement noted that underpinning the educational policies of the majority of countries was the perceived *prime facie* right of a child with SEN and disabilities to be educated in mainstream schools, on the condition that mainstream schools have the capacity to meet those needs (UNESCO, 1996). In the USA, PL 94–142, the Education for All Handicapped Children Act of 1975, Section of 504 of the Rehabilitation Act (PL 93–112) which was passed in 1973 but not implemented until 1977, PL 105–17 and PL 108–446, have also all stressed the need to promote a shift away from educating young disabled people and those with SEN in segregated settings (such as special schools) towards 'including' them in mainstream schools or 'least restrictive environments' (Fitzgerald, 2006; UNESCO, 1996). Political commitment to inclusion in Australia also came to be expressed explicitly in the steady flow of government policies published since the 1980s (see, for example, Australian Labor government, 1988; Victorian Ministerial Review Committee, 1984). The same was also true in France, where the shift towards educating disabled pupils in regular schools under the jurisdiction of the Ministry of Education was repeatedly emphasized in a plethora of national legislation and policy-related initiatives published since the mid-1970s (UNESCO, 1996).

In Britain, the principle of educating young disabled people and those with SEN in mainstream schools has gained growing political support since the introduction of the 1944 Education Act in which these pupils were assigned to medically defined categories such as the 'physically handicapped', 'blind' and 'educationally sub-normal' (Halliday, 1993; Thomas, 2008). Following a medical or psychological assessment pupils were often placed into (segregated) special education in pre-determined categories of impairment which, Halliday (1993) suggests, did not consider their individual needs or competencies. By the mid-1960s however, there was growing support for the need to reverse the segregation of those young disabled people and those with SEN who received their education in special schools towards encouraging their ability to 'access' and be educated alongside their peers in mainstream schools. While this was due in part to educational policy developments at this time, the move towards the inclusion and integration of these pupils in mainstream education needs to be understood in the context of changing power differentials between disability activist groups (for example, the Union of the Physically Impaired Against Segregation; see Chapter 1), disabled people generally and other groups within the wider society since the 1960s. More specifically, in conjunction with the gradual long-term change in the overall distribution of power from greater to smaller power differentials, the campaigning between these groups helped focus attention upon the need for disabled people to have similar opportunities to access, and participate in, education and social life more generally (Smith and Thomas, 2005).

The growing policy emphasis on the desirability of educating young disabled people and those with SEN in mainstream schools was further consolidated by the 1978 Warnock Report and the 1981 Education Act. Based on the recommendations of the Warnock Report which came to be regarded as 'the touchstone of the modern era of SEN provision' (Garner and Dwyfor Davies, 2001: 10), the medically defined categories through which the individual child was perceived as the 'problem' some thirty years previously, were replaced with the concept of SEN in the 1981 Education Act to prevent the sharp distinction between two groups of pupils: the 'handicapped' and the 'non-handicapped' (Halliday, 1993; Thomas, 2008). The introduction of the legally-defined term 'SEN' resulted in a move away from using rigid categories of handicap that had previously been the basis for the provision of special educational services for those pupils who needed them. In this regard, the concept of SEN now refers to the school-based learning needs of pupils that arise from a wider range of difficulties – including cognitive, physical, sensory, communicative or behavioural difficulties as well as those who are perceived to be specially gifted in one way or another – and is used to identify (typically in a statement of SEN) those pupils for whom some kind of special educational provision needs to be made (Audit Commission, 2002; Department for Education and Skills (DfES), 2001). More specifically, while pupils with SEN – like all pupils – are not a homogenous group and 'are part of a continuum of learners' (Garner and Dwyfor Davies, 2001: 26) they are typically considered to have a learning difficulty of one kind or another if they:

(a) have a significantly greater difficulty in learning than the majority of children of the same age; or
(b) have a disability which prevents or hinders them from making use of educational facilities of a kind generally provided for children of the same age in schools within the area of the local education authority; or
(c) are under compulsory school age and fall within the definition at (a) or (b) above or would so do if special educational provision was not made for them.
(DfES, 2001: 6)

While the previous categories of handicap applied to approximately 2 per cent of the school population – many of whom were educated in special schools – this reclassification of pupils, which apparently focused more fully on their individual needs, led to the identification of as many as 20 per cent of children considered to have SEN (some of whom may have disabilities) (DES, 1978). Indeed, although there are real difficulties in trying to arrive at a precise estimate of the number of young disabled people and those with SEN in mainstream schools, recently published data suggests that approximately one in five school children are now considered to have a formally, or informally, identified SEN of one kind or another (Audit Commission, 2002; Vickerman, 2007a).

According to Halliday (1993), the constraints imposed upon teachers and schools by the 1981 Act further encouraged what has been a 'partial and gradual transference' of pupils from special to mainstream schools and thus mainstream PE. It has been partial inasmuch as it was typically those pupils with less severe difficulties who were being educated in mainstream schools, whilst those with more severe difficulties (including those with and without disabilities) tended to remain in the special school sector (Halliday, 1993; Thomas, 2008). By the mid-1990s, however, the commitment towards integrated education (as it had come to be known by this time) and the debate surrounding its feasibility was further expressed by the publication of the 1993 and 1996 Education Acts, the introduction of the Code of Practice and the 1995 Disability Discrimination Act. The political commitment by the current Labour government in Britain to endorsing the recommendations of the Salamanca Statement and developing a 'more inclusive education system' is also made clear in the Green Paper *Excellence for All Children: Meeting Special Educational Needs* (DfEE, 1997). In particular, it was suggested that:

> We want to see more pupils with SEN included within mainstream primary and secondary schools. We support the United Nations Educational, Scientific and Cultural Organization (UNESCO) Salamanca World Statement on Special Needs Education. This calls on governments to adopt the principle of inclusive education, enrolling all children in regular schools, unless there are compelling reasons for doing otherwise. That implies the progressive extension of the capacity of mainstream schools to provide for children with a wide range of needs. (DfEE, 1997: 44)

This commitment to ensuring that all pupils, who were formerly educated in segregated special schools, are now educated alongside their peers in mainstream schools unless this is incompatible with the wishes of the pupil's parents or 'the provision of efficient education for other children' (Stationery Office, 2001), continues to form a mainstay of educational policy in Britain. For example, the White Paper *Meeting Special Educational Needs: A Programme of Action* (DfEE, 1998), the *SEN Revised Code of Practice* (DfES, 2001), *Special Educational Needs and Disability Act* (Stationery Office, 2001), and the publication of the SEN strategy *Removing Barriers to Achievement* (DfES, 2004) are all predicated on the assumption that mainstream schools should not refuse a disabled pupil or those with SEN on the basis that they cannot meet their needs. In this regard, inclusive education policy in many countries is said to be centrally concerned with the 'development of strategies that seek to bring about a genuine equalization of opportunity' (UNESCO, 1994: 11) and improvement in the educational experiences and achievement of young people (UNESCO, 1994).

Given the growing policy emphasis that has come to be placed on inclusion and the provision of equal opportunities for disabled pupils and those with SEN alongside their age-peers in mainstream schools, it is not altogether surprising to find that PE and school sport has become an increasing focus for the achievement of broader social welfare policy goals. In Britain, for example, *A Sporting Future for All* published by the Department for Culture, Media and Sport (DCMS) in 2000, created the expectation that those involved in the development and delivery of PE and sport in schools, especially those working in Specialist Sports Colleges (SSCs) in England, would 'commit themselves to putting social inclusion and fairness at the heart of everything they do' (DCMS, 2000: 20). In relation to the experiences of PE and school sport among young disabled people and those with SEN, it was suggested – as in many other school-based sport policies (see, for example, DfES/DCMS, 2003; DCMS/Strategy Unit, 2002; Sport England, 2006) – that:

> All pupils should have access to physical education and disability should not be a barrier to inclusion in sport programmes. Appropriate arrangements, including teacher support and development if needed, should be in place to support young people with physical and learning disabilities to have good access to physical education and sport, in both mainstream and special school settings. (DCMS, 2000: 31)

It is within this developing social inclusion policy context that the recent re-emphasis on the inclusion of young people, particularly those with disabilities, SEN and those from other minority groups, has emerged. Accordingly, a recognition of these issues and an appreciation of broader changes in social and educational policy are vital pre-requisites for developing an understanding of the ways in which growing concern with inclusion, and the provision of positive worthwhile educational experiences for young disabled people and those with SEN, have come to be featured in contemporary PE and school sport policy. In this context, the next section of this chapter considers how the inclusion policy agenda has come to impact on teachers' and pupils' perceptions and experiences of PE and school sport by focusing, in particular, on the revision of the 2000 National Curriculum for Physical Education (NCPE) for England.

Inclusion, physical education and school sport

In England and Wales, the introduction of a NCPE established a broad and balanced curriculum as a statutory entitlement for all pupils educated in all state schools and was, like other areas of the National Curriculum, 'heralded as a significant step towards, if not a guarantee of, equal opportunities' (Penney, 2002: 110). This having been said, whilst it is intended that all pupils should experience a broad range of involvement in each of the activity areas that comprise the NCPE (namely, team games, athletics, gymnastics, swimming, dance and outdoor and adventurous activities (OAA)), it was recognized by the Working Group prior to the implementation of the NCPE that teachers would experience difficulty in 'fully integrating children with (SEN and disabilities) into all aspects of a physical education programme' (DES/WO, 1991: 36). The Working Group acknowledged, moreover, that 'traditional' team games, rather than more individualized pursuits (such as dance, swimming and OAA), are activities in which teachers might experience particular difficulty in incorporating some young disabled people and those with SEN (DES/WO, 1991). More specifically, it was suggested that:

Modifications to conventional games sometimes facilitate access, but the placing of a child with a visual impairment, or with a severe locomotor disability, in a class learning netball or rugby are not likely to be successful. (DES/WO, 1991: 38)

Despite this early recognition of some of the constraints that the presence of disabled pupils and pupils with SEN in mainstream classes, together with a lack of teacher training (to be discussed in more detail later), might have on teachers' practices, it was the revision of the NCPE 2000 for England – which featured for the first time a detailed statutory policy statement on inclusion (DfEE/QCA, 1999) – where the perceived contribution that PE and school sport could make to the achievement of greater social inclusion of these pupils was explicitly identified. In this regard, in the NCPE 2000 for England, the British government formally re-emphasized the alleged centrality of 'inclusion' and 'inclusive practices' in PE and created an expectation that teachers would ensure that all pupils were 'enabled to participate as fully and effectively as possible within the National Curriculum and the statutory assessment arrangements' therein (DfEE/QCA, 1999: 33). Teachers and other practitioners have, of course, always been expected to employ differentiated strategies that are appropriate and challenging to all pupils regardless of how diverse their needs and abilities are. The emphasis on inclusion in current NCPE policy, however, reaffirms the expectation that teachers should 'ensure that all pupils have the chance to succeed, whatever their individual needs and the potential barriers to their learning may be' (DfEE/QCA, 1999: 3). It also creates the expectation that teachers will design and deliver PE curricula with 'due regard' to three principles of inclusion, namely, setting suitable learning challenges; responding to pupils' diverse learning needs; and overcoming barriers to learning and assessment for individuals and groups of pupils (DfEE/QCA, 1999: 28). These principles of inclusion, and the political and policy emphasis on the supposed need to educate disabled pupils and those with SEN in mainstream schools, will continue to be found in the new NCPE 2008 for England which was published in September 2008 (QCA, 2007).

It is important to note, however, that the ideological commitment to inclusion and the provision of equal opportunities would appear to be at variance with other policy commitments, particularly in Britain, that are part of the growing marketization of education. In this regard, inclusive education policy should not be seen in isolation from other existing policies and, in particular, those which stress the need to raise standards of achievement, promote competition between schools, and the need for cost effectiveness. The growing tendency towards increasing parental and consumer choice, and the publication of league tables should also be seen as part of this overall process which has helped to foster a culture of growing accountability in the education sector and which may help undermine the political aspiration for promoting greater inclusion in schools. The stress placed on improving levels of performance in competitive sports, skill development and excellence in PE and school sport, together with other policy initiatives such as, in England, the Physical Education and School Sport Clubs Links (PESSCL) strategy and the establishment of SSCs (DfES/DCMS, 2003), would appear to be objectives that are not necessarily compatible with those of other inclusive education policies.

But to what extent has the NCPE achieved its stated objective of greater inclusion in schools? What have been the related constraints that have come to be placed on teachers' and pupils' views and experiences of the subject? In other words, has the inclusion of young disabled people and those with SEN in mainstream PE lessons helped to enhance the educational experiences of these pupils? Or have these policies also resulted in consequences that, in the event, may well be the very reverse of what was intended?

Inclusion and equal opportunities in physical education

Despite the apparent consensus among policy-makers and government ministers that inclusive education is about providing young people with equal opportunities, in many countries debate surrounding its nature and purposes – as well as its implications for teachers' practice and pupils' experiences – remains nothing if not a persistent and contentious one. Indeed, there is now a large and expanding literature which suggests that what is understood by inclusion, its viability in mainstream schools, and the impact this has on pupils' learning is rather less clear than the existing policy rhetoric would imply. In their review of existing international studies of teachers' attitudes towards inclusion, Avramidis and Norwich (2002) concluded that although teachers were generally in support of the philosophy of inclusive education, many had serious reservations about the suitability of the widespread placement of young disabled people and those with SEN in mainstream schools. These reservations and variations in teachers' perceptions emanated from several interrelated concerns, and focused, in particular, on how the diverse and complex nature of pupils' needs, quality of previous teaching experiences, inadequate training and professional development, as well as the ethos, resources and organization of individual schools constrained their day-to-day practices (Avramidis and Norwich, 2002). Croll and Moses (2000) have also noted how the education officers and headteachers of special and mainstream schools in their study suggested that whilst 'the principle of inclusion of all children in mainstream . . . schools has achieved widespread support, at least at a rhetorical level' (2000: 4), there 'is a basic belief in the desirability of inclusion but no real thought that this is realisable' (2000: 10). In a not dissimilar way, the teachers and other professionals in Evans and Lunt's (2002) study also concluded that the inclusion of all disabled pupils and those with SEN in mainstream schools was idealistic and unrealistic and, more specifically, was particularly difficult for some pupils who have severe cognitive and physical difficulties that are not easily accommodated in those settings.

As Smith and Thomas (2005, 2006) have noted however, whilst there is a large body of literature on mainstream teachers' and pupils' perceptions and experiences of inclusion, this is an issue that has – until relatively recently – been largely ignored by those within the PE subject-community not only in Britain, but in many other countries too. Indeed, it is clear that apart from the USA where research on inclusion in PE and youth sport is rather more advanced than elsewhere (for a review, see Block and Obrusnikova, 2007), until recently few attempts have been made to examine the outcomes associated with the introduction of policies designed to promote the inclusion of disabled young people and those with SEN in mainstream PE in England and elsewhere in Europe.

Despite this general dearth of research, however, those studies that have examined the ways in which teachers view and experience inclusion in PE have yielded similar findings to those found in the inclusive education literature more generally. A study of teachers in the North of England, for example, concluded that whilst almost all teachers had 'a strongly avowed commitment to the principles of inclusion' (Morley et al., 2005: 92) and perceived it as an 'aspiration' or a 'journey' towards which they were working, the practicalities of fully including pupils with a diverse range of abilities in PE was not thought to be realizable to any great degree. In a similar study conducted in the West Midlands of England, Smith (2004) also reported how the 'underpinning rationale' of the policy of inclusion in the NCPE was to ensure that all pupils, including those with SEN and disabilities, have an 'equal opportunity' to participate in PE. In this way, the teachers suggested that by providing 'as much opportunity as possible' and 'equal opportunities for all pupils' they had, in their view, fulfilled the statutory obligation to include disabled pupils and those with SEN in PE, even though providing pupils with the 'same opportunities' created the opportunity for the experience of PE to become just as or even more unequal (Smith, 2004). Indeed, Smith (2004) concluded that whilst the expressed commitment to providing pupils with 'equal opportunities' was a more-or-less common feature of many of the teachers' views on inclusion, as well as a justification for what they did in practice, upon closer scrutiny what they considered inclusion to 'be' and what they *actually* did in practice was more in keeping with traditional conceptualizations of integration (Avramidis and Norwich, 2002; Barton, 1993). In other words, there was a tendency among teachers to use the terms inclusion and integration interchangeably (Vickerman, 2002, 2007b), and their every day practice seemed to resemble an assimilation process through which young disabled people and those with SEN are required to 'fit into' the existing PE curriculum that was already planned. This process was, therefore, for the most part contingent upon the degree to which teachers adapted and modified the sports and activities typically delivered to pupils (Smith, 2004; Smith and Green, 2004).

These are points which are not confined to England it seems, for as Hodge et al. (2004) have observed in relation to their study in the USA, while all of the teachers in their sample 'believed that inclusion was 'good' conceptually' (Hodge et al., 2004: 407), they expressed particular concern over the extent to which pupils with more severe difficulties could be and were being included in PE lessons (Block, 1999). Consequently, what the teachers in this study claimed to do in the name of inclusion in PE was more reflective of those practices closely associated with integration. Put another way, there existed an expectation among teachers that pupils would fit into existing PE curricula as they were originally planned and that 'successful inclusion practice' (Hodge et al., 2004: 408) was a corollary of their ability to adapt and modify the activities and equipment which were used by other pupils in lessons. In this regard, it is clear that whilst there is a basic belief in the desirability of inclusion and a commitment by teachers to providing 'equal opportunities' for disabled pupils and those with SEN in mainstream PE, this appears in practice to have created the opportunity for the experience of PE to become even more unequal. In particular, insofar as policy towards inclusion in PE and school sport amounts almost to a statement of faith in its effectiveness in promoting pupils' educational experiences, it seems that when some young disabled pupils and those with SEN are educated in the same learning contexts as their age-peers, there is a tendency for them to be taught *separately* (usually with the help of a non-PE qualified teaching assistant) from one another within the same PE class. Thus, the tendency for much inclusion policy to be driven largely by the ideological agendas of policy-makers has meant that the trend towards inclusion in PE has, in fact, resulted in and not gone beyond the existence of *de facto* integration, whereby some young disabled people and those with SEN are required to 'fit into' existing curricula as they are already planned by teachers (Barton, 1993; Morley *et al.*, 2005; Smith, 2004; Smith and Green, 2004).

It is perhaps not altogether surprising, therefore, to find that one corollary of the existence of *de-facto* integration in PE has been a *reduction* in pupils' opportunities to experience a 'broad and balanced' NCPE rather than the 'genuine equalization' hoped for by policy-makers and organizations such as Ofsted (2003) and UNESCO (1994). Indeed, much of the available evidence points towards the ways in which, when compared to their age-peers, young disabled people and those with SEN are typically provided with a more narrowly focused PE curriculum in which they tend to participate in fewer activities than other young people, and spend less time on average when doing so. In a nationwide study of sports participation by young disabled people conducted by Sport England (2001), for example, 45 per cent of 6–16-year-olds reported spending less than one hour per week in PE lessons compared to 18 per cent of the overall school population, and one-third (34 per cent) spent 1 hour-1 hour 59 minutes per week doing so, compared to 40 per cent of pupils without disabilities (Table 5.1). Overall, 20 per cent of disabled pupils claimed to spend the recommended two or more hours per week in PE lessons, compared to 32 per cent of the overall school population (Sport England, 2001).

The study also revealed that, on average, 10 per cent of disabled youngsters did not participate occasionally (defined as less than 10 times in the past year) in any sport or physical activity in school lessons (Sport England, 2001). As Table 5.2

Table 5.1 Average time spent by 6–16-year-old disabled people participating in PE lessons per week in 2000 (%)

Average time spent per week in PE lessons	Young disabled people	Overall school population
Less than 1 hour	45	18
1 hour–1 hour 59 mins	34	48
2 or more hours	20	32
Total	100	100

Source: Sport England (2001)

Table 5.2 Number of sports and physical activities undertaken in PE lessons by 11–16-year-old disabled people in 2000 (%)

Number of activities	Males occasionally	Females occasionally	Males frequently	Females frequently
0	12	11	36	38
1–3	24	22	41	39
4–6	24	22	16	15
7–9	19	20	6	7
10 or more	22	25	2	2
Average	6.0	6.6	2.1	2.2

Source: Sport England (2001)

indicates, among 11–16-year-olds, 48 per cent of disabled males and 44 per cent of disabled females participated in up to six sports and activities occasionally, compared to 41 per cent of males and 45 per cent of females who played seven or more activities occasionally in lessons. The number of sports and physical activities undertaken by young people occasionally decreased as the number of disabilities they had increased; ranging from seven activities undertaken on average by those with one disability to four activities on average for those with seven or more disabilities (Sport England, 2001). In terms of frequent participation in PE (defined as ten times or more in the past year), just over one-third (36 per cent) of all school-aged young disabled people did not participate frequently in lessons (Sport England, 2001). In the secondary age group, 57 per cent of males and 54 per cent of females participated frequently in one to six activities compared to 8 per cent of males and 9 per cent of females who played seven or more sports and activities frequently in lessons (Table 5.2). The average number of sports and activities undertaken frequently by 11–16-year-olds (two on average) was much lower compared to those in which they participated occasionally, whilst those pupils who had one disability were more likely to participate in more sports and physical activities in PE lessons (three on average) compared to those with seven or more disabilities (one on average) (Sport England, 2001).

The evidence from Sport England's (2001) study of sports participation among young disabled people also confirmed a pattern widely reported elsewhere, namely, that in school PE lessons disabled pupils tend to participate in a limited number of more individualized physical activities and adapted variations of team sports, rather than in full versions of competitive sports that tend to form the core of PE curricula within schools (Atkinson and Black, 2006; Fitzgerald and Kay, 2004; Morley et al., 2005; Smith, 2004; Smith and Green, 2004). Indeed, as Table 5.3 indicates, the top five most widely undertaken activities in which 11–16-year-olds participated occasionally in school lessons in Sport England's (2001) study were swimming, football, other games skills, gymnastics and athletics. Similarly, those activities in which males and females participated frequently in schools also featured an amalgamation of team games (for example, football) alongside more individualized 'lifestyle activities' (such as gymnastics) (Sport England, 2001). A

Table 5.3 Most widely undertaken sports and physical activities in PE lessons by 11–16-year-old disabled people in 2000 (%)

Sport	Males occasionally	Females occasionally	Males frequently	Females frequently
Swimming	55	57	37	36
Football	53	26	26	8
Gym	40	44	16	21
Athletics	38	38	11	11
Other games skills	37	46	14	21

Source: Sport England (2001)

more recent study of the experiences of PE and sports participation among school-aged youngsters in Leicestershire and Rutland in England also revealed that whilst most young disabled people were taught all six activity areas or strands that comprise NCPE (athletics, dance, games, gymnastics, outdoor and adventurous activities and swimming), 'the activities offered within each strand tend to be limited' (Atkinson and Black, 2006: 6). Accordingly, the authors concluded that when compared to the overall school population, disabled pupils were typically offered 'a fairly narrow curriculum' (Atkinson and Black, 2006: 33) by teachers and, as a consequence, there was a perceived need 'for a broader range of opportunities for young disabled people within each strand of the curriculum, to engage and motivate, and to stretch their abilities' (Atkinson and Black, 2006: 6). Finally, in a not dissimilar way, the National Disability Authority (NDA) (2005) in Ireland concluded that many of the pupils in their study were offered a 'limited curriculum' (NDA, 2005: 132) in PE, with participation in team games, in particular, being especially limited. In order to improve pupils' participation in and experiences of the subject, the NDA suggested that there was a need for teachers to 'adapt activities and approaches to meeting individual needs in a meaningful way' (NDA, 2005: 132) and to individualize the curricular available to pupils in schools.

On the basis of the available (albeit limited) evidence, therefore, it might be argued that the current *team-based activity structure* of PE curricula, with their apparent emphasis on *competitive sport, performance, excellence and skills*, together with teachers' perceptions of what constitute appropriate activities for pupils, serves to constrain – and, at times, prevent – many pupils from participating fully with their peers in PE and school sport in mainstream settings. The comments of teachers from two studies conducted in England help illustrate the complexities involved:

> I think the difficult ones to include pupils with disabilities and special needs [in] are team games. It's alright in situations when you are developing skills and fitness but when it comes to the actual game there is not a lot you can actually do. (Smith, 2004: 47)

> The team situations . . . (are) okay with the skills that's fine but when they're actually put into a game situation . . . they get confused, it's frustrating for them . . . because they don't know where they're supposed to be within the spatial awareness of things. (Morley *et al.*, 2005: 97–8)

In this regard, it seems that in addition to those constraints related to, among others, teaching style, available facilities, the needs and abilities of the group and group size, and the rather different pattern of social relationships involved in the kinds of activities provided as part of PE curricula can often impact significantly on the extent to which these pupils can be incorporated in mainstream PE (Smith, 2004; Sugden and Talbot, 1996; Wright and Sugden, 1999). More particularly, young disabled people and those with SEN appear likely to participate more fully in those activities where they are able to move in ways that better suit their own physical capabilities and where they are more able to control the intensity and duration of those movements. In more complex performance-oriented team sports however, it is the interweaving of the actions of a large number of players involved and the use of complex movement patterns, alongside the need to use other requisite physical and psychological skills, which comes to limit their participation and inclusion in many aspects of PE programmes in schools (Sugden and Talbot, 1996; Smith, 2004; Wright and Sugden, 1999). As with other subjects taught in schools (Avramidis and Norwich, 2002; Croll and Moses, 2000; Evans and Lunt, 2002), this is especially – though not exclusively – the case for those with more severe emotional and behavioural difficulties (EBD) of one kind or another whom, it has been claimed, tend to 'present teachers and schools with the greatest challenge' to inclusion (Garner and Dwyfor Davies, 2001: 67). This is a point that has been confirmed by the majority of empirical studies conducted in many countries. Writing of the situation in England, Smith (2004) and Morley *et al.* (2005), for example, reported that the majority of teachers in their studies were somewhat apprehensive towards, and had particular difficulty with, the inclusion of pupils with various behavioural difficulties in PE. In the USA, Hodge *et al.* (2004) have also noted how pupils with severe difficulties, especially those with severe EBD, presented the most difficult challenge for teachers when delivering PE programmes generally, and team games in particular. By contrast, the inclusion in PE of pupils with moderate learning difficulties (such as those with dyspraxia) as well as those with difficulties of a more physical and sensory kind, like many other areas of the curriculum, tend to be viewed more favourably by teachers, not least because these pupils are often perceived to pose less constraint upon their teaching and are more easily included in lessons where more individualized activities are taught (Fitzgerald, 2005; Fitzgerald and Kay, 2004; Hodge *et al.*, 2004; Meegan and MacPhail, 2006; Morley *et al.*, 2005; Smith, 2004; Smith and Green, 2004).

In this regard, although it depends upon the particular needs and abilities of pupils, it seems that for some – perhaps even a majority – of young people, their limited experience of the breadth of activities available as part of PE programmes in mainstream schools is something that is said to have had a negative impact on their self-esteem and confidence in PE and sport (Brittain, 2004; Fitzgerald, 2006; Fitzgerald *et al.*, 2003; Goodwin and Watkinson, 2000). More specifically, the findings from studies conducted with both pupils and teachers, it is not uncommon to find that the tendency for pupils to be taught different activities separately from others in the class has the effect of isolating them from other members of the class, and of reinforcing, rather than breaking down, barriers between pupils with different abilities. This informal divide between pupils in mainstream PE classes also appears to have helped construct an implicit hierarchy of acceptable activities in PE where the status and performance of those undertaken by young disabled people and those with SEN are at times perceived, both by teachers and other pupils, as inferior compared to those done by others in the class. Simultaneously, however, there is also some evidence that points to the ways in which PE is believed to be a context (particularly where a disability sport is used) where disabled pupils and those with SEN can demonstrate their physical capabilities to others, where self-esteem and self-confidence can be enhanced, and where the perceptions and attitudes of others can be challenged though participation in sport and physical activity (Brittain, 2004; Fitzgerald, 2006; Fitzgerald *et al.*, 2003; Goodwin and Watkinson, 2000).

Initial teacher training, continuing professional development and the role of support staff

Perhaps one of the most salient issues to have attracted the attention of teachers, other educators and academics since the early 1990s, has been the perceived failure of government and policy-makers to provide adequate resources to realize the desired objectives of greater inclusion of disabled pupils and those with SEN in schools. In particular, there has been growing criticism of the apparent inadequacy of teachers' experiences of initial teacher training (ITT) and continuing professional development (CPD) programmes, and the failure of government and policy-makers to provide adequate resources to help teachers meet pupils' needs and manage the expectations of them as set out in contemporary policy for PE and school sport (Ofsted, 2003; Robertson *et al.*, 2000; Vickerman, 2002, 2007a, b; Vickerman *et al.*, 2003). In this context, Ofsted (2003) have noted that despite the trend towards inclusion in mainstream schools, it is not uncommon for many teachers to claim that they 'were being asked to teach children with significant learning needs and manage difficult situations without enough learning' (Ofsted, 2003: 24) and without sufficient confidence to do so. Writing of the situation in England, Vickerman (2002: 92), for example, has stressed 'a need for the profession to establish a clear and consistent approach to inclusive PE' against the background of what has been described as 'the impoverished nature of special educational needs and inclusive education provision' (Robertson *et al.*, 2000: 61). Within PE teacher training, Robertson *et al.* (2000), among others (see, for example, Morley *et al.*, 2005; Vickerman, 2007a, b; Vickerman *et al.*, 2003) argue that in order to meet more adequately the needs of all pupils, especially those with SEN and disabilities, 'inclusion issues' should be embedded throughout all aspects of such training. That such commentators have made claims of this kind is partly a consequence of the fact that several studies have revealed quite clearly that teachers have frequently attributed their lack of confidence in including young disabled people and those with SEN in PE lessons to what they perceive as the generally 'inadequate', limited and overly theoretical nature of professional training they receive as part of ITT and CPD (Morley *et al.*, 2005; Ofsted, 2003; Robertson *et al.*, 2000; Vickerman, 2007a, b). Three points are of immediate relevance in this regard. The first is that the provision of teacher training (in the form of ITT, CPD or other professional courses such as those organized by the Youth Sport Trust) is, from the perspective of teachers, coaches and other practitioners, often too brief, superficial, inaccessible, inconsistently delivered, and on a short-term basis. The second point is that much of the formal school-based training that is delivered to teachers tends to be oriented primarily towards 'general issues of inclusion' and is often not always specifically related to PE. The third point is that a small, but growing body of evidence seems to be suggesting that where teachers do receive training that they perceive as being more relevant to PE, this tends to be done on a rather informal *ad hoc* basis at departmental level; that is to say, through discussions with fellow colleagues both within and beyond PE departments in schools (Morley et al, 2005; Smith and Green, 2004; Vickerman, 2002, 2007a).

Although there is evidence of an increased availability of training that is focused specifically upon preparing teachers to meet the diverse needs of young disabled people and those with SEN, there has been a tendency to over-emphasize the significance of training as influential on teachers' practice (Green, 2002; Smith and Green, 2004; Smith and Thomas, 2005, 2006). More specifically, despite the existence of claims which relate to the supposed benefits of 'inclusion training', there would appear to exist a number of implicit and almost taken-for-granted assumptions within the existing literature that ITT or CPD which is focused more specifically towards 'inclusion issues' will necessarily influence the 'already established philosophies and practices of would-be (and currently practising) teachers' (Green, 2002: 70). In short, even though it runs counter to the popular view that more training can be one of the most effective ways of improving the degree to which teachers can help promote inclusion, the available evidence is suggestive of the fact that we should, at the very least, be rather more cautious about making claims of this kind and avoid investing so much faith in teacher training as some kind of panacea for the constraints teachers experience when educating disabled pupils and those with SEN in mainstream schools.

An additional and particularly noteworthy feature of the growing political commitment towards inclusion and of recent SEN policy has been the expectation that teachers will work in collaboration with a range of other professionals, including Learning Support (or Teaching) Assistants (LSAs) and other SEN-related staff (such as SEN Coordinators). The achievement of greater inclusion in PE and school sport has, however, allegedly been compromised further by the associated tendency for these support staff, many of whom are not specialists or qualified to teach PE, to place a significant degree of constraint upon the every day activities of teachers. In particular, the ways in which these groups seek to disseminate, where it is available, information regarding the particular abilities of pupils has been a key source of criticism from teachers, not least because that information indicates little, if anything, about the specific needs of young people with disabilities and SEN in PE (Hodge *et al.*, 2004; Morley *et al.*, 2005; Smith and Green, 2004). Among other things, this has had a series of consequences for the experiences of those pupils with whom LSAs work ranging, on the one hand, from the alleged benefits this can have for them in terms of their individual learning and, on the other, the perceived lack of support they receive from support staff compared to other, ostensibly more academic, subjects such as English, maths and science, and the negative impact their presence can have upon pupils' interaction and learning, as well as teacher effectiveness (Atkinson and Black, 2006; Fitzgerald *et al.*, 2003; Hodge *et al.*, 2004; Morley *et al.*, 2005; NDA, 2005; Smith and Green, 2004). This having been said, and notwithstanding the tendency for teachers to be rather critical of the kind and amount of support they receive from LSAs, one study has demonstrated how teachers have been particularly receptive to the involvement of LSAs in lessons, not least because of the practical benefits this had for them (NDA, 2005; Smith and Green, 2004). In this regard, Smith and Green (2004) observed that although the teachers in their study appeared committed to working with LSAs to meet pupils' needs, their primary concern appeared to be one of pragmatism; that is to say, by supporting disabled pupils and those with SEN, LSAs let teachers 'off the hook', as it were, and enabled them to 'get on with teaching the other pupils'. One further way in which LSAs might be viewed as playing a crucial role in this regard is that of assisting teachers with ensuring the safety of pupils generally, and those with SEN and disabilities in particular. In policy terms this is significant, for the constraint on teachers to include pupils with EBD (emotional and behavioural difficulties) and severe learning difficulties alongside those who use mobility devices (such as wheelchairs), for example, is likely to further intensify the pressures experienced by teachers in ensuring the safety of all pupils in lessons, whilst meeting the expectation of them to include pupils of all needs and abilities in PE.

Summary

This chapter has attempted to establish the developing policy context within which the political commitment towards including young disabled people and those with SEN in PE and youth sport in mainstream British schools has emerged. In doing so, we have argued that while inclusion has been uncritically accepted and considered as an unambiguously good and desirable policy response designed to bring about, among other things, more equitable and positive experiences of PE and school sport for all pupils, but particularly those with disabilities and SEN. However, the trend towards educating young disabled people and those with SEN in mainstream schools has been accompanied by what might be held to be a series of unintended, unforeseen outcomes. Perhaps the first point to note in this regard is that the failure of social policies such as the promotion of inclusion in PE to achieve their declared objectives, and to have outcomes that were unplanned and which may even be the opposite of what was intended, is by no means unusual. Indeed, insofar as the formulation and implementation of policy is a complex process, it is a process that almost inevitably has consequences that are not only unplanned but which, as may be the case here, are held to be undesirable by the relevant parties involved (Dopson and Waddington, 1996).

Despite the lack of empirically-grounded studies of how inclusion policy is implemented and exists in practice, it seems fairly clear that the alleged 'privileging' of sport over more individualized physical activities (Penney and Evans, 1999) in PE, alongside the provision of a limited and somewhat narrow range of activities for some pupils, raises serious questions about the extent to which disabled pupils and those with SEN *are* being included – in any meaningful sense – within sport-based PE curricula that were typically designed for non-disabled young people (Barton, 1993). Furthermore, in contrast to the expectations of policy-makers and government ministers, the emphasis on inclusion appears to have had the effect of further alienating some pupils (particularly those with more severe needs) from others in lessons. Simultaneously, from the perspective of pupils and teachers, this appears to have had the effect of limiting the extent to which young disabled people and those with SEN can derive satisfying experiences from PE and sport in schools, especially when these pupils are sometimes taught different activities separately from others in lessons.

At the time of writing, the trend towards including pupils with disabilities and SEN in mainstream schools has also not appeared to have radically altered the content, organization and delivery of PE and sport in schools; it would also appear that insofar as extra-curricular PE and after-school clubs remain heavily dominated by competitive team sports that retain a strong emphasis on performance, excellence and skills, as well as the availability of transport to attend clubs, the opportunities available for those with disabilities and SEN to participate in extra-curricular activities would appear particularly limited (Atkinson and Black, 2006; Fitzgerald and Kay, 2004; Smith, 2004). Indeed, it might be suggested that the growing emphasis on inclusion in schools may do more to reduce, rather than enhance, the opportunities for these pupils to participate in the same activities, and to the same extent, in extra-curricular PE than they might have done in the special school sector (Fitzgerald and Kay, 2004; Smith, 2004; Thomas and Green, 1995). Brittain (2004) also goes as far to say that in England there are some preliminary indications which suggest that the move towards inclusion in schools has made it particularly difficult for those working in disability sport to identify new potential talented athletes with disabilities. This, he argues, may help undermine the competitive strength of future British teams at the elite level of disability sport (Brittain, 2004).

It is important to note, however, that even though the process of inclusion has been met with, at best, only very limited success and does not seem to have generated the desired impact on improving pupils' experiences of PE and sport in mainstream schools, it should *not* necessarily be interpreted as an abject policy failure. Indeed, it would be churlish to deny that the inclusion of pupils with disabilities and SEN alongside their age-peers in mainstream schools has not had *any* impact on challenging dominant perceptions of pupils' abilities, or on improving the experiences and participation of pupils. Indeed, there is some – albeit limited – evidence which indicates that the emphasis on inclusion has enjoyed a measure of success in helping to develop positive experiences of, and participation in, PE and sport among some young disabled people and those with SEN. This is particularly the case where teachers have provided pupils with a range of activities (particularly modified team games and more individualized, recreational activities) from which to choose to participate with their friends, when they were accepted by their peers and felt part of the whole class (Atkinson and Black, 2006; Fitzgerald and Kay, 2004; Goodwin and Watkinson, 2000; NDA, 2005; Smith, 2004). It remains to be seen, however, whether the continued policy commitment to inclusion can, in fact, help make a greater contribution to the promotion of young people's experiences in PE and sport than has been the case hitherto.

Revision questions

1   Why has the inclusion of disabled pupils and those with SEN become a key policy priority of many governments?

2   How does the content, organization and delivery of PE and sport impact on the ways and extent to which teachers are able to facilitate the inclusion of disabled pupils and those with SEN in schools?

3   To what extent has the use of PE and school sport as vehicles of social policies designed to bring about more equitable and positive experiences of PE and school sport for all pupils been successful?

4   What practical insights can teachers and teacher trainees derive from the analysis presented in this chapter?

5   What policies and strategies need to be considered to promote the greater social inclusion of disabled people in sport and in the wider society more generally?

Key readings

Block, M. and Obrusnikova, I. (2007) 'Inclusion in physical education: a review of the literature from 1995–2005', *Adapted Physical Activity Quarterly*, 24: 103–24.

Fitzgerald, H. (2006) 'Disability and physical education', in D. Kirk, D. MacDonald and M. O'Sullivan (eds) *The Handbook of Physical Education*, London: Sage.

Goodwin, D. and Watkinson, E. (2000) 'Inclusive physical education from the perspective of students with physical disabilities', *Adapted Physical Activity Quarterly*, 17: 144–60.

Smith, A. and Thomas, N. (2005) 'Inclusion, special educational needs, disability and physical education', in: K. Green and K. Hardman (eds) *Physical Education: Essential Issues*, London: Sage.

Vickerman, P. (2007a) *Teaching Physical Education to Children with Special Educational Needs*, London: Routledge.

Recommended websites

Department for Children, Schools and Families
www.dcsf.gov.uk

English Federation of Disability Sport
www.efds.net

Qualifications and Curriculum Authority
www.qca.org.uk

6 Elite disability sport
The Paralympic Games

Objectives

This chapter will:

- examine the structure and organization of elite level disability sport, particularly the Summer Paralympic Games;
- discuss the on-going debate surrounding the classification of disabled athletes;
- explore the issues surrounding the inclusion of Paralympic athletes and disability sport events in the Olympic Games; and
- examine the use of technological aids by Paralympic athletes.

Introduction

Elsewhere in this book we have examined the complex structure, organization and provision of disability sport at the local and national levels. In particular, we drew attention to the roles played by disability sport organizations (Chapter 2), local authorities (Chapter 3), national governing bodies of sport (Chapter 4) and schools (Chapter 5), in providing opportunities for disabled people to participate in recreational and competitive sport. The central objective of this chapter is to examine the structure and organization of elite level disability sport by focusing, in particular, on the most well-known elite disability sport competition: the Summer Paralympic Games. In doing so, we shall focus on just three of the contemporary issues associated with the Paralympics, including: the on-going debate surrounding the classification of athletes; the inclusion of Paralympic athletes and disability sport events in the Olympic Games; and the use of assistive technology by Paralympians. We are not, therefore, centrally concerned with other international disability sport competitions such as the Deaflympics or Special Olympics, both of which have been explored in greater detail elsewhere (e.g. DePauw and Gavron, 2005). We will also not attempt to examine the complex issues surrounding the use of drugs by Paralympians, the marketing of the Paralympics in conjunction with the Olympic Games, or the increasing political use of the Paralympics as a tool for achieving sporting and non-sport objectives such as economic regeneration, international development and political relations, the promotion of health and social inclusion.

The organization and structure of elite disability sport

In Chapter 2 we drew attention to the role played by Sir Ludwig Guttmann and the importance of Stoke Mandeville Hospital in the emergence and early development of disability sport in Britain. We also noted that when compared to other forms of sporting competition, disability sport in very many societies has a relatively short history and is a process that has been characterized by, among other things, the *ad hoc* emergence of a range of bodies that have become responsible for the organization of sport for disabled athletes. In order to help understand something about how and why the present organization and structure of elite disability sport developed, we need to revisit the role of Guttmann who, because of his pioneering involvement in the early development of the Paralympics and elite disability sport, was named by the Pope as the 'de Coubertin of the paralysed' (Gold and Gold, 2007).

It has become something of a hackneyed way to begin any analysis of the emergence and development of elite disability sport and the Paralympic Movement, in particular, by tracing the roots of this process to the request made by the British government that Guttmann (a Jewish neurosurgeon) open the National Spinal Injuries Centre (NSIC) at Stoke Mandeville Hospital in Aylesbury, England, in 1944 (DePauw and Gavron, 2005; Gold and Gold, 2007). The NSIC was opened at the end of the Second World War as more traditional methods of rehabilitation were no longer believed to meet adequately the medical and psychological needs of large numbers of soldiers and civilians who were returning home with a range of war-related injuries, and particularly spinal cord injuries. As Gold and Gold have noted, Guttmann helped treat and rehabilitate severely war injured servicemen and challenge the prevailing view that their needs could be met only through permanent hospitalization, by implementing

> a programme of 'total care', having patients turned physically every two hours day and night to prevent sores and improving standards of bladder hygiene to help tackle problems of infection. Physiotherapy assisted limb flexibility and, for some patients, increased mobility. A pre-vocational work regime and various forms of recreation including concepts, visits and *competitive* sports, designed to keep patients busy and create a sense of purpose, complemented the medical regime. (2007: 85–6; emphasis in the original)

More particularly, whilst Guttmann was said to be initially concerned with using sport and physical activity as vehicles of recreation and for the therapeutic recuperation of patients, he quickly acknowledged the perceived benefits that competitive, organized sports could have for war veterans and for challenging attitudes about the abilities of disabled people (Gold and Gold, 2007; Guttmann, 1976). Thus, on 28 July 1948, the same day as the Opening Ceremony of the London Olympic Games, Guttmann and other hospital workers at the NSIC founded the first Stoke Mandeville Games where an archery competition for athletes with spinal cord injuries was held in the grounds of Stoke Mandeville Hospital. From then on, the Stoke Mandeville Games were to be held annually and during the course of their early history Guttmann is alleged to have constantly reinforced the perceived parallels between them and the Olympic Games (Gold and Gold, 2007; IPC, 2007a). In particular, during a speech which he gave at the end of the second Stoke Mandeville Games in 1949, Guttmann is alleged to have suggested that the Games would eventually be seen as the paraplegics' equivalent of the Olympics (IPC, 2007b), whilst athletes and aspects of the media variously described the Games using labels such as 'The Paralympics' or the 'Paraplegic Olympics' (Gold and Gold, 2007; IPC, 2007b). In this regard, whilst the precise origins of the term 'Paralympic' – and, hence, reference to the Paralympic Games – remain largely unknown and unclear, it is often suggested that it derives from the terms 'paraplegic' and 'Olympics' during the 1950s as the Stoke Mandeville Games developed. As we shall explain later, the term 'Paralympics' initially came to be the preferred label by which the IOC referred to the Games.

As we noted in Chapter 2, the growing international representation of participants at the Games from the early 1950s is often attributed solely to the activities of Guttmann as if he somehow operated completely independently of others to meet the needs of disabled patients. It is clear, however, that he was unavoidably dependent on the wider relationships he had developed whilst working at Stoke Mandeville Hospital to expand the sporting opportunities available to patients. That Guttmann was inevitably bound up in a complex web of relationships is evident from the ways in which he drew upon the institutional connections he and other doctors, trainers, physiotherapists and administrators had 'developed through training visiting staff, through staff moving to other hospitals and spreading Stoke Mandeville's characteristic approach to sport, and through ex-patients who pioneered paraplegic sport in their own countries' (Gold and Gold, 2007: 86), to help establish various rules, classifications, policies and procedures in a Handbook of Rules that were used to organize the first International Stoke Mandeville Games. These Games were held in 1952 where a total of 130 wheelchair athletes with spinal cord injuries from Britain and the Netherlands competed in six wheelchair sports (archery, lawn bowling, table tennis, shot putt, javelin and club throw). The number of participating nations, participants and, hence, the complexity of the relationships involved, gradually increased and by the early 1960s the Games incorporated teams from Australia, Canada, Finland, France, Israel, South America and the United States. The range of wheelchair sports similarly increased, with basketball, fencing, snooker, swimming and weightlifting all being added to the full programme during the 1960s (DePauw and Gavron, 2005).

Such was the growing internationalization, globalization and competitiveness of the Games from the mid-1950s, alongside the increasing need to ensure that they were funded, managed and organized along more professional lines, in 1960, the International Stoke Mandeville Games Committee (ISMGC) was founded to oversee the organization of the annual Stoke Mandeville Games and sanction all international competitions for athletes with spinal cord injuries. The ISMGC also became responsible for organizing a four-yearly 'Olympic' style competition – now known as the Paralympics (to be examined later) – until 1972 when its constitution was amended to the International Stoke Mandeville Games Federation (ISMGF). The ISMGF was constituted with a remit to govern the sports which comprised the International Games, and to serve the interests of an increasing number of organizations who were becoming part of its membership as the number of events (e.g. the Paralympics and annual International Stoke Mandeville Games) under its aegis similarly increased. As demand grew for further events to be included within individual competitions and for more sport-specific programmes and competitions for disabled people to be developed, in 1991 the ISMGF subsequently became the International Stoke Mandeville Wheelchair Sports Federation (ISMWSF).

Notwithstanding the growing popularity of sport among those with spinal cord injuries, during the 1960s international disability sport competitions were developed for those elite disabled athletes without spinal cord injury who were, therefore, ineligible to participate in either the International Stoke Mandeville Games or the World Games for the Deaf (DePauw and Gavron, 2005; IPC, 2007a). Following a recommendation by the International Working Group on Sport for the Disabled that an umbrella organization was required to coordinate these additional international disability sport competitions, the International Sports Organization for the Disabled (ISOD) was created in Paris in 1964. To help achieve this a number of sporting federations or International Organizations of Sport for the Disabled (IOSD) developed with the intention of providing athletes with visual impairments, amputations and cerebral palsy an opportunity to participate in sport from the grassroots to the international level (DePauw and Gavron, 2005; IPC, 2007a). In this regard, and in addition to ISOD and the International Committee of Sports for the Deaf (ICSD), the IOSDs were comprised of four additional federations, namely, the ISMGF; Cerebral Palsy International Sport and Recreation Association (CP-ISRA); International Blind Sports Association (IBSA); and International Sports Federation for Persons with Mental Handicaps (INAS-FMH). Currently, there are at least six international federations with responsibility for the organization of elite disability sport and which, unlike Olympic federations, are multi-sport and organized around categories of impairment (DePauw and Gavron, 2005). These include the International Paralympic Committee; CISS; IBSA; CP-ISRA; the International Sports Federation for Persons with an Intellectual Disability (INAS-FID) formerly INAS-FMH; and the International Wheelchair and Amputee Sports Federation (IWAS), which was formed following the merger of ISMWSF and ISOD in 2004. In addition to providing sporting opportunities to athletes under their own jurisdiction, each of these IOSDs is responsible for the governance of a range of sports through their international organizations. Boccia and seven-a-side football for athletes with cerebral palsy, for example, is governed by CP-ISRA; judo and five-a-side football for athletes with visual impairments is governed by IBSA; and IWAS is the international governing body for athletes participating in wheelchair fencing and wheelchair rugby. A further expression of the current complex structure of international disability sport which emerged out of the organizational structure that developed in the 1960s and 1970s relates to the ways in which some sports are governed not by the IOSDs but by their respective International Federations. Wheelchair basketball, for example, is currently governed by the International Wheelchair Basketball Federation and thus provides the link between the Great Britain Wheelchair basketball Association and the IPC. Tennis is governed by the International Tennis Federation; table tennis by the International Table Tennis Federation and rowing by the International Rowing Federation.

In a similar way to the organization of disability sport at a national level (see Chapter 4), there is, therefore, considerable variability in the extent to which elite disability sport was, and still is, governed by sport-specific, rather than impairment-specific organizations. It is also the case that, as Hargreaves has noted, sport generally, and the Stoke Mandeville Games in particular, came increasingly to be seen as a means of physical, psychological and social rehabilitation of disabled people, through which their 'sporting performances . . . were related to their identities as *disabled* people – a reminder of the essential *difference* between disabled sportsmen and women and their able-bodied counterparts' (Hargreaves, 2000: 181; emphases in the original). Hargreaves adds further in this connection that whilst the Games provided disabled athletes with an important opportunity to participate in sport

> it was not the sporting abilities of the athletes that was the *raison d'être* of competition, but rather it was their *disabilities* that created a sportsworld specifically for them – separate, spatially and symbolically, from the 'real' world of sport outside. (2000: 181; emphases in the original)

An appreciation of these socio-historical processes provide an important backcloth for understanding how similar views continue, to a greater or lesser degree, to prevail amongst those currently involved in the provision of sporting opportunities for disabled people at other levels of sport (see Chapters 3 and 4) and the media (Chapter 7). But let us now examine in more detail the processes associated with the development of the Paralympics from the 1960s and, in particular, the role played by the IPC in the organization of the Paralympic Games.

The growth of the Paralympic Games and establishment of the IPC

As we noted above, the first Paralympics were held in 1960 in Rome immediately after the Olympic Games and were organized by the ISMGF, who continued to have responsibility for organizing the Summer Paralympic Games until 1988. We also noted that, although the Paralympics and the concept of competitive disability sport generally was initially developed for athletes with spinal cord injuries only, from 1972 other groups of disabled athletes were gradually integrated into the Games. The gradual incorporation of athletes with impairments other than spinal injuries in the Paralympic Games is perhaps not surprising given the increasing number of international bodies (IOSDs) and their predecessors who came to be involved in, and, in some cases, have some responsibility for, organizing the early Paralympics specifically, and international disability sport more broadly. As we noted earlier, the ISMGF which represented the needs of wheelchair athletes and especially those with spinal cord injuries (SCI), was the first IOSD (beyond the ICSD which was responsible for organizing the separate Deaflympics) to organize the international Summer Paralympics from 1960 to 1972 at which only athletes with SCI participated (see Table 6.1). By 1976, however, amputees and *les autres* (the term used to cater for those with other forms of physical impairment) began participating in the Games as ISOD began to assume some responsibility for organizing the Paralympics, whilst the inauguration of CP-ISRA in 1978 to advance the interests and participation of athletes with cerebral palsy at international level helped foster the inclusion of those athletes in the Summer Games for the first time in 1980. The formation of IBSA in 1981 and its involvement in the organization of international disability sport also strengthened the growing involvement of athletes with visual impairments in the Games since 1976, and after a decade of campaigning by INAS-FMH athletes with intellectual impairments were also included for the first time in the 1996 Atlanta Paralympics.

Given the emergence of this increasingly complex network of IOSDs, each of which were involved in organizing the Paralympics and international competitions for athletes within specific impairments, it is not unsurprising that concern came increasingly to be expressed over the growing duplication of events and overlap in the roles and responsibilities between the vast array of organizations involved. The need to coordinate their activities and improve the effectiveness of the institutional organization of the Paralympics and international disability sport was expressed in 1982, when four IOSDs (ISOD, ISMGF, CP-ISRA and IBSA) entered into discussion to establish a committee the central purpose of which would be to 'to coordinate the existing efforts for disability sport on an international level' (DePauw and Gavron, 2005: 76). By June 1984, the four IOSDs agreed that the International Coordinating Committee of World Sports Organizations for the Disabled (ICC) should be formed to act as the official coordinating body for international disability sport and, in particular, for the Paralympic Games (DePauw and Gavron, 2005; Gold and Gold, 2007; Sherrill, 1993). The ICC,

Table 6.1 Sports events for disabled athletes at the 2002 Manchester Commonwealth Games

Sport	Event	Impairment	Number of athletes (male, female)	Number of British athletes (male, female)
Swimming	Men's 50m, 100m	Multi-disability	38 M	4 M
	Women's 50m, 100m		32 F	4 F
Athletics	Men's 100m	Visually impaired	15 M	2 M
	Women's 800m	Wheelchair	10 F	2 F
Weightlifting	Men's bench press	Multi-disability	15 M	2 M
Lawn Bowls	Men's triples	Physically disabled	27 M	3 M
	Women's singles		10 F	1 F
Table Tennis	Women's singles	Visually impaired Wheelchair	13 F	2 F

which was comprised of senior representatives from the founding IOSDs, was alleged to have given 'the disabled sports movement a single voice for the first time' (Gold and Gold, 2007: 92) in relation to the governance of the Paralympics and international disability sport and was intended to represent the IOSDs in developing relations with the IOC and other global organizations (Gold and Gold, 2007; IPC, 2007a). Indeed, DePauw and Gavron (2005: 76) go as far as saying that 'one of the ICC's most important functions during its short tenure' was the negotiations it undertook with the then IOC President, Juan Antonio Samaranch, regarding the use of the term 'Olympics' by the ICC and other disability sport organizations. In particular, it is alleged that the IOC prevented the ICC from using the word 'Olympics' to refer to the international disability sport competitions that it organized and for which it was responsible, and that the preferred term to be adopted by the IOC, National Olympic Committees and the ICC should be 'Paralympics' since they were seen to run parallel to the Olympic Games (DePauw and Gavron, 2005: 76).

Although the ICC were responsible during its short tenure for organizing the Paralympics in 1988 and 1992, intra- and inter-organizational conflict between member nations over the need for more national and regional representation within the ICC eventually led to the establishment of a single democratically organized body, namely, the IPC which was established on 22 September 1989. As the sole global governing body for the Paralympic Movement, the IPC was established as a counterpart to the IOC and is now responsible for organizing both the Summer and Winter Paralympic Games and other World and Regional Championships in 13 sports (including athletics and swimming), for which it also acts as the International Federation (IPC, 2003). By drawing upon the resources of the four IOSDs with which it now works, the IPC has, according to Howe and Jones (2006: 31), 'arguably turned the Paralympic Games into the most recognizable and possibly most influential vehicle for the promotion of sport for the disabled'. Among the other formally stated objectives of the IPC (2007b) are

> to seek the expansion of sport opportunities from a developmental to an elite level . . . to liaise with the . . . IOC and other international sports bodies . . . and to assist and encourage educational programmes, research and promotional activities.

Indeed, since its inauguration, the IPC has actively and increasingly sought to raise the public and commercial profile of elite disability sport by developing closer links with the IOC and the Olympic Movement, as well as attracting significant media coverage of the Summer and Winter Paralympics (see Chapter 7; Howe and Jones, 2006; Smith and Thomas, 2005). It is important to note, however, that whilst these developments have raised, to some degree at least, the visibility and social significance of elite disability sport, and the Paralympic Movement in particular, the Paralympics have certainly not reached the global prominence achieved by competitions such as the Olympics and soccer's World Cup. These and related issues of sponsoring and marketing of the Paralympics have been discussed in greater detail elsewhere (e.g. Darcy, 2003; Gold and Gold, 2007), but let us consider briefly the trends in participation by athletes at the Summer Games from 1992, since when the Summer Paralympics have been hosted in the same venue as the Olympic Games.

The Summer Paralympics: trends in participation

As Hargreaves (2000: 206) has rightly pointed out, despite their growth as an elite international competition, there is nevertheless 'a recognizable pattern of unequal participation rates of women in comparison to men at the Paralympic Games.' The differential and unequal patterns of participation between athletes participating at the Summer Paralympics since 1992 are presented in Table 6.2, from which it is clear that female athletes have consistently made up approximately one-quarter of all participants involved in the Games. Indeed, whilst there has been a general trend towards increasing numbers of athletes and countries competing at the Paralympics since they were held in 1992 in Barcelona, Spain, the proportion of female athletes has increased marginally from 23 per cent to 24 per cent in 1996, and then to just over one-quarter in 2000 (27 per cent) and 31 per cent at the Athens Games in 2004 (Table 6.2). In this regard, it is clear that in participatory terms at least the Paralympics has remained a heavily male-dominated competition and one in which female athletes have historically participated in a narrower range of sports and have been largely excluded from traditional 'male' sports such as football (soccer) and rugby union (Hargreaves, 2000; Sherrill, 1993), and have only begun to represent their home nations in events such as powerlifting since 2000 (Hargreaves, 2000). It is also the case that, as Hargreaves (2000) observes, those countries with the highest number of female athletes – though the same point applies to males too – in their teams have tended to be from the Western world.

The reasons why more males than females and athletes in Western societies have tended to participate in the Paralympics are, of course, multifarious and linked in a variety of ways to other sources of social division such as age, social class, sexuality, religion, race and ethnicity, to such things as the infrastructure of and available opportunities for engaging in disability sport in individual countries, and 'to ideas about difference, experience, identity and the body' (Hargreaves, 2000: 184). In addition, Hargreaves claims that 'those in positions of power in disability

Table 6.2 Trends in participation in the Summer Paralympic Games: 1992–2004

Year	Location of games	Number of countries	Number of athletes	Number of male athletes	Number of female athletes
1992	Barcelona, Spain	82	3,021	2,324	697
1996	Atlanta, USA	103	3,195	2,415	780
2000	Sydney, Australia	122	3,843	2,798	1,045
2004	Athens, Greece	136	3,808	2,643	1,165

sport organizations are mostly men, (and) they are mostly White and able-bodied. They are not, therefore, properly representative of disabled women [and men] in general, or of those from varied social and ethnic backgrounds'. In this regard, Hargreaves argues that part of the explanation for the differential participation rates between men and women in the Paralympics can be related to the fact that 'in the main, disability sport organizations are organizations *for* the disabled and not *of* the disabled. Regardless of the veracity of these claims, it is nevertheless true that 'despite the existence of an international disability sport movement, very little is known' (Hargreaves, 2000: 207) about the complex ways and extent to which males' and females' participation in the Paralympics is enabled and constrained by 'gendered relations of power, social and cultural barriers and personal choices' (2000: 211). It is, therefore, important that future research seeks to examine systematically and explain more adequately the complex underlying reasons for the differential rates of participation by athletes in the Paralympics. As we outline next, any such explanation should also account for the implications that the various classification systems and related debates surrounding the inclusion of elite disabled athletes in mainstream sports competitions such as the Olympic Games can have for participation in the Paralympics.

The classification of disabled athletes

Competitive sport for disabled people, like many other areas of modern sport, is organized using various systems of classification or rankings. However, whilst various systems of categorizing athletes are widely used in mainstream sport to differentiate them according to things such as age (e.g. 'juniors' to 'vets' in running), gender ('male' and 'female' in most sports), bodyweight (e.g. boxing and judo) and ability (e.g. football leagues and golf handicaps), classification is frequently cited as the central defining characteristic of disability sport (Howe and Jones, 2006; Sherrill, 1999; Steadward, 1996; Vanlanderwijck and Chappel, 1996). This is perhaps not unsurprising because the classification of athletes according to their impairment is a process the roots of which can be traced back to the early days of disability sport at Stoke Mandeville and, in particular, to the inauguration and classification systems of the various IOSDs that help organize disability sport at the elite level. One of the historical legacies of this heritage was that the complex impairment-specific forms of classification that were used by the IOSDs were largely accepted uncritically initially by disability sport administrators and the IPC (Howe and Jones, 2006). However, as Howe and Jones (2006: 36) have noted, since the establishment of the IPC 'constant pressure has been placed on the IOSDs to find alternatives to the disability-specific classification systems in order to facilitate the streamlining of the Paralympic programs' and, as we make clear in Chapter 7, to enhance the marketing of the Paralympics and attract greater media coverage of the Games. The classification of athletes and the methods by which this is to be achieved has, however, been an issue which has generated considerable debate amongst those both inside and outside the disability sport community. As we shall explain below, this has revolved, in particular, around the ways and extent to which the classification of athletes helps ensure 'fair' and equitable competition whilst stimulating participation and preventing the 'drop out' of severely disabled athletes in particular (Howe and Jones, 2006; Steadward, 1996; Vanlanderwijck and Chappel, 1996).

Prior to the early 1990s elite disability sport-specific competitions such as the Paralympics were organized around the use of a particularly complex medical classification system which grouped athletes into categories of similar impairment. Initially, athletes were classified in seven groups according to their impairment only; eight classes were used to group athletes with cerebral palsy, three for athletes with visual impairments, seven for wheelchair athletes, nine were employed to classify amputees, and six were used for *les autres*, with just one classification system being used for athletes with intellectual impairments (Sports Council, 1993a). However, as more sports were introduced to the Paralympic programme for athletes with more severe kinds of impairment than had been the case previously, the correlative increase in the number of classes which resulted from this meant that in some sports as many as 23 categories were required to permit 'equitable competition' between participants. Thus, given the logistical problems that accompanied the expanding number of athletes who needed to be grouped into an increasing number of classes, from 1992 emphasis came increasingly to be placed on the development and implementation of sport-focused classification systems where disabled athletes are grouped according to their functional ability in a particular sport, rather than those that are based on a clinical impairment (Howe and Jones, 2006; Sherrill, 1999; Vanlanderwijck and Chappel, 1996). The then IPC President, Robert Steadward (1996), claimed that this form of classification which focuses more on an athlete's functional capability in their respective sport helped to reward excellence, increase levels of competition and standards of performance. He was also of the view that 'the potential benefit of decreasing classes by using a functional integrated classification system is that it may simplify the integration into the rest of the sports world' (Steadward, 1996: 36). In a not dissimilar way, the supposed efficacy of sport- or functionally-based form of classification was also expressed more recently in the IPC's Classification Code published in November 2007 (IPC, 2007c). In particular, the IPC reaffirmed its commitment in the Code to focusing, among other things, on the sporting abilities of athletes to help improve standards of sporting excellence for all athletes across all sports in the Paralympic Movement (IPC, 2007c). More specifically, the IPC claim that it prefers the sport- rather than impairment-specific form of classification 'on the basis that it will contribute to sporting excellence for all Athletes (sic) and sports in the Paralympic Movement, providing equitable competition, through Classification processes that are robust, transparent and fair' (IPC, 2007c: 6). For Hargreaves (2000: 184), the shift from impairment-specific forms of classification to one that is predicated on the assumption that the functional abilities of athletes is more important than the limits imposed by their impairment is also 'an important symbol that the bodies of disabled people are being redefined as effective rather than defective'.

The functionally-based form of classification has also proven popular with some administrators of disability sport, as well as some academics and personnel within the Paralympic Movement. There is, however, still no uniform approach taken to classification by the various IOSDs affiliated to the IPC (Howe and Jones, 2006). The principles which underpin the functional- and impairment-specific systems also remain heavily contested and there is at present 'a lack of agreement between the IPC and the IOSDs as to what is best for the athletes involved in various sports' (Howe and Jones, 2006: 36). In order to demonstrate the differential ways in which the IOSDs affiliated to the IPC classify disabled athletes at the Paralympics it is useful to draw on the work of Howe and Jones who have shown how in the sport of swimming the functional integration (or sport-specific) system of classification has been adopted since the 1992 Paralympics, whilst in athletics a system that classifies athletes according to their specific impairment continues to be used despite pressure from the IPC to use the sport-specific system.

As Howe and Jones (2006) have noted, the sport of swimming was one of the first Paralympic sports to adopt the IPC's preferred integrated functional classification system where athletes are grouped together so that they compete alongside athletes of a similar ability, but who may have not necessarily have the same impairment as them. In swimming, the shift towards using this kind of classification system has brought about a series of supposed benefits for the athletes themselves and in organizational and logistical terms as well (Howe and Jones, 2006; Wu and Williams, 1999). The first and most widely cited benefit of the functional integrated system is that because the number of classes used to group swimmers together has been reduced from 31 to 10, this has also helped limit the number of events that need to be cancelled and the number of races in which swimmers compete (Howe and Jones, 2006; Wu and Williams, 1999). This, as Howe and Jones (2006: 37) have argued, was important since under the previous impairment-specific system of classification 'if two events needed to be combined, then the athletes from the less impaired class were bound to dominate. By reducing the number of classes, the likelihood of combined classes has also been removed.' Not unsurprisingly, reducing the number of classes and races in swimming has been positively received by the IPC, among others, not least because it helps simplify and speed up events, reduce confusion and may, therefore, enhance its appeal to the media and spectators.

Notwithstanding the use of functionally integrated systems in IPC, swimming is said to have had a series of benefits for athletes, these are believed to have been accompanied by a series of disadvantages and that, in some cases, this has meant that some athletes are no longer able to compete. It has been suggested, for example, that under the functionally integrated system it has become increasingly difficult for administrators to classify swimmers because of the need to consider athletes with a diverse range of impairments simultaneously (Howe and Jones, 2006; Daly and Vanlanderwijck, 1999). These problems are further compounded by the fact that classifiers are being requested to assess the functional ability of athletes using many tests that have not been statistically validated. This often means that some athletes are misclassified and thereby placed at a disadvantage by being placed in a class higher than their impairment warrants (Howe and Jones, 2006; Wu and

Williams, 1999). The final source of concern for some commentators is that under the functionally integrated system some swimmers – though the point also applies to athletes competing in other sports where the functionally integrated system is used – might be penalized for enhancing their personal performance through training and improving technique and be reclassified based on their improved functional ability (Howe and Jones, 2006: 38).

In contrast to the situation in swimming, the impairment-specific system of classification has been retained by the IOSDs in athletics so that athletes of similar impairments can compete against each other within specific events in the discipline (Howe and Jones, 2006). This has meant, however, that unlike in swimming where the number of classes has been reduced as a consequence of the shift towards sport-specific forms of impairment, in athletics the number and complexity of the classification systems within each impairment group has meant that it is increasingly difficult to organize events and competitions in a clear, understandable and logistically feasible way (Howe and Jones, 2006). Howe and Jones (2006: 39), for example, have pointed towards the complexities associated with this form of classification when they note how '[T]here were fifteen 100-m final races for men and eleven for women in the sport of athletics in the 2000 Paralympic Games compared with one final race per sex for the 100 m at the Olympic Games.'

Although the IPC has been locked continuously in a series of power struggles with the various IOSDs in athletics since the early 1990s to reorganize its events using a variant of the integrated form of classification, the IOSDs have thus far been able to retain its preferred impairment-specific system of classification (Howe and Jones, 2006). This has meant, however, that because the IPC stipulate that an event must have at least six competitors from four individual countries to make it viable for inclusion in the Paralympic programme, 'many IPC athletic events for the more severely impaired and women have been canceled (sic) or combined' (Howe and Jones, 2006: 40). Thus, rather than promoting and expanding the participation of athletes who, as we noted above, have traditionally been under-represented – in participatory terms – in the Paralympics, the persistence of impairment-specific classification systems in athletes appear to have done more to reduce still further lower participation rates among severely impaired athletes and women.

Notwithstanding the apparent inconsistencies that characterize the attempts by the various IOSDs towards classifying athletes, it is clear that this is an area of some considerable debate that usually calls forth from many people within the world of disability sport strong emotional feelings about whether or not their own sporting organization, or some other organization, *should* consider the use of particular systems of classification. Whether a particular IOSD *should* adopt some form of impairment- or sport-specific system of classification depends, of course, on one's own ideological position regarding the efficacy of particular classification systems in disability sport. But whichever course of action that organizations such as the IPC and the IOSDs in athletics, for example, take in relation to the future classification of athletes, what we can be certain of is that the implementation of any classification system will inevitably be accompanied by a series of outcomes, some of which may be intended, but others of which will be unplanned and unintended by some, if not all, of the relevant parties involved.

Integration and inclusion in elite disability sport

A closely related – though equally debated and contentious – issue in the world of disability sport is that which surrounds whether disabled athletes should be able to compete in mainstream sporting competitions such as the Olympics (Labanowich, 1989; Steadward, 1996; Vanlanderwijck and Chappel, 1996). Although there is no general consensus between all the major disability and elite mainstream sport organizations regarding this process of mainstreaming (see also Chapter 4), there is at least an official commitment by the IPC to 'increase the integration of sports for athletes with disabilities into the international sports movement for able-bodied athletes, whilst safeguarding and preserving the identity of sports for disabled athletes' (IPC, 2003). In particular, as Robert Steadward, the former President of the IPC, noted in 1996, the IPC are concerned that promoting the achievements of disabled athletes should involve

> the *inclusion of events* for athletes with a disability in major international competitions such as the Olympics, as well as the *inclusion of athletes* with a disability into sport opportunities in which they can participate 'side-by-side' with their able-bodied counterparts. (1996: 27; emphases in the original)

Despite the lack of consensus regarding inclusion, it is nevertheless clear that there has been a growing tendency over the last half-century or more for *some* disabled athletes to participate alongside non-disabled athletes in competitions such as the Olympics and Commonwealth Games. DePauw and Gavron (2005), for example, have pointed out that one of the first disabled athletes to participate in the Olympic Games was Karoly Takacs, who won gold medals in archery in the 1948 and 1952 Games; Liz Hartel also won a silver medal for Dressage whilst representing Denmark at the 1952 Helsinki Olympics; and Neroli Fairhall, a wheelchair athlete from New Zealand, competed in Women's archery at the 1984 Olympics held in Los Angeles. It was also during the 1984 Games that growing numbers of disabled athletes (typically, though by no means exclusively, wheelchair athletes) began to participate in demonstration events as a showcase for the Paralympic Games which preceded the Olympic Games. The inclusion of demonstration events has continued to form part of the Olympic programme ever since and, in more recent years, Marla Runyan from the USA also became the first registered blind person to participate in the full Olympic programme when she reached the finals of the 1,500 metres at the 2000 Sydney Olympics (Hargreaves, 2000). Natalie Du Toit, a South African amputee swimmer, became the first amputee to compete in the Olympic Games held in Beijing in 2008 having qualified for the 10km open water event following her fourth place finish at the 2008 Open Water World Championships.

The inclusion of disabled athletes in mainstream elite sports competitions is not confined to the Olympic Games. In the last decade or so some disabled athletes have begun to participate alongside non-disabled competitors in the Commonwealth Games. In part, the trend towards some disabled athletes participating in the Commonwealth Games emerged in 1990 when the IPC International Committee on Integration of Athletes with a Disability (ICI) was formed with the intention of promoting the inclusion of some full medal events for disabled athletes in international competitions, especially the Commonwealth Games and Olympics. The ICI – which was later renamed the Commission for Inclusion of Athletes with a Disability (CIAD) – was successful in some of its lobbying campaigns with the Commonwealth Games Federation (CGF) when, in 1991, the CGF agreed to include six demonstration events for disabled athletes in the 1994 Games in Victoria, Canada. Four of these events were intended for disabled male athletes (e.g. the open wheelchair marathon and 800m wheelchair race) and two featured disabled women (100m freestyle swimming class S9 and visually impaired lawn bowls singles) (DePauw and Gavron, 2005: 243). In 1997, the CGF formally expressed its commitment to increase the incorporation of disabled athletes and disability sport events within the full medal programme following the perceived success of the demonstration events at the 1994 Games. In particular, following consultation with the Commonwealth Games Associations, the National Paralympic Committees and the international sports governing bodies, the CGF decided to make the inclusion of disabled athletes and disability sport events in the full Commonwealth programme compulsory from 2006. The Manchester Commonwealth Games Organizing Committee (MCGOC), who were responsible for organizing the 2002 Games held in Manchester, England, between 25 July and 4 August sought, however, to comply with the recommendations of the CGF ahead of schedule by including five sports (swimming, athletics, lawn bowls weightlifting and table tennis) for 160 disabled athletes from 20 countries in its programme (CGF, 2003). As a consequence, the XVII Commonwealth Games held in Manchester was the largest Commonwealth Games ever, and the first major international multi-sport event to include disabled athletes in its main sports programme and medal table.

The inclusion of disabled athletes and disability sport-specific events in elite sports competitions is an important policy issue that continues to be raised in discussions between the IPC and IOC and between the various sporting organizations involved. It is likely that these discussions about inclusion will continue to generate considerable debate over a range of issues, including: the implications that the classification of disabled athletes has for the viability of including disabled athletes in elite mainstream competitions; the impact that inclusion will have on the participation of disabled sportswomen and those with more severe impairments in particular; and the extent to which disabled athletes' participation in competitions such as the Olympics may come to impact on their identities and the identity of disability sport more generally. As we explain in Chapter 7, it is likely that the media coverage, sponsorship and marketing of disabled athletes and disability sport will also form part of discussions between the IPC and IOC. But let us consider one final aspect of the debate surrounding the inclusion of disabled athletes in elite mainstream sports competitions by drawing on the recent discussions about the use of technological aids by some disabled athletes to facilitate their performance in elite sport.

Inclusion, technology and performance-enhancement: Oscar the 'cheetah'?

An additional and increasingly significant dimension of the on-going debate about whether disabled athletes should be allowed to compete alongside non-disabled athletes in mainstream sports competitions has been their use of various technologies and assistive devices to participate in sport. Perhaps the most recent and high profile athlete who uses technological aid to assist performance in disability sport and who has generated substantial debate in the sporting world is the South African double amputee sprinter, Oscar Pistorius, popularly known as the 'Blade Runner'. Pistorius, who was born without fibula bones and had the lower part of both legs amputated when he was 11 months old, uses two J-shaped carbon-fibre Össur Cheetah Flex-Foot prosthetics to enable him to run. He won the gold medal in the 200m and bronze in the 100m at the Athens Paralympics and is also the world record holder in both events. Although Pistorius regularly trains with, and competes against, non-disabled athletes in competitions in South Africa, his application to compete in the 400m at the Beijing 2008 Olympic Games and other mainstream sports events recognized by the International Association of Athletics Federations (IAAF) generated substantial debate about whether the use of his prostheses constituted a technical aid that contravenes IAAF competition rule 144.2 and which gives him an unfair advantage over other athletes not using the same prosthetics (*Guardian*, 10 January 2008; *The Times*, 31 December 2007). In particular, concern was expressed about the extent to which Pistorius's use of the 'Cheetah' prosthetics made him taller – than he would have been had he been born with fibula bones – thereby increasing his stride length, and whether the energy they released, and the fact that lactic acid does not build up as it does in the legs of non-disabled athletes, enables him to distribute speed over the whole lap and run faster than other athletes (*Guardian*, 10 January 2008). To establish whether the prosthetics did, in fact, give Pistorius an unfair advantage over other athletes in these ways, the IAAF filmed his performances in a series of competitions and also required Pistorius to undertake a series of biomechanical tests conducted in November 2007 by Professor Gert-Peter Brüggemann at the German Sports University in Cologne. On the basis of the findings presented by Professor Brüggemann, the IAAF concluded in January 2008 that the 'Cheetah' prosthetics gave Pistorius 'considerable advantage' over other athletes not using the device and banned him from competing against non-disabled athletes in the Olympics or any other event recognized by the IAAF. The IAAF explained that the use of the prosthetics contravened its rules regarding the use of technical aids because:

> It is evident that an athlete using the 'Cheetah' prosthetic is able to run at the same speed as able-bodied athletes with lower energy consumption. Running

with prosthetic blades leads to less vertical motion combined with less mechanical work for lifting the body. As well as this, the energy loss in the blade is significantly lower than in the human ankle joints in sprinting at maximum speed. An athlete using this prosthetic blade has a demonstrable mechanical advantage (more than 30 per cent) when compared to someone not using the blade. (*Guardian*, 14 January 2008)

Despite the IAAF's decision, Pistorius subsequently challenged the scientific findings of Professor Brüggemann and filed an appeal to the Court of Arbitration for Sport (CAS) in Lausanne, Switzerland. On 16 May 2008 the CAS upheld the appeal filed by Pistorius and concluded in a press release that

the IAAF did not meet its burden of proof that Rule 144.2 (e) is contravened by Oscar Pistorius. On the basis of the evidence brought by the experts called by both parties, the Panel was not persuaded that there was sufficient evidence of any metabolic advantage in favour of a double-amputee using the Cheetah Flex-Foot. Furthermore, the CAS Panel has considered that the IAAF did not prove that the biomechanical effects of using this particular prosthetic device gives Oscar Pistorius an advantage over other athletes not using the device. (CAS, 2008)

The Panel went on to emphasize that its decision was 'limited to the eligibility of Oscar Pistorius only and, only, to his use of the specific prosthesis in issue in this appeal' (CAS, 2008) and did not exclude the possibility that

with future advances in scientific knowledge, and a testing regime designed and carried out to the satisfaction of both Parties, the IAAF might in the future be in a position to prove that the existing *Cheetah Flex-Foot* model provides Oscar Pistorius with an advantage over other athletes. (CAS, 2008; emphases in the original)

The verdict of the CAS came just as the manuscript of this book was being completed so the implications of its decision to allow Oscar Pistorius to compete in the Olympics and other events recognized by the IAAF should he have qualified were not known. The initial reaction by parts of the British media, however, was that the CAS Panel had made 'an historic legal decision' (*Times*, 17 May 2008) that represented 'a huge breakthrough for disabled athletes' (*Guardian*, 17 May 2008), whilst Pistorius himself was quoted as saying that 'It is a battle that has been going on for far too long. It's a great day for sport. This day is going to go down in history for the equality of disabled people' (*Guardian*, 17 May 2008). But what might we take to learn about the Pistorius case and similar cases in the future? Perhaps the first point to note is that within the sporting context the decision by the CAS Panel is likely to open serious debate on the future use of prosthetics and other assistive devices in sport that will not be limited to the case of Pistorius case, but is likely to raise serious questions about the eligibility of many disabled athletes to participate in any mainstream elite sports competition under IAAF rules (Lippi and Mattiuzzi, 2008). In this regard, the use of prosthetics may begin to be seen increasingly in a similar light as performance-enhancing drugs in sport, namely, as a technological form of cheating and means of obtaining an unfair advantage over other athletes. It might also reasonably be expected that the successful challenge of Pistorius will stimulate considerable debate on the impact that the participation of some disabled athletes in the Olympics may have for the future of the Paralympic Movement and, in particular, the Paralympics. It may also come to impact not only on the relationships between disabled and non-disabled athletes, but also on those within both groups of athletes too. Reflecting on these issues in the immediate aftermath of the decision to allow Pistorius to compete in IAAF recognized events, Dame Tanni Grey-Thompson, Britain's most successful Paralympian, was quoted as saying that:

> For Oscar, it is huge and I can understand why he is doing it. He will be the first Paralympian who is truly known worldwide and the movement will benefit from it. But the argument goes much deeper than Oscar. What happens is that, if he runs at the Olympics, they have to take his event out of the Paralympics because I would not want the Paralympics race becoming the 'B' event or the 'B' final. It is never going to happen in wheelchair racing because there is no way we could ever drop into the women's 800m. If Oscar is seen to be making the jump from Paralympics to Olympics, then the Paralympics is immediately B finals. I don't ever want it to be that. He has always said he wants to run both but there is something about that which does not feel quite right. It is a much wider debate about whether he runs or not. It is the whole future of his event at the Paralympics Games which is under discussion. (*Guardian*, 17 May 2008)

Within the context of the wider society the use of technological devices in disability sport will continue to add further weight to the on-going debates about the use of biotechnologies and new genetic engineering techniques which are becoming increasingly available and, perhaps more importantly, which are becoming increasingly used. As Swartz and Watermeyer (2008: 188) have rightly noted, it also raises fundamental questions about the social relationships and 'boundaries between disabled and non-disabled groups' and reminds us of 'what it means to be human' (2008: 187). The fact that the disabled body continues to draw attention 'by its difference and otherness' (Swartz and Watermeyer, 2008: 187) may also stimulate debate about what it means socially to be disabled, and what means to be non-disabled. Another possibility is that the presence of disabled athletes such as Pistorius competing against non-disabled athletes in sport may raise further questions about the expectations and abilities of disabled people more generally. More specifically, as we discuss in Chapter 7, might it be that the presentation – particularly in the media – of disabled people (such as Pistorius) who may be perceived as 'super-crips', as having '"overcome adversity" in a heartwarming manner and not been restricted by his or her "flaws", but [who believe] that "everything is possible" for those who work hard' (Swartz and Watermeyer, 2008: 189), alongside those who may be viewed as 'invalid, dependent, incapable, damaged both inside and out' (Swartz and Watermeyer, 2008: 189), reinforces stereotypical perceptions of disabled people and their lives? Or may it help challenge taken-for-granted expectations about the lives and capabilities of disabled and non-disabled people? These are just some of the fundamental questions that are raised by the case of Pistorius and that deserve to be researched and taken seriously.

Summary

It is clear from the analysis presented in this chapter that the organization and structure of elite sport for disabled people has a relatively short history and remains particularly fragmented, complex and confusing. We have also noted that the emergence and development of elite disability sport and, in particular, the Paralympics can only be conceptualized adequately if it is located within the context of broader social processes, and especially the politicization, commercialization, globalization and internationalization of modern elite sport, all of which have been occurring at an accelerating rate since the immediate post-1945 period. In the elite disability sport context, however, we have attempted to show how these processes appear to have accelerated most rapidly since the establishment of the IPC in 1989, which has since come to play an increasingly significant organizational role. We have also explored how the on-going debates surrounding the classification of disabled athletes in the Paralympics, the inclusion of Paralympic athletes and disability sport events in the Olympic Games, and the use of technological aids by Paralympians all provide a number of opportunities and challenges to the IPC and others within the elite disability sport community who are concerned with promoting Paralympic sport. In a similar vein, the next chapter explores the growing media coverage of disabled athletes that has accompanied the growth of elite disability sport that we have examined here.

Revision questions

1   If we are to explain how elite level disability is currently organized and structured, why is it important to understand something of its origins at Stoke Mandeville Hospital and the role of Sir Ludwig Guttmann?

2   What are the roles and responsibilities of the IPC and IOSDs in the organization of elite level disability sport?

3   Using the IPC's Classification Code (2007c) as a case study, what are the key opportunities and challenges of grouping athletes together according to sport- rather than impairment-specific systems of classification in the Paralympics?

4   If you worked for the IOC and IPC, what issues need to be considered if more elite disabled athletes wished to participate in the Olympics?
5   What are the different outcomes that may result from the decision by the CAS to allow Oscar Pistorius to compete in all mainstream sports events recognized by the IAAF?

Key readings

DePauw, K. and Gavron, S. (2005) *Disability Sport*. (2nd edn), Champaign, IL: Human Kinetics.

Gold, J. and Gold, M. (2007) 'The rise of the Paralympics', in J. Gold and M. Gold (eds) *Olympic Cities: City Agendas, Planning, and the World's Games, 1896 to 2012*, London: Routledge.

Hargreaves, J. (2000) *Heroines of Sport: The Politics of Difference and Identity*, London: Routledge.

Howe, D. and Jones, C. (2006) 'Classification of disabled athletes: (Dis)empowering the Paralympic practice community', *Sociology of Sport Journal*, 23: 29–46.

Steadward, R. (1996) 'Integration and sport in the Paralympic Movement', *Sport Science Review*, 5: 26–41.

Recommended websites

Commonwealth Games Federation
www.thecgf.com/getflash.asp

Court of Arbitration for Sport
www.tas-cas.org

International Paralympic Committee
www.paralympic.org

7   Disability sport and the media

Objectives

This chapter will:

- examine media coverage of disabled athletes participating in the Paralympics and Commonwealth Games;
- suggest that media coverage of disabled athletes has not always been as positive as is sometimes assumed; and
- argue that the media coverage of disability sport has tended to focus on particular athletes, with particular impairments, competing in particular sports.

Introduction

In the previous chapter we examined the emergence and development of modern elite disability sport-specific competitions such as the Paralympic Games, as well the growing involvement of disabled people in mainstream sports events such as the Commonwealth Games. Accompanying the development and, in particular, the growing commercialization and professionalization of these events, there has been a correlative increase in the media coverage and attention devoted to those competitions and the athletes who participate in them. The central object of this chapter is to examine the changes and degrees of continuity that characterize the ways and extent to which the media (in particular, newspapers) in Britain and elsewhere have reported on the involvement of disabled athletes in the Paralympics and the 2002 Commonwealth Games. In doing so, it begins to question the largely uncritically held assumption that the growing media coverage of such competitions is a 'positive' development in the evolution of modern elite disability sport. It also suggests that, in many ways, such coverage may have done more to reinforce, than challenge, socially constructed stereotypical perceptions of impairment, disability and the sporting and non-sporting abilities of disabled people.

Whilst we are primarily concerned in this chapter with the social representation of disabled athletes in the media, such an analysis also holds out the possibility of shedding light not only on dominant present-day perceptions of, and attitudes towards, disabled athletes, but also of disabled people, impairment and disability more generally. It is, of course, in the absence of detailed empirical research, difficult to know the precise impact that the media coverage of disabled people and disability sport is interpreted and perceived by the intended audience. It may challenge their pre-conceived perceptions about the sporting capabilities of disabled athletes and of their experience of impairment and disability; alternatively, it may have the effect of reinforcing existing thoughts the audience has about the lives of disabled people. Another possible scenario is that the coverage of disability sport will challenge *and* reinforce the public's perceptions of athletes and their abilities, while other aspects of the media's treatment of the phenomenon may be rejected and ignored entirely by the recipients. These and more variations are possible. It is not a profound thing to suggest, therefore, that it is important to continually remind ourselves of these provisos when interpreting the coverage of the Paralympic and Commonwealth Games outlined below, and to keep in mind the realization that we do not, and cannot, have a complete understanding (or anything approaching it) of the reasons why the media report on these issues in the ways they do. It is also crucial that the coverage to which we refer is not accepted uncritically, for the accounts provided therein are unlikely to be more-or-less adequate representations of the events being described. More specifically, insofar as the press are not simply neutral and passive observers of disability sport and the societies in which it is undertaken, one needs to be vigilant and alive to the possibility that the coverage has been characterized by varying degrees of conscious intent and has served to express the more-or-less perceived self-interests and ideologies of journalists and their editors, the majority of whom are often White, non-disabled males. As will become clear however, on occasions the phenomenon of disability sport, particularly in more recent years, has also been the subject of more circumspect and analytical treatment by the press.

Representations of disability and disabled people in the press

Before we examine these issues, it is useful to examine how the press have reported upon disabled people, impairment and disability generally (Barnes and Mercer, 2003; Barnes *et al.*, 1999; Shakespeare, 1997), for this forms an important back-cloth for understanding the representation of disabled athletes to be discussed later on. As Barnes (1992) has noted, in the context of the various campaigns for equal rights for disabled people, there has been since the 1980s growing interest in the cultural representation and characterization of disabled people and disability in the media, particularly in relation to television (see, for example, Barnes, 1992; Barnes and Mercer, 2003; Cumberbatch and Negrine, 1992; Karpf, 1988) and the written press (see, for example, Barnes, 1992; Cooke *et al.*, 2000; Smith and Jordan, 1991). While such media treatment has been characterized by significant spatio-temporal variations that can be interpreted as one expression of the struggles over the differential power chances available to different groups of disabled and non-disabled people (see, for example, Barnes, 1992; Shakespeare, 1997), focusing on these variations should not preclude an analysis of the equally important similarities. In this regard, it has been claimed that in many Western societies, in particular, disabled people have historically been presented as passive objects of aid to whom charity and pity can be directed by 'normal', non-disabled members of the wider society. More particularly, the socio-cultural stereotypes of disabled people and the experience of impairment and disability that are evident in the press are said to have the effect of evoking from readers emotions of pity and fear. These stereotypes and emotions, it has been claimed, help to express and construct perceptions of disabled people as 'tragic', 'brave', 'helpless' and 'superhuman' members of a deviant minority group whose lives are bedevilled by experiences of extreme pain caused by the presence of impairment (Barnes, 1992; Barnes and Mercer, 2003; Barnes *et al.*, 1999; Cooke *et al.*, 2000; Cumberbatch and Negrine, 1992; Shakespeare, 1997; Smith and Jordan, 1991).

In the study *What the Papers Say and Don't Say about Disability*, Smith and Jordan (1991), for example, reported that the tabloid newspapers in their sample focused on a limited number of issues related to disability, with articles discussing health, fund-raising and charity appeals, as well as the personal lives and stories of disabled people accounting for over one-third (35 per cent) of all coverage. The marked tendency by the tabloid press to ignore other aspects of disabled people's lives and to conceptualize disability as a medical or individual problem also characterized the treatment given by the broadsheets or 'quality' press too. However, the coverage in the broadsheet or 'quality' newspapers also featured a wider consideration of other aspects of disabled people's lives, with participation in education, sport, the arts and employment among the issues discussed (Smith and Jordan, 1991). In this regard, the authors concluded that 'much of the language used by (the) newspapers (was) both "pejorative" and "prejudicial"' (Smith and Jordan, 1991: 8) and that 'the press contravene(d) the newspaper industry's own . . . "Code of Conduct"' (Smith and Jordan, 1991: 23).

A follow-up study to Smith and Jordan's (1991) original investigation conducted eight years later revealed that there had been a 400 per cent increase in the number of articles relating to disabled people since 1991 and some notable changes in their treatment by the press treatment (Cooke *et al.*, 2000). In particular, aspects of the coverage was said to be more 'balanced' and 'less prejudiced' than in the previous study, with 'many examples of good practice' (Cooke *et al.*, 2000: 12) evident in the work of some journalists, particularly those working for local (regional) newspapers. Despite the perceived improvement in the press treatment given to disability issues, there was nevertheless a strong element of continuity in the coverage which indicated that 'disabled people are still stereotyped and appear only in selected areas of news' (Cooke *et al.*, 2000: 23) (such as health, medical research, welfare and benefits, and fundraising) that indicate further the alleged dominance of thinking about impairment and disability in highly medicalized and individualized ways (Cooke *et al.*, 2000). Indeed, given this often narrow focus of newspaper coverage, it is not uncommon to hear that the press treatment of disabled people and experiences of impairment and disability is perceived to be characterized 'by always taking an individualized perspective, focusing on disability as personal misfortune' (Shakespeare, 1997: 219). It is also the case that, as Cooke *et al.*'s findings reveal, and as we shall see later in the press coverage of the Paralympic and Commonwealth Games, several aspects of the recent press treatment of disabled people continue to contravene the newspaper and periodical industry's Code of Practice, that was ratified again recently, and which states that:

*   The press must avoid prejudicial or pejorative reference to an individual's race, colour, religion, gender, sexual orientation or to any physical or mental illness or disability.
*   Details of an individual's race, colour, religion, gender, sexual orientation, physical or mental illness or disability must be avoided unless genuinely relevant to the story. (Press Complaints Commission, 2007: 1)

Finally, it is important to note that as well as the tendency for the press to portray and reproduce particular stereotypical views of disabled people and their life experiences, the press is also believed to reinforce other sources of social division, particularly in relation to gender, and especially women (Barnes, 1992; Barnes *et al.*, 1999; Meekosha and Dowse, 1997; Morris, 1991). The gendered nature of press coverage of disabled people is said to be indicated by the tendency for newspapers to focus disproportionately on disabled men and, in particular, the ways in which they attempt to manage their perceived loss of masculinity and associated qualities of strength, courage and physicality because of the existence of their impairment. In this regard, some disabled men are typically presented in the press as endeavouring to 'reclaim' their lost sense of masculinity and sense of self-identity through 'superhuman' effort and 'triumphing over the tragedy' that characterizes their lives (Barnes 1992; Meekosha and Dowse, 1997; Morris, 1991). By contrast, it has been argued that since many women are represented in the press as 'vulnerable, passive and dependent, there is less artistic interest in portraying disabled women, unless it is as tragic or saintly figures' (Barnes *et al.*, 1999: 196), or as asexual beings who do not conform to other supposedly desirable forms of femininity (Barnes and Mercer, 2003; Meekosha and Dowse, 1997; Morris, 1991).

We shall return to the gendered nature of the media treatment of disabled people later. However let us now examine in greater detail the press coverage of disabled athletes participating at the elite level.

Press coverage of disability sport since the 1980s

In the years before the Paralympic Games were held in 1984 (New York and Aylesbury) and 1988 (Seoul), interest in the Paralympics among the press in many countries was said to be almost non-existent and that which did exist was perceived by athletes and other interested parties as reinforcing popular negative stereotypes of disabled athletes and disabled people more generally (Brittain, 2004; Stein, 1989). Reflecting on the 1984 Games, one of the male athletes in Brittain's (2004) study of the Great Britain Paralympic track and field squad who competed at the Sydney 2000 Paralympics, said:

> They were very low key, and I know that BBC had a 45-minute programme on them [1984, New York] and it was very . . . I was going to say derogatory, derisive, but they were just demeaning, really. (Brittain, 2004: 447)

When asked in what sense the coverage was perceived as 'demeaning', the same athlete replied:

> In an, 'Oh look at these disabled people, aren't they marvellous ... getting out there and doing something,' (way) and it was the same after Seoul with Cliff Morgan. Patronising, I think, is probably the best description. (Britain, 2004: 447)

Although media coverage generally – including both print and TV coverage – of the Paralympics has increased gradually since the 1980s, the press treatment and social significance of the sporting performances of disabled athletes remains considerably lower than that afforded non-disabled athletes, and global sporting events such as the Olympics and football (soccer) World Cup. The media representation of disabled athletes is also a very much under-developed area of study among academics, especially when compared to the abundance of existing literature which examines other aspects of the sports media (Schantz and Gilbert, 2001; Schell and Duncan, 1999; Sherrill, 1993, 1997; Smith and Thomas, 2005; Thomas and Smith, 2003). It is, therefore, not unsurprising that there have been calls by those inside and outside the disability sport community to increase further the media coverage of disability sport events such as the Paralympics not least because, as the Great British Paralympian Tanni Grey-Thompson (2001: 112) has noted, it is believed that 'the press can be useful in helping to raise the profile of disability sport and the wider issue of disabled rights'. Writing in 2000, Peter White, the BBC's disability affairs correspondent, for example, argued in this connection that:

> Despite the little burst of interest which accompanies every Paralympic Games, sport for disabled people might just as well be taking place on another planet in the intervening four years. Attempts to establish a continuity of coverage, to build up a consistent level of interest, to enable readers to identify with the personalities which disability sport always throws up regularly fall on stony ground. I know, I've tried. The lines of rejection are familiar enough 'our readers don't seem to be interested', 'they can't identify with the athletes', 'people find disability sport uncomfortable'. (Cooke *et al.*, 2000: 30)

Brittain (2004: 448) has also claimed in a similar way that 'the interest from the media is very fleeting and dies away completely within two to three weeks of the Paralympic closing ceremony'; a point that, he suggests, provides an indication of 'the low regard in which the media hold disability sport and the performances of athletes with disabilities' (Brittain, 2004: 448). In a not dissimilar way, Nixon (2007: 424) has noted that:

> The fact that the 2004 Athens International Paralympic Games were broadcast in the United States on the Outdoor Life Network nearly 2 months after the competition ended, long after the extensively covered 2004 Athens Olympics, is an indication that disability sport is not invisible but remains far outside the mainstream public's eye.

Against this backdrop of sporadic media coverage of disability sport, many disability sport organizations such as the British Paralympic Association (BPA) and the English Federation of Disability Sport (EFDS) have repeatedly campaigned for greater and more regular sustained media coverage of disabled athletes on the assumption that such coverage will necessarily be a 'good' or 'positive' development for the disability sport community, and for both disabled and non-disabled audiences. The BPA (2003), for example, have claimed that 'with greater media coverage than ever before more people in Great Britain appreciated the world class quality of the (disabled) athletes' competing at the 2002 Manchester Commonwealth Games. Similarly, the EFDS claimed that the inclusion of disabled athletes in the Manchester Games provided further opportunity for 'much needed' media coverage of disability sport and that 'for the games to be considered a success where disability sport is concerned . . . the disabled athletes must be positively portrayed' (EFDS, 2002: 55). More specifically, it was hoped that:

> If the 2002 Games can avoid the public 'awww' and 'bless them' factor, and accusations of tokenism it will, *without doubt*, help to further change public perceptions of disability sport in this country and build on the positive work of the Paralympics. (EFDS, 2002: 55; emphases added)

Even among more critical observers there has been a tendency to extol, somewhat uncritically, the ways in which the same event was 'a positive example of athletes with disabilities competing at the same venue as mainstream competitors' (Vickerman *et al.*, 2003: 58). But to what extent, if any, has the growing and slowly changing media coverage of events such as the Paralympics helped to raise the profile of disability sport? Has the limited coverage of elite disabled athletes, in fact, helped to challenge dominant perceptions of, and the issues surrounding, impairment, disability and disabled people's lives? Or has it also resulted in consequences that, in the event, may well be the very reverse of what was intended by the advocates involved?

Descriptions of impairment, disability and disabled athletes

Perhaps the first point to note is that aspects of the visual and print media coverage of disabled athletes competing in the Paralympics from the 1980s and, since 2002, in the Commonwealth Games, has to varying degrees been characterized by a tendency to discuss the performances of disabled athletes in terms more-or-less consistent with a medicalized or individualized understanding of disability and impairment. That is, disabled athletes have tended to be portrayed as 'victims' who overcome the 'painful' individualized experience of disability in order to participate in sport (Darcy, 2003; Schantz and Gilbert, 2001; Schell and Duncan, 1999; Smith and Thomas, 2005; Thomas and Smith, 2003). In their study of American television coverage of the 1996 Paralympic Games Schell and Duncan (1999), for example, noted that aspects of the coverage emphasized the ways and extent to which disabled athletes were perceived 'as less-than-capable athletes' (1999: 35) and as 'transcending human limitations' by 'overcoming nearly insurmountable obstacles' (1999: 37). An analysis of French and German press coverage of the same event also revealed that most of the eight newspapers analysed contained articles that 'marginalized and trivialized' (Schantz and Gilbert, 2001: 86) the Paralympics by suggesting that it was, in a variety of ways, a less serious sporting event compared to other mainstream sports competitions, whilst the athletes themselves were frequently presented as having 'beaten all odds to "overcome their disability"' (Schantz and Gilbert, 2001: 81). Similarly, Thomas and Smith's (2003) study of British press coverage of the 2000 Paralympic Games indicated that in just under one-quarter (23 per cent) of articles athletes were depicted as 'victims' or 'courageous' people who 'suffer' from 'personal tragedies'; indeed, in some instances, Paralympic athletes were described as demonstrating 'great dedication and courage . . . despite . . . [the] . . . hurdles or misfortune put in their way' (Thomas and Smith, 2003: 172–3), and as offering 'an even more inspiring illustration of the indestructible nature of the human spirit' (Thomas and Smith, 2003: 173). Similar portrayals of athletes' personal experiences of impairment were also used by tabloid newspapers, in particular, when describing the achievements of Great Britain's most well-known Paralympian, Tanni Grey-Thompson. One reporter for the *Daily Mail* newspaper cited in Thomas and Smith's (2003) study, for example, explained how 'Anyone who spends time in her [Tanni Grey-Thompson's] company quickly ignores the ravages of spina bifida' (Thomas and Smith, 2003: 173), before going on to suggest that disability sport releases 'Runners . . . from the solitary confinement of autism . . . [and] . . . swimmers . . . from the chrysalis of a broken body' (Thomas and Smith, 2003: 173).

The tendency to describe athletes who were perceived to have 'overcome the personal misfortune' of having an impairment and thus the experience of disability was also a particularly enduring theme of the British press coverage of the inclusion of disabled athletes in the mainstream 2002 Manchester Commonwealth Games (Smith and Thomas, 2005). The British bowler Richard Coates, for example, was said to have 'overcome the tragedy of losing both his hands' and shown 'true courage' and 'determination' to participate at the Games (Smith and Thomas, 2005: 57), whilst the South African swimmer Natalie Du Toit was frequently described as the 'bravest girl at the Games' (Smith and Thomas, 2005: 57). In this regard, Du Toit's participation in Manchester was believed to speak 'multiple volumes for her tenacity, mental strength and an extraordinary will both to win and to place her life back where it was' (Smith and Thomas, 2005: 57). As in other studies (Darcy, 2003; Schantz and Gilbert, 2001; Thomas and Smith, 2003), Smith and Thomas (2005) also noted that in addition to describing disabled athletes in highly medicalized terms, aspects of the British press coverage – as in many other countries – continued to express the longstanding and uncritically accepted view that sports participation is perceived to play a central role in the physical and social rehabilitation of disabled people (see Chapter 2). It is, therefore, perhaps unsurprising that this kind of press treatment has been considered to have the effect of doing more to reinforce, than to challenge, traditional stereotypical perceptions of the role of sport for disabled people and of a more individualized and medicalized understanding of disability among members of the intended audience (Schell and Duncan, 1999; Schantz and Gilbert, 2001; Thomas and Smith, 2003).

The significance of gender and impairment type

As Hargreaves (2000: 203) has noted, a related feature of the press treatment of disability sport has been the 'tendency for disabled sportsmen to get more coverage than disabled sportswomen, and for wheelchair sport to be prioritized' over other events. The differential press coverage of males and females relates both to the written and photographic coverage athletes receive, with the general pattern being that males are more likely to receive greater coverage overall and be photographed in more active competitive situations. With the exception of several high profile disabled female athletes (such as Natalie Du Toit, Tanni Grey-Thompson and Louise Sauvage), many disabled women by comparison tend to receive significantly less press coverage than their male counterparts, and non-disabled men and women, and often feature in photographs which present them in more passive, non-competitive situations. Thomas and Smith's (2003) study, for example, revealed that of the 76 per cent of articles that included a photo of athletes participating in the Sydney 2000 Paralympics, 80 per cent of those photographs featured disabled sportsmen in active, competitive situations, with the purpose being, it seemed, to convey to the reader images of physicality and strength said to be strongly associated with popular socio-cultural perceptions of particular kinds of masculinities (DePauw, 1997, 2000; Hargreaves, 2000; Shakespeare, 1996; Sherrill, 1993, 1997). Simultaneously, however, in the remaining photographic coverage similar proportions of males (48 per cent) and females (52 per cent) were photographed in non-competitive and passive situations (Thomas and Smith, 2003), which reflects aspects of the traditional media presentation of disabled people, particularly disabled women, discussed earlier.

A further similarity between the sports and general media coverage of disabled people appears to lie in the ways and extent to which wheelchair athletes, and those with impairments that are acquired and appear more recognizable and understandable to non-disabled people (for example, amputees), typically receive greater coverage than athletes with congenital (such as cerebral palsy) and learning disabilities. As Nixon (2007) has noted, although explanations for this disproportionate media coverage are not entirely clear, one interpretation of this trend relates to the existence of an apparent 'hierarchy of acceptability' among the media, which has resulted in greater written and visual coverage being afforded those athletes with impairments that are not perceived to deviate substantially from dominant perceptions of able-bodiedness (Schantz and Gilbert, 2001; Schell and Duncan, 1999; Sherrill, 1997; Smith and Thomas, 2005; Thomas and Smith, 2003). Indeed, such a view would appear to have been accepted by some disabled athletes themselves. Writing in her autobiography, *Seize the Day*, Tanni Grey-Thompson, for example, claimed that the tendency by the media to focus on wheelchair athletes can be seen as a further expression of 'the fact that athletes in wheelchairs don't look too disabled' (Grey-Thompson, 2001: 58) to non-disabled people, many of whom, she claims, 'aren't comfortable with other categories [of impairment] because the athletes look different' (Grey-Thompson, 2001: 195). Regardless of the veracity of these claims, the emphasis on wheelchair athletes in the media would appear to express further narrow stereotypical and uncritically accepted views of disability as being synonymous with physical immobility and, according to Barnes (1992: 37), perpetuate 'widespread ignorance about the realities of impairment' experienced by other disabled people. Let us explore this apparent pre-occupation with able-bodiedness further.

Emulating able-bodiedness and ignoring impairment and disability

Despite the evident continuities in the press treatment of disabled athletes, the consistency of coverage has been accompanied by some equally apparent changes in the kind of commentary offered by the press upon disability sport at the elite level. In particular, there has been a recent tendency in some aspects of press coverage in a range of countries to present disabled athletes as 'aspiring to or emulating the *able*-bodiedness of athletes without disabilities' (Thomas and Smith, 2003: 179; original emphasis). It is, of course, not uncommon in the sports media for new and emerging athletes to be compared to other more established sports stars and celebrities (such as David Beckham and Tiger Woods). In the disability sport context, however, one outcome of the trend towards emphasizing the sporting abilities of disabled athletes has been the tendency to compare them to other non-disabled athletes. In our own media analysis of the 2000 Sydney Paralympics, for example, just over one quarter (26 per cent) of the articles we analysed explicitly compared British Paralympians to those non-disabled athletes who had competed in the Olympics that began one month or so previously (Thomas and Smith, 2003). Simon Jackson, a blind British judo fighter, for example, was frequently labelled 'the Paralympian equivalent of Steve Redgrave' (Thomas and Smith, 2003: 174), and Tanni Grey-Thompson was typically described as 'the Paralympic equivalent of American sprint ace Marion Jones' (Thomas and Smith, 2003: 174). These comparisons did not appear to just be an expression of the reporter's own personal views however, for several disabled athletes themselves were often quoted directly as being concerned with emulating the efforts of Olympic athletes. Nigel Capewell, the then Great British cycling team rider, for example, was widely quoted as saying that he 'had hoped to emulate Olympian Jason Queally' (Thomas and Smith, 2003: 174) who had earlier won the 1km Olympic time trial. In a similar way, Simon Jackson was also said to have repeatedly emphasized, in both the press and during television interviews, that he was 'after (Steve) Redgrave's record' (Thomas and Smith, 2003: 174) of winning gold medals at five consecutive Olympic Games.

The emphasis that came (and has increasingly come) to be placed on the *sporting* achievements of disabled athletes could also be interpreted as being one expression of the ways in which the press actively sought to further reinforce the perceived success of British athletes at the Olympics. It was also claimed that the coverage may have been used as part of a deliberate strategy by journalists to add further emphasis to the prevailing and largely media-generated view that Britain was, at the time, re-emerging as a successful sporting, specifically Olympic, nation (Thomas and Smith, 2003). In the course of presenting disabled athletes' attempts to demonstrate their sporting achievements and capabilities during this and other competitions, there has been a parallel tendency within the press not only in Britain, but elsewhere, too, to ignore, or at least downplay, the presence of their impairment and the impact that disability has on their lives, and to report upon their achievements in ways that are consistent with the approach taken in sports journalism generally. More particularly, on occasions the press coverage of disability sport has often focused predominantly upon the sporting performances of disabled athletes by emphasizing the significance of records, medals, times and the success of athletes whilst offering little or no comment on the athletes' experience of impairment and disability (Thomas and Smith, 2003). On the one hand, this style of coverage might appear to represent the commitment to acknowledge disabled athletes as *athletes* without reference to the presence of their impairment and disability. This style of coverage might be deemed by many as a 'positive' development in the evolution of disability sport since it focuses primarily upon the athlete and their sporting ability. Simultaneously, however, focusing only on the *sporting* achievements of disabled athletes and juxtaposing them to those of able-bodied athletes may lead us to conclude that this style of press coverage would appear to perpetuate, rather than help break down, particular stereotypical perceptions of disability and dominant pre-occupations with able-bodiedness. In this regard, it might be argued that those aspects of the press coverage of disability sport which are characterized by the apparent tendency to deny the existence of an athlete's disability and impairment also perpetuates the view that an impairment, as a biological condition, is not central to a disabled person's life experiences and self-identity (see Chapter 1; Hughes and Paterson, 1997).

A third possibility may be that sports media coverage which portrays disabled athletes as aspiring to, or emulating, the able-bodiedness of non-disabled athletes, provides an illustration of the ways in which disabled athletes (especially males) are increasingly socialized and encouraged into imitating those characteristics of bodily strength and physical wholeness that are typically associated with able-bodiedness, particularly in Western societies (Hahn, 1984; Hargreaves, 2000; Shilling, 2005). That this explanation appears to have a degree of adequacy is indicated by the findings of Hargreaves's (2000) study of the sporting experiences and lives of disabled sportswomen. In this regard, Hargreaves noted that many of the women to whom she spoke were particularly 'concerned with their able-bodiedness' (Hargreaves, 2000: 198), wanted 'to be able to participate in sport without being viewed as objects of pity or represented as victims' (Hargreaves, 2000: 198), and frequently described their attempts to demonstrate their *physical* capabilities through participating in sport. Similarly, Smith and Sparkes (2002) have noted that one consequence of the perceived growing pressure on disabled people, and particularly men with physical impairments, to demonstrate their able-bodiedness to others in the wider society is that sport has come increasingly to be seen as a particularly important enclave in which they are able to challenge dominant perceptions of the 'imperfection' of their bodies. In this context, it has been claimed that for many disabled men participation in sport is seen as a particularly useful means through which to make their disabled bodies appear 'normal' as possible, and to help 'reclaim' their lost sense of masculinity through the expression of physicality and strength required by participating in sport (DePauw, 1997; Hargreaves, 2000; Smith and Sparkes, 2002). Whether such a view is one that prevails among consumers of the sports media is, of course, an empirical question and in the absence of detailed empirical research which examines these issues, it is difficult to draw any firm conclusions regarding the audience effects of this kind of media presentation of disabled athletes. But in what other ways have the press tended to report on the growing participation and presence of disabled people in sport? Let us examine some of the issues involved by considering the ways and extent to which the press in Britain reported upon the presence of disabled athletes in the 2002 Manchester Commonwealth Games as a case study (Smith and Thomas, 2005).

The inclusion of disabled athletes in mainstream elite sports competitions

As we noted in Chapter 6, there has been over the last three decades or so a growing tendency, particularly at the elite level, for some disabled athletes to participate alongside non-disabled athletes in mainstream sports competitions such as the Olympics and Commonwealth Games. Perhaps unsurprisingly, the decision by the MCGOC to incorporate some disabled athletes and disability sport-specific events in the full medal programme at the 2002 Commonwealth Games was met with particular enthusiasm by those inside and outside the disability sport movement. Indeed, it was not uncommon at the time to read in both the academic and popular press that, among other things, 'the Manchester 2002 Commonwealth Games were a positive example of athletes with disabilities competing at the same venue as mainstream competitors' (Vickerman *et al.*, 2003: 58). But how did the British press, in fact, report upon the participation of disabled athletes? In what ways and to what extent did the coverage portray athletes? Were disabled athletes presented in ways other than that which the various disability sport bodies and others expected? The findings of a recent study that explored the coverage afforded disabled athletes by six national British newspapers provides some useful clues in this respect (Smith and Thomas, 2005).

As Smith and Thomas (2005) have noted, around the time that the 2002 Manchester Games were held, particular emphasis was placed by some journalists and politicians upon how the incorporation of disabled athletes within the Games represented a significant step towards the 'inclusion' of those athletes in mainstream sports events. Maria Eagle, the then British Minister for Disabled People, for example, claimed that the 2002 Games had 'addressed the issues of inclusiveness' (*Sunday Telegraph*, 28 July 2002: 22) and helped meet the perceived moral obligation to enable disabled athletes to participate alongside their non-disabled counterparts in sport. Mike Todd, the Disability Advisor to the Manchester

Games, was also widely cited in the press as being of the view that the decision by the MCGOC to include disabled athletes in the main programme, rather than as participants in demonstration events, was 'not done as a favour for the athletes – we are doing it because it's the *right* thing to do' (*The Times*, 25 July 2002a; emphasis added). Indeed, many of the articles in Smith and Thomas's study (2005) repeatedly emphasized the significance of this point and were particularly concerned with reinforcing the view that 'the disabled athletes are taking part in the Commonwealth Games, not the Crippled-Games-we-had-to-tag-on-for-the-sake-of-political-correctness-Games' (*Times*, 25 July 2002b: 3). One journalist writing for the *Daily Telegraph* (25 July 2002) claimed, for example, how:

> inclusion is not before time . . . Disabled athletes have been included in demonstration events at the World Athletics Championships and Olympic Games for 10 years, but it was seen as tokenism . . . this latest development represents a great step forward, with Manchester having been at the heart of an inclusive strategy from the initial planning stages.

Wilson, another journalist working for the *Daily Mail* (26 July 2002), was of the view that:

> For the first time, it makes no difference whether a competitor is able-bodied or disabled at these Commonwealth Games. The barriers that kept them in a parallel universe are down. And if Manchester's Games achieve nothing else, they have ended that sporting apartheid.

Thus, for many British press reporters at the time, the Games provided for the first time a forum in which disabled athletes were 'rightly' able to perform – because of their *sporting* ability – alongside their fellow able-bodied athletes in mainstream sports events (Smith and Thomas, 2005). The inclusion of disabled athletes in the main programme was also widely and uncritically perceived as being part of a broader process in which there is a trend towards the growing acceptance of disabled people in the wider society. More specifically, much of the media coverage examined by Smith and Thomas (2005) endorsed the view that the Games

> mark(ed) a departure from past attitudes towards athletes with disabilities. Not because they are being treated differently but precisely because . . . society is starting to treat them just the same. (Maria Eagle, cited in *The Times*, 25 July 2002)

In particular, the South African swimmer Natalie Du Toit, who became the first disabled swimmer to compete in the final of an able-bodied sports event in the Commonwealth Games, was typically portrayed as 'the symbol not only of these revolutionary Commonwealth Games, but of the times we live in' (*The Times*, 25 July 2002b: 1). Since she participated alongside able-bodied athletes, Du Toit was also widely considered to have helped '(tie) an indissoluble bond between the able bodied and disabled' (*Guardian*, 3 August 2002: 4). Reflecting the complexity and differential press coverage of disability sport more generally, other aspects of the press treatment of disabled athletes participating at the Games was much less uncritically accepting. One reporter in Smith and Thomas's (2005) study, for example, suggested that far from being premised upon notions of inclusion, 'able-bodied athletics is not at all about inclusiveness, but the opposite' (*Sunday Telegraph*, 28 July 2002: 22). For him, the whole purpose of able-bodied sport at the elite professional level is 'about the best meeting and beating the best' (*Sunday Telegraph*, 28 July 2002: 22) where athletes are *excluded* on the basis of ability and the inherently competitive nature of modern sport. In this regard, and in contrast to those aspects of press coverage outlined above, the same journalist was of the view that:

> Truly competitive world-class sport is not about endeavour or heroism, or overcoming advantages; it's about being the best. By running contests for and awarding medals to the disabled alongside the real contests, and giving them equal validity, the Commonwealth Games organisers are simply acknowledging how fundamentally irrelevant the Games are as a sporting contest. True contests could not allow such meaningless parities. (*Sunday Telegraph*, 28 July 2002: 22)

As we have noted elsewhere, however, there is little, if any, evidence to support many of the claims offered by many journalists and editors in this context; that is to say, the somewhat crude and simplistic assumption that the incorporation of disabled athletes in the 2002 Commonwealth Games was an expression of the growing inclusion, acceptance and improved life-chances of disabled people within the wider society. Indeed, as we noted in Chapter 1, when compared to some other members of the non-disabled population, disabled people continue to experience lower levels of education, have poorer housing and fewer employment opportunities and are more likely to live in poverty (see, for example, Barnes and Mercer, 2003; Campbell and Oliver, 1996; Thomas, 2008). A recognition of these and other issues should, therefore, warn us against the prevailing tendency among parts of the media to accept the view that disabled people's circumstances and position in the wider society are improving in the manner described above, for these are at best very partial and distorted representations of the reality of many disabled people's lives.

The classification of disabled athletes and public understanding

As we noted in Chapter 6, it has been widely suggested that the various classification systems used to group disabled athletes in a particular sport or event to permit 'fair' and 'equitable' competition between them is said to be a, if not *the*, central issue facing those within the disability sport movement (Howe and Jones, 2006; Nixon, 2007; Sherrill, 1999; Vanlanderwijck and Chappel, 1996). We also drew attention to how since its establishment in 1989, the IPC has sought to establish a closer partnership with the IOC to help generate much needed long-term financial resources, provide athletes and coaches with access to high quality facilities during the Paralympics, as well as securing a whole range of additional commercial benefits that may be derived from being strongly associated with the Olympic Movement. On 25 August 2003, for example, the President of the IPC, Phillip Craven and Jacques Rogge, the President of the IOC, signed an amendment to the IPC-IOC Agreement previously established on 19 June 2001 that helped formalize the developing partnership between both organizations (IPC, 2003). It also helped formally transfer the 'broadcasting and marketing responsibilities of the 2008, 2010 and 2012 Paralympic Games to the Organizing Committees of these Olympic and Paralympic Games' (IPC, 2003: 1) so that both competitions are marketed as a single entity. Notwithstanding the perceived benefits this deliberate attempt to enhance the commercialization and professionalization of the Paralympics may have for the relevant parties involved, the IOC has since required the IPC to restrict the number of athletes participating in the Paralympic Games to 4,000. According to Howe and Jones (2006), this attempt to limit the number of participants in the Paralympics has been predicated on the premise that it helps make it a more marketable product to manage and improve media interest in the performances of disabled athletes.

However, one of the central problems those in the Paralympic community have faced in achieving greater media coverage and the assumed improvement this will bring in public understanding of the Paralympics and disabled athletes' achievements, has been the very existence of 'a complex classification system that many in the IPC now regard as cumbersome and logistically problematic' (Howe and Jones, 2006: 36). Indeed, as we noted in Chapter 6, since its inauguration the IPC has persistently attempted to constrain the IOSDs to develop more appropriate classification systems with the objective of helping to find better ways of improving the marketability of the Paralympics and attract attention from international sports media. Although this encouragement to modify existing classification systems has impacted on the activities of the IOSDs differentially and been met with mixed enthusiasm (see Chapter 6), perhaps one of the most recent and clearest expressions of the IPC's attempt to obtain greater – perhaps even complete – control over the classification process was the publication of the IPC Classification Code in 2007 (IPC, 2007c). The scope of the Code is wide-ranging and its overall purpose is to support and coordinate the development and implementation of sport-focused classification systems that are designed to help improve standards of sporting excellence for all athletes across all sports in the Paralympic Movement (IPC, 2007c). Its publication may also be interpreted, however, as a further attempt by the IPC to reduce the potential for confusion among the public by simplifying and speeding up competitions and reducing the number of classes used to group athletes together in existing classification systems. At the time of writing it is not clear what impact, if any, attempts to harmonize the approaches to classification by the various IOSDs will have in helping the IPC achieve their desired outcomes. Nevertheless, it seems reasonable to suppose even at this stage that the Code does, indeed, provide a clear indication of the IPC's continued desire to deliberately stimulate media and public interest in the Paralympics, as well as attract additional sponsorship and revenues that may accompany its increasing commercialization in the future. It is also clear, however, that despite the continued emphasis that members of the IPC and other bodies place on the importance of media coverage in raising the profile of disability sport, the various classification systems that help define disability sport can simultaneously come to limit public understanding of it.

Although responsibility for encouraging media interest in the Paralympics remains largely under the jurisdiction of the IPC and IOC, the media attention afforded disabled athletes who compete in mainstream sports competitions at the elite level such as the Commonwealth Games is, of course, a matter for the relevant organizations involved (such as the CGF). These organizations are faced with broadly similar constraints to the IPC and IOC when seeking to stimulate interest in the performances of disabled athletes among the media and the general public. There are, however, several other ways in which these organizations face problems of avoiding spectator confusion particularly when, as in the Commonwealth Games, disabled athletes compete alongside non-disabled athletes. As we explained in Chapter 6, a common feature of all the classification systems employed in the Paralympics is that the athlete who finishes first in an event would be awarded the gold medal in the same manner as non-disabled athletes, even if this simple outcome may not be known for several minutes. At the 2002 Commonwealth Games – which, as we explained above, was marketed as the first Commonwealth Games to incorporate some disabled athletes and disability sport-specific events in the main competition – this system of classifying athletes was not employed in every disability sport event included in the full programme. In the multi-disability swimming events, for example, the swimmer's final placing was determined by their time relative to the current world record in their classification group. This, it was alleged, occurred because the MCGOC and CGF were particularly concerned to ensure the 'maximum inclusion (of athletes with different impairments) across all of the participating nations' (Manchester 2002 Ltd, 2002: 13) and to ensure greater levels of participation by disabled athletes. Consequently, since the winner in each disability sport-specific event was the competitor who finished closest to the world record for their sport, and where the athlete who finished last could feasibly win their event, such moves were potentially very confusing for the audience and media reporters (Smith and Thomas, 2005). This was certainly the opinion of the then chairman of British Blind Sport, Nikhil Nair, who argued that: 'It's going to be horrendous for spectators, who just won't have a clue who is winning' (cited in *The Times*, 25 July 2002: 31). Similar views were also to be found among many parts of the British press at the time, and it was claimed, in particular, that if one of the aims of including disabled athletes in the Manchester Games was, indeed, to improve public understanding of disability sport through the media coverage afforded those events, then this may have done more to increase, rather than reduce, confusion among the audience (Smith and Thomas, 2005).

When planning for the inclusion of disabled athletes within the main programme of the Games, the MCGOC and CGF also sought to ensure that a mixture of individual and team sports were provided for disabled athletes and that these ensured, insofar as it was possible, parity between male and female athletes and athletes with particular impairments (Manchester 2002 Ltd, 2002). However, the CGF did decide against selecting events such as wheelchair basketball and archery that required 'prohibitively expensive equipment' or 'events for EADs (elite athletes with disabilities) that were absent from the overall programme' (Manchester 2002 Ltd, 2002: 13). Those athletes with more severe impairments were also largely excluded from the programme. The decision to focus on what some may consider more aesthetically pleasing classifications of impairment did not go unrecognized by some officials and athletes. Gordon Neale, then Chief Executive of Disability Sport England, pointed out, for example that: 'There are severe classifications – people in electric wheelchairs or people with no arms or legs – who are just as competitive in sport but who are not in these Games' (*Times*, 25 July 2002: 31). Despite the formally stated policy commitment of the MCGOC and CGF towards ensuring that the Games were 'inclusive' in order to help raise the media profile of disability sport, it was clear that whilst some disabled athletes were included at the Games, other athletes were simultaneously *excluded* because of the sport in which they participate and, perhaps most significantly, because of the severity of their particular impairment. This is not to deny the possibility, of course, that the ways in which disabled athletes were portrayed in the media coverage of the Games did not impact upon perceptions of disability sport in the manner desired by the MCGOC, CGF and other groups involved in the Manchester Games. It may well have been the case that, as athletes such Tanni Grey-Thompson claimed, being included in the Commonwealth Games for the first time in Manchester provided athletes with a 'chance to showcase what (they) can do' (*Daily Mail*, 26 July 2002: 93). However, as we noted at the outset of this chapter, the lack of empirical research on the ways and extent to which, if any, such coverage is received by the audience prevents us from making many firm conclusions about the efficacy of the media in enhancing understanding of the sporting performances of disabled athletes, disabled people and their experiences of impairment and disability.

Summary

In this chapter we have attempted to identify the changes and continuities that have characterized media coverage of modern elite level disability sport competitions, and specifically the Paralympics and Commonwealth Games. It is clear that although there has been growing coverage of disabled athletes participating in elite disability sport-specific competitions, as well as in mainstream events where they compete alongside non-disabled athletes, such coverage may not have been as positive as is sometimes uncritically assumed by those inside and outside the disability sport community. It is also the case that aspects of the reported press coverage of disabled athletes clearly contravene the British newspaper and periodical industry's Code of Practice in which the press are expected to avoid using prejudicial or pejorative reference to, for example, a person's disability, and that any such reference to this must only be included if it is genuinely relevant to the article being published (Press Complaints Commission, 2007). The IPC have also issued similar guidelines for 'reporting on persons with a disability' (IPC, 2007d) where the media are expected to avoid using emotional wording such as 'tragic' and 'victim' and portraying disabled people as 'superhuman' or 'recipients of charity or pity' (IPC, 2007d). However, it is quite clear from the analysis presented in this chapter that, once again, press coverage of elite disability sport is, to some extent at least, characterized by a tendency to perpetuate stereotypical views of disability and the lives of disabled people which is not uncommon in the press coverage of disabled people more generally.

We have also noted that whilst some elite disabled athletes are becoming increasingly visible and known to the wider public through the disproportionate media coverage they receive, for many disabled athletes and especially women and those with more severe impairments who compete in less popular sports, such coverage has been in short supply. In this regard, we might reasonably conclude that in many societies – particularly Western societies – the media coverage of disability sport has tended to focus on *particular athletes, with particular impairments, competing in particular sports*. Such coverage has also been characterized by varying degrees of conscious intent on the part of journalists and their editors, and the self-interests and ideologies of these groups often means that the audience is presented with a one-sided perception of impairment, disability and disability sport that simply expresses and reinforces existing social divisions between disabled and non-disabled people both inside and outside sport. But what are the implications of this analysis? Perhaps the first point worthy of note is that 'simply increasing the amount of coverage athletes with a disability receive in the media is unlikely, by itself, to bring about major wholesale changes in societal perceptions' (Brittain, 2004: 450) of disabled people in the ways expected by those who advocate such a position. The second – and very important – point that needs to be considered is that:

> For media coverage to have any real, major, positive effects in this area, it is not only the amount of coverage that needs to improve but also the content of that coverage and the underlying perceptions upon which it is formulated. Although it could be argued that some coverage is better than no coverage at all, if that coverage is only going to reinforce negative perceptions of disability, it has to be questioned . . . whether it is actually doing more harm than good. (Brittain, 2004: 450)

Finally, if we are to understand better the media treatment of disability sport, it is important that future media analyses of disability sport takes into account – more than has been the case hitherto – how the representation of athletes, their disabilities and impairments are not static phenomena, but are dynamic and constantly in flux and subject to change over time and space. More specifically, as in sports media studies more generally, a vital prerequisite for helping to explain the social representation of disabled athletes is an understanding not only of the multifarious and complex processes underlying the ways and extent to which impairment, disability and disabled athletes are constructed and presented in the media, but also the central contribution (both intentionally and unintentionally) made by the media to the construction of sports competitions such as the Paralympic and Commonwealth Games.

Revision questions

1   How would you summarize the main features of the media coverage given to disabled athletes competing in elite level sport?
2   How can the style and kinds of media coverage given to elite disabled athletes be explained?
3   What are the main opportunities and challenges facing those who wish to generate more media interest in disability sport?
4   If you worked for the IPC, what policies and strategies need to be considered if you wished to 'improve' the style and kind of media coverage given to disabled athletes participating in the Paralympics?
5   How would you go about marketing and securing appropriate media coverage for the London 2012 Paralympics?

Key readings

Barnes, C. and Mercer, G. (2003) *Disability*, Cambridge: Polity.
Press Complaints Commission (PCC) (2007) *Newspaper and Magazine Publishing in the U.K. Editors' Code of Practice*, London: PCC.
Schantz, O. and Gilbert, K. (2001) 'An ideal misconstrued: newspaper coverage of the Atlanta Paralympic games in France and Germany', *Sociology of Sport Journal*, 18: 69–94.
Smith, A. and Thomas, N. (2005) The 'inclusion' of elite athletes with disabilities in the 2002 Manchester Commonwealth Games: an exploratory analysis of British newspaper coverage. *Sport, Education and Society*, 10: 49–68.
Thomas, N. and Smith, A. (2003) 'Pre-occupied with able-bodiedness? An analysis of the British media coverage of the 2000 Paralympic games', *Adapted Physical Activity Quarterly*, 20: 166–81.

Recommended websites

BBC Sport
www.bbc.co.uk/disabilitysport

BBC Ouch! Disability Magazine
www.bbc.co.uk/ouch

London 2012 Paralympic Games
www.london-2012.co.uk/paralympic-games

International Paralympic Committee
www.paralympic.org

Conclusion

Perhaps the most obvious way to conclude an introductory text on *Disability, Sport and Society* would be simply to reflect upon the main observations that we made in each of the preceding chapters. It may be rather more helpful and interesting, however, to briefly reconsider some of the main themes that have emerged throughout the whole book and then begin to speculate, somewhat tentatively, upon how some of these are likely to feature in the future of disability sport. It is, of course, notoriously difficult to predict the future but attempting to anticipate the outcomes of trends and developments that we have examined in this book may hold out the possibility of stimulating further discussion and research on the complex relationships between modern sport, disability and aspects of the wider society.

The organization of disability sport: separation and segregation

As we noted in Chapters 2 and 3, the early emergence and development of disability sport occurred in the context of medical-based segregated settings and institutions (e.g. Stoke Mandeville Hospital) away from mainstream sports settings. Historically, therefore, disabled people have, for the most part, tended to participate in sport and physical activity separately from non-disabled people. It is clear, however, that during the course of the last half century or more, the opportunities for disabled people with a range of impairments to participate in sport and physical activity have increased considerably. Disabled people are also now able to participate in a wider range of activities that are provided more regularly, and in a wider variety of mainstream organizational contexts, at the local (Chapter 3), national (Chapters 2 and 4) and international (Chapter 6) levels than previously. Notwithstanding the increasingly important role that these mainstream sports organizations have come to play in the provision of sport for some disabled people, in many respects much of the organization of disability sport remains as it originated: different, separate and segregated from mainstream sport. In Britain, for example, whilst local authorities and governing bodies of sport play a crucial role in providing opportunities for disabled people to participate in sport and physical activity, there also continues to exist a separate, fragmented, complex and cumbersome organizational structure for disability sport that is comprised of many disability sports organizations (DSOs). In Chapter 2, for example, we noted that the formation of the English Federation of Disability Sport (EFDS) in 1998 was intended to act as the umbrella organization for disability sport in England, whilst other DSOs such as CP Sport, BBS and Disability Sport Events (DSE) continue to have significant responsibility for organizing national events.

At lower levels of sport, it is also clear that DSOs continue to organize sport and physical activity for disabled people in isolation and often without support from mainstream governing bodies. At local authority level, many schemes designed to promote the participation of disabled people are delivered separately from those provided for the non-disabled. On an international scale, the Paralympic Games and other events such as the World Games for the Deaf also continue to exist and be organized separately from competitions such as the Olympics. In these and other respects it seems reasonable to conclude that despite the growing political interest in disability sport amongst government and the role played by local authorities and governing bodies – discussed in more detail later – all the signs are that, while this is not necessarily an undesirable situation, sport and physical activity for disabled people will continue to be offered in largely segregated settings away from non-disabled people.

The relationship between disability and disability sport organizations

A second notable theme that can be identified from the analysis presented in this book is that whilst there are a diverse range of organizations involved in the development of sport and physical activity for disabled people, and in setting the disability sport policy agenda, these organizations are almost exclusively sport- rather than disability-focused in orientation. Indeed, at almost all levels, disability sport is delivered by organizations that have a specific interest in one or more sports for disabled people who have one or more particular impairments. These sports organizations, it should be noted, are not directly influenced by the disabled people's movement or organizations that are led and run by disabled people (such as the UK's Disabled People's Council and Disabled People International), for these groups do not generally appear to be interested in sport. Indeed, although disability organizations may have had an indirect impact on promoting disabled people's participation in sport and physical activity through the various legislation and changes in mainstream educational and social policy brought about by their campaigning and lobbying activities, they cannot generally be regarded as constituting a central part of the disability sport policy network.

It is also the case, however, that neither the DSOs, Sport England and, for that matter, other mainstream governing bodies of sport, have actively sought to deliver sport and physical activity for disabled people by developing relationships with organizations led and ran by disabled people and the disabled people's movement more generally. Given the increased legislation surrounding disabled people's access to 'services', it might be that a closer alliance between organizations concerned with disability sport (such as the EFDS) and those concerned with disability policy more generally (such as the UK's Disabled People's Council) may hold out the possibility that more effective policies designed to promote disabled people's participation in sport and physical activity than has been the case hitherto could be developed in the future. At the time of writing, however, there is little reason to believe that the longstanding and deeply-entrenched tendency for DSOs, Sport England and governing bodies to work largely in isolation from disability organizations that have been traditionally concerned with advancing the interests of disabled people in contexts other than sport is likely to change radically in the near future.

Increasing government interest in disability sport

As noted in Chapter 2, prior to the establishment of the Sports Council in 1972, the British government demonstrated little, if any, interest in and enthusiasm towards disability sport policy from grassroots to higher levels of sport. Since that period, however, government interest in disability sport began to increase slowly, particularly in the context of using sport and physical activities as vehicles of promoting mass participation ('Sport For All') among 'target groups' such as disabled people, and in the promotion of equity and equal opportunities. It might be recalled from Chapters 2 and 3, for example, that these policy objectives were very much at the heart of much national Sports Council policy during the 1980s, including *Sport in the Community: the Next Ten Years* and *Sport in the Community – Into the Nineties*, and then again in the early 1990s following the publication of *People with Disabilities and Sport: Policy and Current/Planned Action*. Despite the emphasis which government placed on the process of mainstreaming disability sport and raising levels of participation among disabled people in these initiatives, between the 1970s and mid-1990s government had, to varying degrees, retained a preference for adopting a largely hands-off approach to the delivery of its disability sport policy goals by leaving the responsibility for doing so to other DSOs and organizations such as the British Sports Association for the Disabled (BSAD). This having been said, our study of disability sport in local authorities (Chapter 3), governing bodies of sport (Chapter 4) and in physical education and school sport (Chapter 5) suggests, as a consequence of mainstreaming policy, and perhaps ironically, whilst disability sport has rarely been the focus of any sustained or clearly defined political and policy commitment in Britain, it is the non-disability focused sporting organizations who have tended to help deliver the disability sport policy goals of government rather than DSOs. As we noted in Chapter 2, the marginal and limited impact that the generally less powerful DSOs and organizations such as the EFDS have had on influencing and delivering the disability sport policy agenda has typically resulted from the lack of coordination between those groups, as well as their weak lobbying activities.

Since the late 1990s, and particularly following the publication of *A Sporting Future for All* and *Game Plan*, government intervention in the disability sport policy process has become increasingly apparent, but it has continued to do so with little interest and without assuming full responsibility for disability sport. Indeed, whilst the current Labour government has continued to support the process of mainstreaming, raising levels of participation and promoting the international success of elite disabled athletes, it has also placed increasing emphasis on the role of local authorities in delivering disability sport policy goals and on using sport and physical activity to achieve broader social inclusion objectives. In this regard, local authorities are once again being seen as important deliverers of sporting opportunities and facilities for disabled people. Those working in local authority disability sport development are, however, also being constrained to maintain their sports development activities for disabled people whilst managing conflicting pressures generated within a rapidly changing social and political policy climate where social inclusion goals, in particular, are becoming increasingly prioritized. In the present political climate, it is likely that the shift away from the development of sport, towards the increasing use of sport to achieve other desired social objectives in local authority sport development activity will mean that the historical tendency for disability sport to be loosely integrated – at best – into the sports development activities of some local authorities will continue, at least in the short- to medium-term. Indeed, despite the increasing political interest in, and support of, disability sport development at all levels, it is likely that this level of interest and support will remain, by degrees, limited; policy commitment is likely to remain marginal; and responsibility for the organization and delivery of disability sport will be kept at arms length from direct government involvement.

The rhetoric and reality of 'inclusion'

Perhaps the most enduring theme that can be identified as running throughout many of the chapters in this book is that of inclusion and mainstreaming. Whether it is in the context of mainstreaming disability sport at the local (Chapter 3) and national (Chapter 4) level, in the educational policies and practices of schools (Chapter 5), and internationally within the context of the debates surrounding the involvement of disabled athletes in the Paralympics and Olympic Games (Chapters 6 and 7), inclusion and mainstreaming have over the past three decades, in particular, become an increasingly central characteristic of disability sport and of broader government policy in many countries. Indeed, as we noted in many of the preceding chapters, the emphasis which has come to be placed on including disabled people and disability sport in mainstream settings, sports organizations and competitions has generated substantial debate among a variety of interested parties – including politicians, sports administrators, sportsmen and women, the media, teachers and policy-makers – who often have deeply held, often highly polarized, views about the appropriateness of inclusion and mainstreaming. Rather than seek to engage in an ideologically driven debate about the desirability or otherwise of inclusion and mainstreaming, we have endeavoured in this book to identify the differential outcomes that have emerged from the trend towards including disabled people in mainstream settings. In Chapter 5, for example, we noted that whilst the inclusion of young disabled pupils and those with special educational needs (SEN) in mainstream (or regular) schools has helped, to some degree, enhance their experiences of PE and school sport, there is evidence to suggest that the opposite has been the case. In particular, it seems fairly clear that when compared to their non-disabled peers, some disabled pupils and those with SEN typically tend to be provided with a limited and somewhat narrow range of sports and physical activities in which to participate in almost all aspects of PE; in some lessons they are often taught separately from other pupils or sometimes do not participate at all; and on balance, both teachers and pupils have expressed particular concern over the extent to which the policy of inclusion is, in fact, generating the desired impact on improving pupils' experiences of PE and sport in mainstream schools. And yet, despite evidence of this kind there are no signs to suggest that many governments will reconsider their commitment to the policy of inclusion. Indeed, it is probable that this policy commitment will be strengthened in the future and this may raise questions about the extent to which governments are serious about using inclusion as a policy vehicle for helping to make a greater contribution to the promotion of young people's experiences in PE and school sport.

Mention has already been made above of the trend towards mainstreaming disability sport and disabled athletes within the activities of national governing bodies. However, as we have explained in Chapter 4, limited and variable progress towards the full inclusion and mainstreaming of disabled people has been made in many sports, not least because of the fear amongst DSOs that mainstreaming may mean that they will lose valuable resources and control over the organization of disability sport. The various governing bodies are also particularly reluctant to relinquish their existing roles and accept new responsibilities for disability sport because of an alleged combination of financial constraints, a lack of political will within and outside the organizations, and a general lack of agreed vision on what constitutes mainstreaming and how to go about achieving it. Put simply, the primary interests of mainstream governing bodies do not lie in non-disabled sport; it is not a high priority for many of them; few are deeply committed to mainstreaming; and for most governing bodies it is at best a sideline to what they consider to be their core sports development business. The evidence that we cite in our various case studies of governing bodies leads us to believe that while some sports (such as swimming and tennis) provide examples of what may be deemed 'good practice', unless their activities become much more closely regulated and constrained by government policy agendas, in particular, then it is likely that responsibility for mainstreaming disability sport will remain nothing other than peripheral to the core activities of many governing bodies.

Finally, in our studies of elite disability sport that are presented in Chapters 6 and 7, we noted that since the Paralympics were first held in 1960, the Games have become increasingly politicized and commercialized on an international and global scale so much so the Paralympics have become the most well-known disability sport event. It is clear that as a consequence of these developments the size of the Games has increased rapidly. The number of competitors has expanded and now includes athletes from a wider range of countries than previously. The standards of athletes' performances have increased and become more professionalized. Media interest in and attendances at the Games have grown, and there has been a deliberate attempt to align the activities of the Paralympics more closely with the Olympic Games. At the same time, however, these developments have been accompanied by what have been seen as a series of potential threats to the Paralympic Movement and disability sport more broadly. As we explain in greater detail in Chapter 6, the use of particular classification systems in the Paralympics has meant that the opportunities for women, those athletes with more severe impairments, and Paralympians from small countries to participate in the Games are becoming increasingly limited. This process has been accompanied by the perceived need by the International Paralympic Committee to ensure that the Paralympics continues to attract more media coverage and sponsorship to facilitate the growth of the Games. However, Chapter 7 points out that whilst greater media coverage may help promote, among other things, public understanding of disability sport and demonstrate the high standards of disabled athletes' performances, such coverage may not always be as positive as is sometimes uncritically assumed by those inside and outside the disability sport community. Indeed, whilst aspects of the media (particularly press) coverage of the Paralympics does, in the eyes of some people, promote positive images of disability sport, this is typically limited to athletes competing at the elite level and often focuses on those with what are perceived as more aesthetically pleasing or less obvious impairments that do not deviate substantially from the able-bodiedness of non-disabled people. Such coverage can also, to some extent at least, be characterized by a tendency to perpetuate stereotypical one-sided views of disability, and the lives of disabled people, which simply expresses and reinforces existing social divisions between disabled and non-disabled people both inside and outside sport.

A final – though perhaps most controversial – issue that has emerged out of the complex debates related to inclusion and mainstreaming is that which surrounds the inclusion of some disabled athletes in the Olympic Games. In this connection, we cited in Chapter 6 the decision by the Court of Arbitration for Sport to uphold the appeal filed by Oscar Pistorius against the International Association of Athletics Federations (IAAF) who had previously claimed that the use of his Össur Cheetah Flex-Foot prosthetics would give him a considerable advantage over other athletes should he apply to participate in the Olympic Games, which he intended to do. The decision to allow Pistorius to compete in the Olympics will doubtless generate considerable debate on the impact that the participation of some disabled athletes in the Olympics may have for the future of the Paralympic Movement and, in particular, the Paralympics. Indeed, for some commentators, this may have signalled the beginning of the end of some disabled people's participation in segregated disability sport provision. It may also be interpreted in some quarters within the disability sport movement as a sign that the boundaries between disability and mainstream sport are, in some respects, blurring and that this may come to threaten the future and identity of the Paralympic Games and, perhaps, disability sport in general. Whether that and the other possible scenarios outlined above is seen as a good or bad thing depends entirely on one's own preferred ideological view of the future of disability sport.

References

Amateur Swimming Association (ASA) (1997) *Swimming for People with Disabilities.* (Notes of a meeting held at Harold Fern House 8/10/97), Loughborough: ASA.
—— (2002) *Disability Development Plan*, Loughborough: ASA.
Amateur Swimming Federation of Great Britain/Amateur Swimming Association (1997) *Constitutional Review: Swimming for People with Disabilities.* (Notes of a meeting held at Harold Fern House 8/11/97). Loughborough: Author.
Atkinson, H. and Black, K. (2006) *The Experiences of Young Disabled People Participating in PE, School Sport and Extra-Curricular Activities in Leicestershire and Rutland,* Loughborough: Institute of Youth Sport/Peter Harrison Centre for Disability Sport, Loughborough University.
Audit Commission (2002) *Special Educational Needs: A Mainstream Issue*, London: Audit Commission.
Australian Labor Government (1988) *Towards a Fairer Australia: Social Justice Under Labor*, Canberra: Australian Government Publishing Service.
Avramidis, E. and Norwich, B. (2002) 'Teachers' attitudes towards integration/inclusion: a review of the literature', *European Journal of Special Needs Education*, 17: 129–47.
Barnes, C. (1992) *Disabling Imagery and the Media*, Halifax, UK: Ryburn/BCODP.
—— (1997) 'A legacy of oppression: a history of disability in western culture', in L. Barton and M. Oliver (eds) *Disability Studies: Past, Present and Future*, Leeds: The Disability Press.
—— (1998) 'The social model of disability: a sociological phenomenon ignored by sociologists?', in T. Shakespeare (ed.) *The Disability Reader: Social Science Perspectives*, London: Cassell.
Barnes, C. and Mercer, G. (1995) 'Disability: emancipation, community participation and disabled people', in G. Craig and M. Mayo (eds) *Community Empowerment: A Reader in Participation and Development*, London: Zed Books.
—— (2003) *Disability*, London: Polity Press.
Barnes, C., Mercer, G. and Shakespeare, T. (1999) *Exploring Disability: A Sociological Introduction*, Cambridge: Policy Press.
Barrow Borough Council (2008a) *General Statistics for Barrow-in-Furness Census 2001.* Online. Available: http://www.barrowbc.gov.uk (accessed 3 June 2008).
—— (2008b) *Deprivation Statistics at a Borough Level 2007 Indices of Multiple Deprivation.* Online. Available: http://www.barrowbc.gov.uk (accessed 3 June 2008).
Barrow Borough Sports Council (2006) *Barrow Borough Sport and Physical Activity Strategy 2006–2011*, Barrow: Barrow Borough Sports Council.

—— (2008) *Accessibility*. Online. Available: http://www.barrowsportscouncil.org.uk (accessed 2 June 2008).
Barrow Community Regeneration Company (2005) *Four Year Development Plan*, Barrow: Barrow Community Regeneration.
Barton, L. (1993) 'Disability, empowerment and physical education', in J. Evans (ed.) *Equality, Education and Physical Education*, London: The Falmer Press.
Block, M. (1999) 'Did we jump on the wrong bandwagon? Problems with inclusion in physical education', *Palaestra*, 15: 3–17.
Block, M. and Obrusnikova, I. (2007) 'Inclusion in physical education: a review of the literature from 1995–2005', *Adapted Physical Activity Quarterly*, 24: 103–24.
British Blind Sport (2002) *Target: the Newsletter of British Blind Sport*, 37: February.
—— (2003) *Who We Are*. Online. Available http://www.britishblindsport.org.uk (accessed 1 September 2003).
British Paralympic Association (2003) Press Release. History of the Paralympic Games. Online. Available http://www.paralympic.org.uk (accessed 26 March 2004).
British Sports Association for the Disabled (BSAD) (1985) *Isle of Man Think-Tank (11–14 December)*, Aylesbury: BSAD.
—— (1987) *Sporting Opportunities for Disabled People in Britain: A Survey of Provision and Need*, Aylesbury: BSAD.
—— (1989) *1989 Year Book*, London: BSAD.
—— (1990) *Compulsory Competitive Tendering: Policy Guidelines for Leisure Management: 'To Safeguard Provision for People with Disabilities'*, London: BSAD.
—— (1995) *Review 95*, London: City Print.
British Swimming (2004a) *British Swimming: Corporate Plan 2005–2009*, Loughborough: British Swimming.
—— (2004b) *A Vision for Swimming: Swimming's Game Plan – the Next Ten Years*, Loughborough: British Swimming.
British Tennis Foundation (2001) *Programme of Tennis for People with Disabilities*, London: BTF.
British Wheelchair Sports Foundation (2003) *General Information*, History of the Paralympic Games. Online. Available http:// www.bwsf.co.uk. (accessed 4 September 2003).
Brittain, I. (2004) 'Perceptions of disability and their impact upon involvement in sport for people with disabilities at all levels', *Journal of Sport and Social Issues*, 28: 429–52.
Campbell, S. (2006) 'Pathways through Sport', Paper delivered at the English Federation of Disability Sport Count Me in Conference, 3 May 2006, Manchester.
Campbell, J. and Oliver, M. (1996) *Disability Politics: Understanding Our Past, Changing our Future*, London: Routledge.
Court of Arbitration for Sport (2008) Press Release. *Athletics – Case of Oscar Pistorius v/IAAF*, Lausanne: Court of Arbitration for Sport.
Centre Council of Physical Recreation (1960) *Sport and the Community*, London: CCPR.
Cerebral Palsy Sport (2001) Triumph of Sydney. *Sports Scene*, 6, Online. Available http://www.cpsport.org (accessed 1 September 2003).
—— (2002) Start of Something Special. *Sport Scene*, 4, Available http://www.cpsport.org. (accessed 1 September 2003).
—— (2003) *CP Sport: A Potted History*, Online. Available http://www.cpsport.org. (accessed 1 September 2003).
Coalter, F. (2007) *A Wider Social Role for Sport*, London: Routledge.

Collins, D. (1997) *Conference Report: National Disability Sport Conference. Report from Conference held on 22/06/97 at King's Fund Centre, London*, London: Sports Council.

Collins, M. and Kay, T. (2003) *Sport and Social Exclusion*, London: Routledge.

Commonwealth Games Federation (2003) *Post Games Report*, Online. Available http://www.thecgf.com (accessed 10 June 2003).

Cooke, C., Daone, L. and Morris, G. (2000) *Stop Press! How the Press Portrays Disabled People*, London: Scope.

Croll, P. and Moses, D. (2000) 'Ideologies and utopias: education professionals' views of inclusion', *European Journal of Special Needs Education*, 15: 1–12.

Crow, L. (1992) 'Renewing the social model', *Coalition*, 5–9.

Crowther, N. (2007) 'Nothing without us or nothing about us?', *Disability and Society*, 22: 791–4.

Crozier, A. (2002) *An Eye for The Bigger Picture: Inclusive Sport*, Crewe: English Federation of Disability Sport.

Cumberbatch, G. and Negrine, R. (1992) *Images of Disability on Television*, London: Routledge.

Daly, D. and Vanlandewijck, Y. (1999) 'Some criteria for evaluating the "fairness" of swimming classification', *Adapted Physical Activity Quarterly*, 16: 271–89.

Darcy, S. (2003) 'The politics of disability and access: the Sydney 2000 games experience', *Disability and Society*, 18: 737–57.

Department for Culture, Media and Sport (DCMS) (1999) *Policy Action Team 10 (Arts and Sport): A Report to the Social Exclusion Unit*, London: DCMS.

—— (2000) *A Sporting Future for All*, London: DCMS.

—— (2001) *The Government's Plan for Sport*, London: DCMS.

Department for Culture, Media and Sport (DCMS)/Strategy Unit (2002) *Game Plan: A Strategy for Delivering Government's Sport and Physical Activity Objectives*, London: DCMS/Strategy Unit.

Department for Education and Employment (DfEE) (1997) *Excellence for All Children: Meeting Special Educational Needs*, London: Stationery Office.

—— (1998) *Meeting Special Educational Needs: A Programme of Action*, London: DfEE.

Department for Education and Employment/Qualifications and Curriculum Authority (DfEE/QCA) (1999) *Physical Education: The National Curriculum for England*, London: HMSO.

Department for Education and Skills (DfES) (2001) *Special Educational Needs Code of Practice*, London: DfES.

—— (2004) *Removing Barriers to Achievement: The Government's Strategy for Special Educational Needs*, London: DfES.

Department for Education and Skills (DfES)/Department for Culture, Media and Sport. (DCMS) (2003) *Learning through PE and Sport*, London: DfES/DCMS.

Department of Education and Science (1978) *Special Educational Needs: Report of The Committee of Enquiry into the Education of Handicapped Children and Young People (The Warnock Report)*, London: HMSO.

Department of Education and Science/Welsh Office (DES/WO) (1991) *Physical Education for Ages 5–16: Proposals of the Secretary of State for Education and the Secretary of State for Wales*, London, DES/WO.

Department of National Heritage (1995) *Sport: Raising the Game*, London: DNH.

DePauw, K. (1997) 'The (in)visibility of disability: cultural contexts and "sporting bodies"', *Quest*, 49: 416–30.

—— (2000) 'Social-cultural context of disability: implications for scientific inquiry and professional preparation', *Quest*, 52: 358–68.

DePauw, K. and Gavron, S. (2005) *Disability Sport*, 2nd edn, Champaign, IL: Human Kinetics.

Disability Rights Commission (1999) *Disability Rights Commission Act*, London: HMSO.

Dopson, S. and Waddington, I. (1996) 'Managing social change: a process-sociological approach to understanding change within the National Health Service', *Sociology of Health and Illness*, 18: 525–50.

Drake, R.F. (1994) 'The exclusion of disabled people from positions of power in British voluntary organisations', *Disability and Society*, 9: 461–80.

—— (1996) 'Charities, authority and disabled people: a qualitative study', *Disability and Society*, 11: 5–23.

Ducket, P. (1998) 'What are you doing here? Non-disabled people and the disability movement. A response to Fran Barnfield', *Disability and Society*, 13: 625–8.

Elias, N. and Scotson, J. (1994) *The Established and the Outsiders*, London: Sage.

Elvin, I (1993) *Sport, and Physical Recreation*, Essex: Longman.

England Basketball (2006) *EB Policies: Equal Opportunities and Equity*. Available http://www.englandbasketball.com (accessed 13 May 2008).

—— (2008) *Aims and Objectives*. Online. Available http://www.englandbasketball.com (accessed 13 May 2008).

English Basketball (2007) *Aims and Objectives*. Online. Available http://www.englandbasketball.com (accessed 19 September 2007).

English Basketball Association (2001) *England Basketball Equal Opportunities*. Online. Available http://www.englandbasketball.com (accessed 18 September 2002).

—— (2002) *England Basketball Development Plan 2002–2006*. Online. Available http://www.englandbasketball.com (accessed 18 September 2003).

English Federation of Disability Sport (2000) *Building a Fairer Sporting Society: Sport for Disabled People in England: A Four Year Development Plan 2000–2004*, Crewe: English Federation of Disability Sport.

—— (2001) *Inclusive Sport*, Crewe: EFDS.

—— (2002) Manchester (2002) – *The Inclusive Games: Inclusive Sport*, Spring 2002, Crewe: EFDS.

—— (2004) *EFDS Development Framework: Count Me In: 2004–2008*. Crewe: EFDS.

—— (2007) *Swimmers Smash Record at National Short Course*. Online. Available http://www.efds.net (accessed 12 September 2007).

Evans, J. and Lunt, I. (2002) 'Inclusive education: are their limits?', *European Journal of Special Needs Education*, 17: 1–14.

Equality and Human Rights Commission (2008) *Vision, Mission and Priorities*, Online. Available http://www.equalityhumanrights.com (accessed 11 June 2008).

Fitzgerald, H. (2005) 'Still feeling like a spare piece of luggage? Embodied experiences of (dis)ability in physical education and school sport', *Physical Education and Sport Pedagogy*, 10: 41–60.

—— (2006) 'Disability and physical education', in D. Kirk, D. MacDonald and M. O'Sullivan (eds) *The Handbook of Physical Education*, London: Sage.

Fitzgerald, H. and Kay, T. (2004) *Sports Participation by Disabled Young People in Derbyshire: A Report for the Derbyshire and Peak Park Sport and Recreation Forum*, Loughborough: Institute of Youth Sport, Loughborough University.

Fitzgerald, H., Jobling, A. and Kirk, D. (2003) 'Valuing the voices of young disabled people: exploring experiences of physical education and sport', *European Journal of Physical Education*, 8: 175–201.

Football Association, The (n.d.) *Coaching Players with Learning Disabilities*, London: FA.

—— (2001) *The Football Development Strategy 2001–2006*, London: FA.

—— (2004) *Football for Disabled People*, London: FA.

—— (2006) *Football For Disabled People: Strategy Update*, London: FA.

—— (2007) *Football for Disabled People*, Online. Available http://www.thefa.com (accessed 28 September 2007).

—— (2008) *Football for All*. Online. Available http://www.thefa.com (accessed 9 June 2008).

Garner, P. and Dwyfor Davies, J. (2001) *Introducing Special Educational Needs: A Companion Guide for Student Teachers*, London: David Fulton.

Goffman, E. (1961) *Asylums: Essays on the Social Situation of Mental Patients and Other Inmates*, New York: Doubleday.

—— (1963) *Stigma: Some Notes on the Management of Spoiled Identities*, Harmondsworth: Penguin.

Gold, J. and Gold, M. (2007) 'The rise of the Paralympics', in J. Gold and M. Gold (eds) *Olympic Cities: City Agendas, Planning, and the World's Games, 1896 to 2012*, London: Routledge.

Goodwin, D. and Watkinson, E. (2000) 'Inclusive physical education from the perspective of students with physical disabilities', *Adapted Physical Activity Quarterly*, 17: 144–60.

Great Britain Wheelchair Basketball Association (2002) *A World History of Wheelchair Basketball*. Online. Available http://www.gbwba.org.uk. (accessed 23 September 2002).

—— (2007) *GBWBA New Constitution*. Online. Available http://www.gbwba.org.uk. (accessed 14 May 2008).

—— (2008) *GBWBA – Governing the Sport*. Online. Available http://www.gbwba.org.uk. (accessed 14 May 2008).

Green, K. (2002) 'Physical education teachers in their figurations: a sociological analysis of everyday "philosophies"', *Sport, Education and Society*, 7: 65–83.

Green, M. (2006) 'From "sport for all" to not about "sport" at all: interrogating sport policy interventions in the United Kingdom', *European Sport Management Quarterly*, 6: 217–38.

—— (2008) 'Non-governmental organisations in sports development', in V. Girginov (ed.) *Management of Sports Development*, Oxford: Butterworth-Heinemann.

Green, M. and Houlihan, B. (2006) 'Governmentality, modernisation and the "disciplining" of national sporting organisations: athletics in Australia and the United Kingdom', *Sociology of Sport Journal*, 23: 47–71.

Grey-Thompson, T. (2001) *Seize the Day: My Autobiography*, London: Hodder & Stoughton.

Guttmann, L. (1976) *Textbook of Sport for the Disabled*, Oxford: HM & M Publishers.

Hahn, H. (1984) 'Sport and the political movement of disabled persons: examining non-disabled social values', *Arena Review*, 8: 1–15.

Halliday, P. (1993) 'Physical education within special education provision', in J. Evans (ed.) *Equality, Education and Physical Education*, London: The Falmer Press.

Hargreaves, J. (2000) *Heroines of Sport: The Politics of Difference and Identity*, London: Routledge.

Henry, I. (2001) *The Politics of Leisure Policy*, 2nd edn, Basingstoke: Palgrave.

HMSO (1995) *Disability Discrimination Act*, London: HMSO.

—— (2005) *Disability Discrimination Act*, London: HMSO.

Hodge, S., Ommah, J., Casebolt, K., LaMaster, K. and O'Sullivan, M. (2004) 'High school general physical education teachers' behaviours and beliefs associated with inclusion', *Sport, Education and Society*, 9: 395–420.

Houlihan, B. (2002) 'Political involvement in sport, physical education and recreation', in A. Laker (ed.) *The Sociology of Sport and Physical Education: An Introductory Reader*, London: Routledge Falmer.

Houlihan, B. and White, A. (2002) *The Politics of Sports Development: Development of Sport or Development Through Sport?*, London: Routledge.

Houlihan, B. and Green, M. (2006) 'The changing status of school sport and physical education: explaining policy change', *Sport, Education and Society*, 11: 73–92.

Howe, D. and Jones, C. (2006) 'Classification of disabled athletes: (dis)empowering the Paralympic practice community', *Sociology of Sport Journal*, 23: 29–46.

Hughes, B. and Paterson, K. (1997) 'The social explanation of disability and the disappearing body: towards a sociology of impairment', *Disability and Society*, 12: 325–40.

International Paralympic Committee (IPC) (2003) *Spirit in Motion*, Bonn: IPC.

—— (2007a) *History of the Paralympic Movement*. Online. Available http://www.paralympic.org (accessed 15 June 2007).

—— (2007b) *History and Use of the Term 'Paralympic'*. Online. Available http://www.paralympic.org (accessed 15 June 2007).

—— (2007c) *IPC Classification Codes and International Standards*, Bonn: IPC.

—— (2007d) *Guidelines – Reporting on Persons with a Disability*. Online. Available http://www.paralympic.org (accessed 15 June 2007).

Jackson, D. (2008) 'Developing sports practice', in K. Hylton and P. Bramham (eds) *Sports Development: Policy, Process and Practice*, 2nd edn, London: Routledge.

Karpf, A. (1988) *Doctoring the Media*, London: Routledge.

Kent County Council (2004) *Kent Disability Sports Strategy 2004–2008*. Kent: Kent County Council's Sports Development Unit.

—— (2007a) *Kent 2006 Mid-Year Population Estimates*. Online. Available www.kent.gov.uk (accessed 3 June 2008).

—— (2007b) *2005 Ethnic Population Estimates*. Online. Available www.kent.gov.uk (accessed 3 June 2008).

—— (2008) *Release of Indices of Deprivation 2007*. Online. Available www.kent.gov.uk (accessed 3 June 2008).

Kent Sports Development Unit (2008) *Disability Sport*. Online. Available http://www.kentsport.org/disability (accessed 3 June 2008).

Labanowich, S. (1989) 'A case for the integration of the disabled into the Olympic games', *Adapted Physical Activity Quarterly*, 5: 264–72.

Lawn Tennis Assocaition (2006). *LTA Annual Report 2006*. London: LTA.

Lippi, G. and Mattiuzzi, C. (2008) 'Pistorius ineligible for the Olympic Games: the right decision', *British Journal of Sports Medicine*, 42: 160–1.

Long, J., Welch, M., Bramham, P., Hylton, K., Butterfield, J. and Lloyd, E. (2002) *Count Me In: The Dimensions of Social Inclusion through Culture and Sport*, London: Department of Culture, Media and Sport.

Manchester 2002 Limited (2002) *Our Games: The Inclusive Games, Issue 6*, Manchester: Manchester 2002 Limited.

Meegan, S. and MacPhail, A. (2006) 'Irish physical educators' attitude toward teaching students with special educational needs', *European Physical Education Review*, 12: 75–97.

Meekosha, H. and Dowse, L. (1997) 'Distorting images, invisible images: gender, disability and the media', *Media International Australia*, 84: 91–101.

Minister for Sport's Review Group (1989) *Building on Ability*, Leeds, Department of Education: The Minister's Review Group.

Morley, D., Bailey, R., Tan, J. and Cooke, B. (2005) 'Inclusive physical education: teachers' views of teaching children with special educational needs and disabilities in physical education', *European Physical Education Review*, 11: 84–107.

Morris, J. (1991) *Pride Against Prejudice*, London: The Women's Press.

National Disability Authority (NDA) (2005) *Promoting the Participation of People with Disabilities in Physical Activity and Sport in Ireland*, Dublin: NDA.

Nixon, H. (2000) 'Sport and disability', in J. Coakley and E. Dunning (eds) *Handbook of Sports Studies*, London: Sage.

—— (2007) 'Constructing diverse sports opportunities for people with disabilities, *Journal of Sport and Social Issues*, 27: 417–33.

Nottinghamshire County Council (2005a) *Building a Better Future Part 1*, Nottingham: Nottinghamshire County Council.

—— (2005b) *The Inside Out Project*, Nottingham: Nottinghamshire County Council

—— (2006) *Sports Disability Unit Newsletter No. 54*. May 2006, Nottingham: Nottinghamshire County Council.

—— (2007a) *Sports Disability Unit Newsletter No. 57*. Spring 2007, Nottingham: Nottinghamshire County Council.

—— (2007b) *Sports Disability Unit Newsletter No. 59*. Autumn 2007, Nottingham: Nottinghamshire County Council.

—— (2008) *Disability Sport*. Online. Available http:// www.nottinghamshire.gov.uk/ home/leisure/l-sport (accessed 2 June 2008).

Office for Disability Issues (2008) *About the Office for Disability Issues*. Online. Available http://www.officefordisability.gov.uk (accessed 7 June 2008).

Office for National Statistics (2008a) *Barrow-in-Furness (Local Authority) Ethnic Group*. Online. Available http://www.neighboroughood.statistics.gov.uk.co.uk>(accessed 3 June 2008).

—— (2008b) *Ashfield (Local Authority) Ethnic Group*. Online. Available http://www.neighboroughood.statistics.gov.uk.co.uk (accessed 3 June 2008).

—— (2008c) *Newark and Sherwood (Local Authority) Ethnic Group*. Online. Available http://www.neighboroughood.statistics.gov.uk.co.uk (accessed 3 June 2008).

—— (2008d) *Mansfield (Local Authority) Ethnic Group*. Online. Available http://www.neighboroughood.statistics.gov.uk.co.uk (accessed 3 June 2008).

—— (2008e) *Nottingham (Local Authority) Ethnic Group*. Online. Available http://www.neighboroughood.statistics.gov.uk.co.uk (accessed 3 June 2008).

—— (2008f) *Barrow-in-Furness (Local Authority) Ethnic Group*. Online. Available http://www.neighboroughood.statistics.gov.uk.co.uk (accessed 3 June 2008).

Office for Standards in Education (Ofsted) (2003) *Special Educational Needs in the Mainstream*, London: HMSO.

Office of the Deputy Prime Minister (ODPM) (2006) *Indices of Deprivation 2004 – summary (revised)*, London: ODPM.

Oliver, M. (1986) 'Social policy and disability: some theoretical issues', *Disability, Handicap and Society*, 1: 5–18.

—— (1990) *The Politics of Disablement*, Basingstoke: Macmillan.

—— (1992) 'Changing the social relations of research production?', *Disability, Handicap and Society*, 7: 101–114.

Oliver, M. and Barnes, C. (2008) 'Talking about us without us?' A response to Neil Crowther', *Disability and Society*, 23: 397–99.

Penney, D. (2002) 'Equality, equity and inclusion in physical education and school sport', in A. Laker (ed.) *The Sociology of Sport and Physical Education: An Introductory Reader*, London: Routledge Falmer.

Penney, D. and Evans, J. (1999) *Politics, Policy and Practice in Physical Education*, London: E & FN Spon.

Press Complaints Commission (PCC) (2007) *Newspaper and Magazine Publishing in the UK Editors' Code of Practice*, London: PCC.

Qualifications and Curriculum Authority (QCA) (2007) *National Curriculum for Physical Education 2008*, London: QCA.

Robertson, C., Childs, C. and Marsden, E. (2000) 'Equality and the inclusion of pupils with special educational needs in physical education', in S. Capel and S. Piotrowski (eds) *Issues in Physical Education*, London: Routledge Falmer.

Roche, B. (2002) *BBC News*. Online. Available. http://www.bbc.co.uk (accessed 15 February 2002).

Schantz, O. and Gilbert, K. (2001) 'An ideal misconstrued: newspaper coverage of the Atlanta Paralympic games in France and Germany', *Sociology of Sport Journal*, 18: 69–94.

Schell, L. and Duncan, M. (1999) 'A content analysis of CBS's coverage of the 1996 Paralympic games', *Adapted Physical Activity Quarterly*, 16: 27–47.

Shakespeare, T. (1996) 'Disability, identity and difference', in C. Barnes and G. Mercer (eds) *Exploring the Divide: Illness and Disability*, Leeds: The Disability Press.

—— (1997) 'Cultural representation of disabled people: dustbins for disavowal?', in L. Barton and M. Oliver (eds) *Disability Studies: Past, Present and Future*, Leeds: The Disability Press.

Shakespeare, T. and Watson, N. (1997) 'Defending the social model', *Disability and Society*, 12: 293–300.

Sherrill, C. (1993) 'Paralympics 1992: excellence and challenge', *Palaestra*, 9: 25–42.

—— (1997) 'Paralympic games 1996: feminist and other concerns: what's your excuse?', *Palaestra*, 13: 32–8.

—— (1999) 'Disability sport and classification theory: a new era', *Adapted Physical Activity Quarterly*, 16: 206–15.

—— (2004) *Adapted Physical Activity, Recreation and Sport*, 6th edn, Boston: McGraw-Hill.

Shilling, C. (2005) *The Body in Culture, Technology and Society*, London: Sage.

Simmonds, K. (2006) *Football For Disabled People: Strategy Update*, London: Football Association.

Smith, A. (2004) 'The inclusion of pupils with special educational needs in secondary school physical education', *Physical Education and Sport Pedagogy*, 9: 37–54.

Smith, A. and Green, K. (2004) 'Including pupils with special educational needs in secondary school physical education: a sociological analysis of teachers' views', *British Journal of Sociology of Education*, 25: 593–608.

Smith, A. and Thomas, N. (2005) 'Inclusion, special educational needs, disability and physical education', in K. Green and K. Hardman (eds) *Physical Education: Essential Issues*, London: Sage.

—— (2006) 'Including pupils with special educational needs and disabilities in National Curriculum Physical Education: a brief review', *European Journal of Special Needs Education*, 21: 69–83.

Smith, B. and Sparkes, A. (2002) 'Men, sport, spinal cord injury and the construction of coherence: narrative practice in action', *Qualitative Research*, 2: 143–71.

Smith, S. and Jordan, A. (1991) *What the Papers Say and Don't Say about Disability*, London: Spastics Society.

Sport England (2000) *Making English Sport Inclusive: Equity Guidelines for Governing Bodies*, London: Sport England.

—— (2001) *Young People with a Disability and Sport: Headline Findings*, London: Sport England.

—— (2004) *The Equality Standard: A Framework for Sport*, London: Sport England.

—— (2006) *Sport Playing Its Part: The Contribution of Sport To Meeting the Needs of Children and Young People*, London: Sport England.

Sports Council (1982) *Sport in the Community: The Next Ten Years*, London: Sports Council.

—— (1988) *Sport in the Community: Into the 90's. A Strategy for Sport 1988 – 1993*, London: Sports Council.

—— (1993a) *People with Disabilities and Sport: Policy and Current/Planned Action*, London: Sports Council.

—— (1993b) *Sport in the Nineties: New Horizons. Part 2 The Context*, London: Sports Council.

—— (1993c) *Sport and People with Disabilities: Guidelines for Governing Bodies of Sport*, London: Sports Council.

—— (1996) *Annual Report*, London: Sports Council.

—— (1997) *Conference Report: National Disability Sports Conference*, 22 June 1997, King's Fund Centre, London, London: Sports Council.

Sports Council Disability Task Force (1997) *Recommendations of the Future Structure and Integration of Disability Sport in England*, London: Sports Council.

Sports Council Research Unit (1991) *National Demonstration Projects: Major Lessons and Issues for Sports Development*, London: Sports Council.

Stafford, I. (1989) 'Everybody active: a Sports Council national demonstration project in England', *Adapted Physical Activity Quarterly*, 6: 100–8.

Staffordshire Football Association (2008) *Disability Football*. Online. Available http://www.staffordshirefa.com (accessed 9 June 2008).

Stalker, K., Baron, S., Riddell, S. and Wilkinson, H. (1999) 'Models of disability: the relationship between theory and practice in non-statutory organisations', *Critical Social Policy*, 19: 5–19.

Stationery Office (2001) *Special Educational Needs and Disability Act (2001)*, London: Stationery Office.

Steadward, R.D. (1996) 'Integration and sport in the Paralympic movement', *Sport Science Review*, 5: 26–41.

Stein, J.U. (1989) 'US media – where were you during the 1988 Paralympics?', *Palestra*, 5: 45–7.

Steventon, J. (2004) *An Audit of Sport Opportunities for Children and Adults with Disabilities in Cumbria*, Cumbria: English Federation of Disability Sport/Cumbria.

Strategy Unit (2005) *Improving the Life Chances of Disabled People*, London: Strategy Unit.

Strohkendle, H. (1996) *The 50th Anniversary of Wheelchair Basketball*, New York: Waxman.

Sugden, D. and Talbot, M. (1996) *Physical Education for Children with Special Needs in Mainstream Education*, Leeds: Carnegie National Sports Development Centre.

Swain, J., Finkelstein, V., French, S. and Oliver, M. (1993) *Disabling Barriers: Enabling Environments*, London: Sage.

Swartz, L. and Watermeyer, B. (2008) 'Cyborg anxiety: Oscar Pistorius and the boundaries of what it means to be human', *Disability and Society*, 23: 187–90.

Thomas, N. (2004) 'An examination of the disability sport policy network in England: an examination of the English Federation of Disability Sport and mainstreaming in seven sports', Unpublished PhD thesis, Loughborough: Loughborough University.

—— (2008) 'Sport and disability', in B. Houlihan (ed.) *Sport and Society: A Student Introduction*, 2nd edn, London: Sage.

Thomas, N. and Green, K. (1995) 'The integration of children with disabilities into mainstream physical education: an unintended consequence and a cause for concern', *Bulletin of Physical Education*, 31: 30–37.

Thomas, N. and Smith, A. (2003) 'Pre-occupied with able-bodiedness? An analysis of the British media coverage of the 2000 Paralympic games', *Adapted Physical Activity Quarterly*, 20: 166–181.

UK Deaf Sport (2008) *Inside EFDS: Craig Crowley*. Online. Available http://www. UKDeafsport.org (accessed 25 March 2008).

UK Sport (2006) *Athlete Recruitment the Priority for Paralympics*, UK Sport Press Release. Online. Available http://www.uksport (accessed 27 June 2006).

—— (2008) *Investing in Sport*. Online. Available http://www.uksport (accessed 27 May 2008).

Union of the Physical Impaired Against Segregation (1976) *Fundamental Principles of Disability*, London: Union of the Physically Impaired Against Segregation.

United Nations Educational, Scientific and Cultural Organization (UNESCO) (1994) *The Salamanca Statement and Framework for Action*, Paris: UNESCO.

—— (UNESCO) (1996) *UNESCO Survey on Special Needs Education Law 1996*, Paris: UNESCO.

Vanlanderwijck, Y. and Chappel, R. (1996) 'Integration and classification issues in competitive sports for athletes with disabilities', *Sport Science Review*, 5: 65–88.

Vickerman, P. (2002) 'Perspectives on the training of physical education teachers for the inclusion of children with special educational needs – is there an official line view?', *Bulletin of Physical Education*, 38: 79–98.

—— (2007a) *Teaching Physical Education to Children with Special Educational Needs*, London: Routledge.

—— (2007b) 'Training physical education teachers to include children with special education needs: perspectives from physical education initial teacher training providers', *European Physical Education Review*, 13: 385–402.

Vickerman, P., Hayes, S. and Whetherly, A. (2003) 'Special educational needs and National Curriculum physical education', in S. Hayes and G. Stidder (eds) *Equity and Inclusion in Physical Education and Sport*, London: Routledge.

Victorian Ministerial Review Committee (1984) *Integration in Victorian Education: Report of the Ministerial Review of Educational Services for the Disabled*, Melbourne: Education Department of Victoria.

Walmsley, J. (1997) 'Including people with learning difficulties: theory and practice', in L. Barton and M. Oliver (ed.) *Disability Studies: Past, Present and Future*, Leeds: The Disability Press.

Warnock Report (1978) *Report of the Committee of Enquiry into the Education of Handicapped Children and Young People*, London: HMSO.

Winnick, J. (2005) *Adapted Physical Education and Sport*, 4th edn, Champaign, IL: Human Kinetics.

World Health Organization (1980) *The International Classification of Impairments, Disability and Handicap*, Geneva: World Health Organization.

—— (2000) *The International Classification of Impairments, Disability and Handicap 2*, Geneva: World Health Organization.

—— (2001) *The International Classification of Human Functioning and Disability*, Geneva: World Health Organization.

—— (2008) *Disability and Rehabilitation: WHO Action Plan 2006–2011*, Geneva: World Health Organization.

Wright, H. and Sugden, D. (1999) *Physical Education for All: Developing Physical Education in the Curriculum for Pupils with Special Educational Needs*, London: David Fulton.

Wu, S. and Williams, T. (1999) 'Paralympic swimming performance, impairment, and the functional classification system', *Adapted Physical Activity Quarterly*, 16: 251–70.

Index